Law Society of Ireland

Banking & Corporate Financial Services

Cavendish
Publishing
Limited

London • Sydney • Portland, Oregon

Law Society of Ireland

Banking & Corporate Financial Services

Editor
Dr Anne-Marie Mooney Cotter

Authors
John Breslin
Dermot Cahill
Anne-Marie Mooney Cotter
John Darby
Tara Doyle
Joseph Gavin
Tracy Gilvarry
Niamh Moloney

Cavendish
Publishing
Limited

London • Sydney • Portland, Oregon

First published in Great Britain 2003 by
Cavendish Publishing Limited, The Glass House,
Wharton Street, London WC1X 9PX, United Kingdom
Telephone: + 44 (0)20 7278 8000   Facsimile: + 44 (0)20 7278 8080
Email: info@cavendishpublishing.com
Website: www.cavendishpublishing.com

Published in the United States by Cavendish Publishing
c/o International Specialized Book Services,
5824 NE Hassalo Street, Portland,
Oregon 97213-3644, USA

Published in Australia by Cavendish Publishing (Australia) Pty Ltd
3/303 Barrenjoey Road, Newport, NSW 2106, Australia

© Law Society of Ireland   2003

All rights reserved. No part of this publication may be reproduced, stored in a retrieval system, or transmitted, in any form or by any means, electronic, mechanical, photocopying, recording, scanning or otherwise, without the prior permission in writing of Cavendish Publishing Limited, or as expressly permitted by law, or under the terms agreed with the appropriate reprographics rights organisation. Enquiries concerning reproduction outside the scope of the above should be sent to the Rights Department, Cavendish Publishing Limited, at the address above.

You must not circulate this book in any other binding or cover and you must impose the same condition on any acquirer.

British Library Cataloguing in Publication Data

Banking & corporate financial services professional practice guide
1 Banking law – Ireland 2 Financial services industry – Law and legislation – Ireland
I Law Society of Ireland
346.4'17082

Library of Congress Cataloguing in Publication Data
Data available

ISBN 1-85941-801-5

1 3 5 7 9 10 8 6 4 2

Printed and bound in Great Britain

ABOUT THE AUTHORS

John Breslin is a barrister in the chancery/commercial area. He is the author of *Banking Law in the Republic of Ireland* (Gill & MacMillan, 1998). In the past, he has worked in the UK Securities and Investments Board (now the Financial Services Authority), a practising solicitor in the City of London and in Dublin. He is a graduate of Trinity College, Dublin and Christ's College, Cambridge.

Dermot Cahill is author of *Corporate Finance Law* (Round Hall, Sweet and Maxwell), covering a diverse range of topics ranging from insider dealing, debt factoring, debt subordination, merger regulation at Irish and EU level, offers to the public, liabilities arising out of prospectuses, admission and listing rules of the Stock Exchange. Recent publications include his co-authorship of *European Law* ((2000), with Mr Vincent Power (A & L Goodbody) and TP Kennedy (Law Society), 2nd edn, Oxford University Press, 2003).

Dermot specialises in the laws of the European Union, in particular commercial law. A graduate of the College of Europe, the National University of Ireland, and the Law Society, Dermot holds a tenured lectureship in the Faculty of Law, University College Dublin, where he lectures in corporate finance law, European Union, competition and merger control law. He has published and lectured widely on European and corporate law issues. Dermot was Visiting Professor to De Paul University Law School in Chicago, United States, in 1997 and 2003, and has been Visiting Professor in common law at University of Paris X (Nanterre) in 2000–03.

Dermot's recent publications include: 'Cross border financial services: the Treaty Rules and EC Competition Rules and financial services' (co-published by the Polish Institute for European Affairs/Academy of European Law (Trier) in Prawo Dotyczace ustug finansowych w Unii Europeskiej) (*Financial Services and European Law*, Witold Rotkowski (ed), 1998, pp 37–52 and 59–84); 'The EC Merger Regulation – a review of recent developments' [1999] CLP 272; and 'Assignment of debts and the rule in *Dearle v Hall*: the journey from equity to law – and back again', *Liber Memorialis*, in honour of the late Professor James C Brady (Breen, Casey and Kerr (eds), 2001, pp 121–38).

Anne-Marie Mooney Cotter is a Montrealer, fluent in both English and French. She earned her Bachelors degree from McGill University at the age of 18, her Juris Doctor law degree from one of the leading Civil Rights Institutions, Howard University School of Law, and her Doctorate degree (PhD) from Concordia University in political economy international law on the issue of equality. Her work experience has been extensive, acting as Chief Advisor and later Administrative Law Judge appointed by the Prime Minister to the Veterans Review and Appeals Tribunal in Canada; Supervising Attorney in Alaska for the Legal Services Corporation in the United States, and later Executive Director; National Director for an Environmental Network in Canada; and is now Course Co-ordinator for Business Law at the Law Society of Ireland. Anne-Marie is a gold medallist in figure skating. She is also the editor of this book.

John Darby qualified as a solicitor in 1997. He practises in the Corporate and Commercial Department of McCann FitzGerald, solicitors in Dublin. He also lectures on various aspects of commercial law in the Law Society of Ireland.

Tara Doyle is a partner in the Banking and Financial Services Group of Matheson Ormsby Prentice in Dublin. Tara is a graduate of Trinity College Dublin (LLB, 1993) and the London School of Economics (LLM (International Business Law), 1994). Tara acts for a wide range of Irish and international financial institutions in relation to structured finance transactions, including securitisations, bond repackagings and note issues. She also advises Irish and international clients in relation to the regulation of investment services in Ireland and the establishment of investment funds. Tara has spoken at the Global Asset-Backed Securities Summit on the Irish law in relation to securitisations and has contributed articles to financial services and investment industry journals. Tara is a member of the Incorporated Law Society of Ireland and the International Bar Association. She has tutored private international law and lectured on banking, corporate and financial services law on the Law Society's Professional Practice Course.

Joseph Gavin, BCL (1980), MBA (1986), JD (1988) was admitted as an attorney at law in Massachusetts in 1989 and as a solicitor in Ireland in 1995. Since 1989, he has specialised and developed experience in a wide variety of financing transactions and related banking and financial services issues. He joined LK Shields, Solicitors, as a partner in June 1995, having spent four years with Bingham Dana in Boston, Massachusetts and three years with McCann FitzGerald. He regularly advises investment banks, asset managers, credit institutions and stockbrokers in relation to all aspects of their business. In June 2002, he was elected head of the Business Law Department of LK Shields, Solicitors.

Tracy Gilvarry is a trainee solicitor with LK Shields, Solicitors. She graduated from University College Dublin in 2001 with a Bachelor of Business and Legal Studies and an LLM in Commercial Law. She is currently working in the Banking and Financial Services Department.

Niamh Moloney holds degrees from Trinity College Dublin (LLB, 1992) and Harvard Law School (LLM, 1993). After a period of time in practice, she joined the School of Law at the University of Nottingham and subsequently University College London, where she ran the postgraduate securities regulation course. She is now based in Ireland and is a member of the School of Law, Queen's University. She has published widely on securities and financial services regulation in international journals and has spoken at international conferences on this subject. She is the author of *EC Securities Regulation* (Oxford EC Law Library, Oxford University Press, 2002).

CONTENTS

About the Authors		v
Table of Cases		xi
Table of Legislation		xv

1 INTRODUCTION TO BANKING LAW — 1
John Breslin
- 1.1 The statutory regulation of banks — 1
- 1.2 The 1992 Regulations — 5
- 1.3 Financial regulation — 6
- 1.4 Regulatory powers and duties — 7
- 1.5 Building societies and credit unions — 7
- 1.6 Money laundering — 7
- 1.7 Miscellaneous regulatory issues — 10

2 RELATIONSHIP BETWEEN CREDIT INSTITUTIONS AND CUSTOMERS — 13
John Breslin
- 2.1 The bank/customer relationship — 13
- 2.2 Payment systems — 24

3 FORMS OF SECURITY — 29
Joseph Gavin and Tracy Gilvarry
- 3.1 Introduction — 29
- 3.2 Legal issues for companies granting security — 30
- 3.3 Security over land — 39
- 3.4 Charges — 42
- 3.5 Set-off and netting — 45
- 3.6 Registration of a security over intellectual property rights — 48

4 STRUCTURED FINANCE – SECURITISATION — 51
Tara Doyle
- 4.1 Introduction — 51
- 4.2 Taxation regime — 53
- 4.3 Insolvency law issues — 54
- 4.4 Securities law issues — 59
- 4.5 Banking law — 61

		4.6	Irish Stock Exchange listing	63
		4.7	Conclusion	65
5	**INTRODUCTION TO FINANCIAL SERVICES**			**67**
	John Darby			
		5.1	Overview of the regulatory structure	67
		5.2	Role of the CBI	67
		5.3	Authorisation requirements	67
		5.4	Application of authorisation requirements to affiliates	71
		5.5	The authorisation process	71
		5.6	Overview of substantive regulation	75
		5.7	Enforcement	85
		5.8	Extra-territorial application	89
6	**THE REGULATION OF INVESTMENT BUSINESS SERVICES**			**91**
	John Darby			
		6.1	Introduction	91
		6.2	The types of investment firms or services regulated under Irish law as a result of the implementation of the ISD	91
		6.3	Distinct authorisation for each type of investment firm (or service)	94
		6.4	The rules of the two-men management	94
		6.5	Investment firms covered by the ISD that are natural persons and that provide services involving the holding of third party assets	95
		6.6	Conditions set with regard to the shareholders or members of an investment firm covered by the ISD which applies for an authorisation to do business	96
		6.7	Capital requirements	96
		6.8	Appeal against refusal to grant the authorisation	97
		6.9	Conditions additional to or stricter than those contained in the ISD for granting an authorisation to do business	97
		6.10	Application to investment firms other than those covered by the ISD of any of the conditions and rules regarding the authorisation to do business laid down in the ISD	98
		6.11	The prudential rules drawn up in compliance with Art 10 of the ISD	99
		6.12	Member States shall make adequate arrangements for instruments belonging to investors with a view to safeguarding the latter's ownership rights	100
		6.13	Investment firms are to be structured and organised so as to minimise the risk of conflicts of interest	101
		6.14	Prudential rules additional to, or stricter than, those laid down in the ISD	101
		6.15	The prudential rules applicable to any other investment firm not covered by the ISD	102
		6.16	Rules of conduct drawn up by your country in compliance with Art 11 of the ISD	102

6.17	Rules of conduct additional to or stricter than the rules of conduct laid down by the ISD	105
6.18	Applicability to investment firms other than those covered by the ISD of any of the rules of conduct applicable as a result of the implementation of the ISD	105
6.19	Obligation to take account of the professional nature of the person for whom the service is provided. Clear distinction between professional and non-professional investors	105
6.20	Branch of an investment firm having its registered office outside the EU or the European Economic Area that carries on investment services in Ireland on a cross-border basis	106

7 OFFERS TO THE PUBLIC 109
Dermot Cahill and Anne-Marie Mooney Cotter

7.1	Introduction	109
7.2	Choice of legal regime governing the offer to the public	109
7.3	Offer to the public	111
7.4	Relaxation of requirement for a prospectus	114
7.5	Penalties for failure to publish a prospectus	116
7.6	Companies incorporated outside the State (Pt XII of the CA 1963) and the subsequent adoption of the principle of mutual recognition under the Prospectus Directive	117
7.7	Proposals for reform – EU Directive proposal on offers to the public	118
7.8	The American perspective	119
7.9	Recent events	120

8 INSIDER DEALING 123
John Darby

8.1	Introduction	123
8.2	The statutory regime	123
8.3	Definitions	123
8.4	The prohibition	125
8.5	Exemptions	126
8.6	Liability	127

9 THE IRISH STOCK EXCHANGE 133
John Darby

9.1	Introduction	133
9.2	Function	133
9.3	Equity markets	134
9.4	ITEQ® – the technology market of the Exchange	134
9.5	Irish Government bond market	134
9.6	Regulation of the Exchange background	135
9.7	Summary of the Stock Exchange Act 1995	135

10 MUTUAL FUNDS — 147
Joseph Gavin and Tracy Gilvarry

- 10.1 The main categories of Irish mutual funds — 147
- 10.2 Key features of unit trusts and investment companies — 148
- 10.3 Retail funds established as UCITS funds — 149
- 10.4 Non-UCITS retail and institutional funds — 151
- 10.5 Authorisation procedure for mutual funds — 154
- 10.6 Continuing requirements for mutual funds — 156
- 10.7 Taxation of mutual funds in Ireland — 157
- 10.8 Listing of mutual funds on the Irish Stock Exchange — 159
- 10.9 Prime brokers — 161
- 10.10 UCITS III — 162

11 INTERNATIONAL BANKING AND FINANCIAL SERVICES — 165
Niamh Moloney

- 11.1 Developments in EC financial services law — 165
- 11.2 International developments — 177

Index — 181

TABLE OF CASES

Ireland

AIB v Glynn [1973] IR 188	3.3.1
Bank of Ireland v Martin [1937] IR 189	3.5
Curran Construction Ltd v Bank of Ireland Finance Ltd (8 September 1976, unreported)	3.2.5.1
Deering v Hyndman (1886) 18 LR (IR) 323	4.3.1
Dempsey v Bank of Ireland (1963–93) Irish Company Law Reports 328	3.5.1
Forshall v Walsh (High Court, 18 June 1997, unreported, Shanley J)	2.1.3.3
Glow Heating Ltd v The Eastern Health Board [1988] IR 110	3.5.1, 4.3.1
Irish Shipping Ltd, Re [1986] ILRM 518	2.2.4
Keenan Bros, Re [1986] BCLC 2542	3.4.6
Kennedy v Allied Irish Banks plc [1998] 2 IR 48	2.1.3.4
Kinlan v Ulster Bank Ltd [1928] IR 171	2.1.1
McSweeney v Bourke and Investment Bank of Ireland (High Court, 24 November 1980, unreported, Denham J)	2.1.3.1
Northern Bank Finance Corp Ltd v Quinn & Achates Investment Co [1979] ILRM 221	3.2.1.1
Pyke v Hibernian Bank Ltd [1950] IR 195	2.1.3.2
Towey v Ulster Bank Ltd [1987] ILRM 142	2.1.3.1
Wogans Drogheda Ltd, Re [1993] 1 IR 154	3.4.6

Europe

Council Decision 99/468/EC (Comitology Decision)	11.1.3

England and Commonwealth

A Ltd, Re [2001] Lloyd's Law Rep: Banking 73–84	1.6.2
AG Hong Kong v Reid [1994 1 AC 324	1.6.2

Agip Africa v Jackson [1990] Ch 265	1.6.2
Agnew and Another v Commissioner of Inland Revenue (also known as Brumark Investments, Re) [2001] 3 WLR 454	3.4.5, 3.4.6
Allen v Hyatt (1914) 30 TLR 444	8.6.4.1
Baker v Australian and New Zealand Bank Ltd [1958] NZLR 907	2.1.3.2
BCCI v Akindele [2000] Lloyd's Law Rep: Banking 292	1.6.2
Bell Houses Ltd v Citywall Properties Ltd [1996] 2 All ER 674	3.2.1
Boardman v Phipps [1967] 2 AC 46	8.6.4.4
Bray v Ford [1896] AC 44	8.6.4.4
Brightlife Ltd, Re [1987] Ch 200	3.4.5
British Eagle International Airlines Ltd v Compagnie Nationale Air France [1975] 1 WLR 758	3.5.1, 4.3.1
Brumark Investments, Re [2001] 3 WLR 454	3.4.5, 3.4.6
Chase Manhattan Bank NA v Israel-British Bank (London) Ltd [1980] 2 WLR 202	2.2.4
Coleman v Myers [1977] 2 NZLR 225	8.6.4.3
Corporate Affairs Commission (South Australia) and Another v Australian Central Credit Union (1985) 59 ALJR 785	7.3
Cotman v Brougham [1918] AC 514	3.2.1
Derry v Peek (1889) 14 App Cas 337	8.6.4
Director General of Fair Trading v First National Bank plc [2000] 1 All ER 240	2.1.2.1–2.1.2.6
Falch v London and South Western Bank Ltd (1915) 31 TLR 334	2.1.3.2
Finers v Miró [1991] 1 WLR 35	1.6.2
Foley v Hill (1848) 2 HL Cas 28	2.1.1
Henderson v Merrett Syndicates Ltd [1994] 3 WLR 761	2.1.3.4
Illingsworth v Holdsworth [1904] AC 355	3.4.4
Interfoto Picture Library Ltd v Stiletto Visual Programmes Ltd [1989] QB 433	2.1.2
Introductions (Introductions Ltd v National Provincial Bank Ltd), Re [1968] 3 All ER 1221	3.2.1.1
Jayson v Midland Bank Ltd [1967] 2 Lloyd's Rep 563; [1968] 1 Lloyd's Rep 409	2.1.3.2
Joachimson v Swiss Bank Corp [1921] 3 KB 110	2.1.1
Kinwatt Holdings Ltd v Platform Ltd (1982) 6 ACLR 398	8.3.4
KPMG v Prince Jefri Bolkiah [1999] 2 AC 222	2.1.4
Kpohraror v Woolwich Building Society [1996] 4 All ER 119	2.1.3.2
Lee v Evans (1964) 112 CLR 276	7.3
Maxwell Communications Corp plc (No 2), Re [1994] 1 BCLC 1	4.3.1, 4.3.2

National Bank v Silke [1891] 1 QB 435	2.2.1.3
National Provincial Bank Ltd v Liddiard [1941] 1 Ch 158	
National Westminster Bank Ltd v Halesowen Presswork and Assemblies Ltd [1972] AC 785	4.3.1
New Bullis Trading, Re [1994] 1 BCLC 385	3.4.5
Nocton v Lord Ashburton [1914] AC 932	8.6.4.1
Percival v Wright [1902] 2 Ch 431	8.6.4.1, 8.6.4.2
Public Prosecutor v Allan Ng Poh Meng [1990] 1 MLJ v	8.3.5
Raafbye Corp Pty Ltd v Westpac Banking Corp Ltd (Supreme Court of New South Wales, 21 October 1994, unreported, Levine J)	2.1.3.2
Rogers v Challis (1859) 27 Beav 175	2.1.1
Sherwell v Combined Incandescent Mantle Syndicate (1907) 23 TLR 482	7.3
Siebe Gorman & Co Ltd v Barclays Bank Ltd [1979] 2 Lloyd's Rep 142	3.4.5
Smith New Court Securities Ltd v Scrimgeour Vickers (Asset Management) Ltd [1994] 1 WLR 1271	2.1.3.3
South of England Natural Gas, Re [1911] 1 Ch 573	7.3
Tai Hing Cotton Mill Ltd v Liu Chong Hing Bank Ltd [1986] AC 80	2.1.3.4
Telford Motors Ltd, Re (27 January 1978, unreported)	3.2.4.2
Tournier v National Provincial Bank [1924] 1 KB 461	2.1.5
Turner v Royal Bank of Scotland (1999) 143 SJ LB 123	2.1.5
Verity and Spindler v Lloyds Bank plc [1996] Fam Law 213	2.1.3.1
Westdeutsche Landesbank Girozentrale v Islington London Borough Council [1996] 2 All ER 961	2.2.4
Williams & Glyn's Bank Ltd v Barnes (English High Court, 26 March 1980, unreported, Gibson J)	2.1.1
Woods v Martins Bank Ltd [1959] 1 QB 55	2.1.4
Yorkshire Woolcombers Association Ltd, Re [1903] 2 Ch 284	3.4.4

International

Johnson v Wiggs 433 F 2d 803 (1971)	8.3.4
Nanus Asia Ltd v Standard Chartered Bank [1990] 1 HKLR 396	1.6.2
Strong v Repide 213 US 419 (1909)	8.6.4.2

TABLE OF LEGISLATION

Ireland

Statutes

Agricultural Credit Corporation Bank Act 1992	1.1
Asset Cover Securities Act 2001	1.7
Bankers' Books Evidence Act 1879	2.1.5
Bankruptcy Act 1988—	
s 57	3.5.3
s 58	3.5.3
s 59	3.5.3
Bills of Exchange Act 1882	2.2.1.5
s 73	2.2.1.1
Building Societies Act 1989	1.5.1
Central Bank Acts 1942–98	1.1
Central Bank Acts 1971–97	4.5
Central Bank Act 1942	1.1.1
Central Bank Act 1971	1.1.1, 1.1.2
s 2	1.1.1
s 8(2)	4.5
s 8(2)(a)	1.1.1
s 17	1.4
s 18	1.4
s 21	1.4
s 24	1.4
s 27	1.4
s 28A	1.4
Central Bank Act 1989	1.1.1, 1.1.2
s 16	1.7
s 36	1.4
s 37	1.4
s 38	1.4
s 44	1.4
s 47	1.7
s 117	2.1.6
Central Bank Act 1997	1.1.1, 1.1.2
s 70(b)	1.1.1
s 70(e)	1.4
s 74	1.4
Central Bank Act 1997 (contd)—	
s 75	1.4
Central Bank Act 1998	1.1.1, 1.1.2
Cheques Act 1959	2.2.1.4
Companies Acts 1963–2001	4.3.2, 9.1, 9.7.2
Companies Act 1963—	
s 2(1)	7.2.1
s 8(1)	3.2.1.2
s 19	4.4
s 33(1)(c)	4.4
s 43	4.6
s 44	7.2.2, 7.3
s 44(1)	4.6, 7.2.1
s 44(3)	7.2.1
s 44(4)(a)	7.3, 7.4.1, 7.4.1
s 44(7)(b)	7.4.1
s 44(8)	7.5.1, 7.5.3
s 45	4.6
s 47	4.6, 7.5.1, 7.5.2
s 47(1)	4.4
s 47(1)(c)	4.4
s 47(2)	4.4
s 49	4.6
s 50	4.6, 7.5.1, 7.5.2, 7.5.3
s 56(1)	4.4
s 57(1)	4.4
s 60	3.2.3
s 60(4)	3.2.3
s 61	7.4.1
s 61(2)	7.3
s 61(3)	4.4, 4.6
s 99	3.2.4.3, 3.6
s 99(1)	3.2.4
s 99(2)	3.2.4
s 106	3.2.4.2
s 109	3.2.4.3
s 111	3.2.4.3
s 139	3.5.3
s 180	8.5
s 216(1)	4.3.2
s 275	4.3.1

Companies Act 1963 (contd)—		Consumer Credit Act 1995	2.1.7
s 286	3.2.5.1, 3.2.5.2, 3.5.3	Pt III	2.1.7.1
s 286(5)	3.2.5.1	Pt V	5.6.3
s 288	3.2.4.1, 3.2.5.4	Pt XII	1.7
s 361(2)	4.6	Conveyancing Act 1881—	
s 362	4.6	s 16	3.3.4
s 363	4.6	s 19	3.3.3
Sched 3	7.1, 7.2.1, 7.2.2, 7.4.1, 7.5.1	s 20	3.3.3
Pt III	4.4	s 24	3.3.3
Pt IV	3.2.4	Conveyancing Act (Ireland) 1634	3.2.5.3
Pt XII	7.1, 7.6	Copyright and Related Rights Act 2000	3.6
Companies Act 1990	4.3.2, 8.3.5, 10.4.1	Credit Union Act 1997	1.5.2
s 25	3.2.2.1	Criminal Justice Act 1994	1.6.1, 5.6.10, 6.17, 10.3.5
s 25(3)	3.2.2.1	s 31	1.6.1
s 26	3.2.2.2	s 31(8)	1.6.1
s 31	3.2.2, 3.2.2.3, 3.2.2.4	s 32	1.6.1
s 32	3.2.2.3	s 57	1.6.1, 2.1.5
s 34	3.2.2.3	s 58(2)	1.6.1
s 35	3.2.2.3	Criminal Justice (Theft and Fraud Offences) Act 2001—	
s 36	3.2.2.3	s 21	1.6.1
s 37	3.2.2.3		
s 38	3.2.2.4	Data Protection Act 1998	2.1.5
s 38(2)	3.2.2.4	Family Home Protection Act 1976—	
s 39	3.2.2.4	s 7	3.3.3
s 40	3.2.2.4	Finance Act 1991	4.2
s 107	8.3.1, 8.3.2, 8.6.1	Finance Act 1995—	
s 108	8.3.3, 8.6.2	s 36	10.7.1
s 108(1)	8.4.1	Finance Act 2000	10.7.1, 10.7.4, 10.7.5
s 108(2)	8.4.1	Financial Transfers Act 1992	1.7
s 108(3)	8.4.2	Industrial Designs Act 2001	3.6
s 108(7)	8.5.1	Insurance Act 2000—	
s 108(8)	8.5.2	s 16(2)	1.1.1.1
s 108(10)	8.5.6	Investment Intermediaries Act 1995	5.1.1, 5.2, 5.3.1–5.3.5, 5.4, 5.5.1.1–5.5.1.3, 5.5.2.1–5.5.2.3, 5.5.3.1, 5.5.3.2, 5.6.1, 5.6.2, 5.6.2.4, 5.6.6.1, 5.6.7, 5.6.7.1, 5.6.8, 5.6.9, 5.7.1, 5.7.1.1, 5.7.12, 5.7.13, 5.7.1.5– 5.7.1.8, 5.7.2, 5.8.1, 6.1, 6.2.3, 6.6, 6.10, 6.11, 6.14, 6.17, 6.18
s 109	8.6.1		
s 111	8.6.2		
s 112	8.6.2		
s 113	8.5.5		
s 122	3.6		
s 132	4.3.1		
s 135	3.2.5.1		
s 136	3.2.5.4		
s 139	3.2.5.2		
s 140	4.3		
s 223	8.5.3		
Pt III	3.2.2		
Pt V	8.2, 8.3, 8.5.4	s 9(2)	6.19, 6.20
Pt XIII	5.3.5, 10.7.2	s 10	6.9
Company Law Enforcement Act 2001	3.2.2.2	s 10(3)	6.8
s 75	3.2.2.1	s 10(5)	6.6
s 76	3.2.2.2	s 10(5)(a)	6.4
s 78	3.2.2.3	s 10(5)(d)	6.4
s 79	3.2.2.3	s 10(7)	6.7
ss 75–79	3.2.2		
Pt IX	3.2.2		

TABLE OF LEGISLATION

Investment Intermediaries Act 1995 (contd)—	
s 10(10)	6.3
s 15	6.14
s 18	6.14
s 23	6.19
s 24	6.19
s 37	6.11, 6.16, 6.19
s 37(1)	6.16
s 37(1)(f)	6.13
s 52	6.5, 6.11
Investment Limited Partnerships Act 1994	5.3.5, 10.4.1
Investor Competition Act 1998	5.6.8
Larceny Act 1861—	
s 84	7.5
Netting of Financial Contracts Act 1995	3.5.3
s 4	3.5.3
Patents Act 1992—	
s 85(1)	3.6
Registry of Deeds (Ireland) Act 1707	3.3.5
Registration of Title Act 1964	3.3.1
Statute of Limitations 1957	2.1.8
Stock Exchange Act 1995	5.2, 6.1, 6.2, 6.2.2, 6.10, 6.11, 6.14, 6.15, 6.17, 6.18, 9.6, 9.7
s 8	9.7.1
s 9	9.7.2
s 11	9.7.3
s 12	9.7.4
s 13	9.7.5
s 14	9.7.6
s 15	9.7.7
s 17	9.7.8
s 18	9.7.9
s 18(3)	6.8
s 18(5)(d)	6.4
s 18(5)(e)	6.6
s 18(11)	6.3
s 20	9.7.10
s 21	9.7.11
s 22	9.7.12
s 23	6.14, 9.7.13
s 24	9.7.14
s 25	9.7.15
s 26	6.14, 9.7.16
s 27	9.7.17
s 28	9.7.18
s 29	9.7.19

Stock Exchange Act 1995 (contd)—	
s 30	9.7.20
s 31	6.19, 9.7.21
s 32	6.19, 9.7.21
s 33	9.7.22
s 34	9.7.22
s 37	9.7.23
s 38	6.11, 6.16, 6.19, 9.7.24
s 38(1)(f)	6.13
s 40	9.7.25
s 41	9.7.25
s 42	9.7.25
s 44	9.7.25
s 45	9.7.25
s 46	9.7.25
s 48	9.7.25
s 51	9.7.26
s 52	6.5, 6.11, 9.7.27
s 56	9.7.28
s 57	9.7.29, 9.7.30
s 62	9.7.30
s 63	9.7.30
s 64	9.7.31
s 65	9.7.31
Sched 1	9.7.19
Sched 2	9.7.31
Taxes Consolidation Act 1997—	
s 110	4.2
Trade Marks Act 1996—	
s 29(1)	3.6
s 29(2)	3.6
s 29(3)	3.6
Trustee Savings Bank Act 1989	1.1
Unit Trusts Act 1990	5.3.5

Statutory instruments

Companies (Recognition of Countries) Order 1964 (SI 1964/42)	7.6
Contracts Negotiated Away from Business Premises Regulations	2.1.7
European Communities (Companies) Regulations 1973 (SI 1973/163)—	
Reg 6	3.2.1.2
European Communities (Deposit Guarantee Schemes) Regulations 1995 (SI 1995/168)	1.7
European Communities (Finality of Settlement in Payment and Securities Settlement Systems) Regulations 1998 (SI 1998/539)	2.2.3

European Communities (Licensing and
    Supervision of Credit Institutions) 1992
    (SI 1992/395) 1.1.1, 1.1.2, 1.4, 1.5.1, 1.5.2
  Reg 16   1.2, 1.3
European Communities (Stock Exchange)
    Regulations 1984 (SI 1984/282)   4.6, 9.3
  Reg 6(2)   7.5.3
  Reg 6(3)   7.5.3
  Reg 12   4.6
  Reg 12(2)   7.2.3
  Reg 12(3)   7.2.3, 7.5.3
  Reg 13   4.6
European Communities (Stock Exchange)
    (Amendment) Regulations 1991
    (SI 1991/18)   4.6
European Communities (Transferable
    Securities and Stock Exchange)
    Regulations 1992 (SI 1992/202)   4.4, 7.2.3,
                                      7.3, 7.4.1, 7.4.2
  Reg 7   4.2
  Reg 8   7.2.2
  Reg 8(2)   7.2.2
  Reg 11   7.5.2
  Reg 20   7.5.2
  Reg 21(3)   7.2.2, 7.6
  Reg 21(4)   7.2.2, 7.5.2
European Communities (Undertakings
    for Collective Investments in
    Transferable Securities) Regulations
    1989 (SI 1989/78)   6.2.2
European Communities (Unfair Terms
    in Consumer Contracts Regulations)
    1995 (SI 1995/27)   2.1.1, 2.1.2, 2.1.2.1,
                              2.1.6, 10.1.1, 10.3
  Reg 3(2)   2.1.2
  Reg 4   2.1.2
  Reg 69   10.1.1.1, 10.3.1, 10.3.6.2, 10.3.6.3
  Pt VII   10.1.1.1, 10.3.2, 10.3.6.2, 10.3.6.3
  Sched 2   2.1.2
  Sched 3   2.1.2

Trade Marks Rules 1996 (SI 1996/199)   3.6

Europe

Treaties and Conventions

Basle Accord 1988   1.3, 11.2.2

Treaty of Rome Establishing the
    European Communities 1957—
  Art 251   11.1.3

Directives

64/225/EEC (Insurance Undertakings
    Directive)   5.3.5
73/239/EEC (activity of direct
    insurance other than life assurance)—
  Art 1   5.3.5
77/780/EEC (First Banking
    Directive)   1.1.1, 5.3.5
79/267/EEC (activity of direct life
    assurance)—
  Art 1   5.3.5
79/279/EEC (Admissions Directive)   4.6
  Art 3(e)   7.2.2
80/390/EEC (Listing Particulars
    Directive)   4.6, 7.2.3, 7.7, 9.3
82/121/EEC (Interim Reports Directive)   4.6
85/611/EEC (UCITS
    Directive)   5.3.5, 10.1.1, 10.3, 11.2
87/345/EEC (co-ordinating the
    requirements for the drawing-up,
    scrutiny and distribution of the
    listing particulars to be published
    for the admission of securities to
    official stock exchange listing)   7.2.3
88/220/EEC (investment policies
    of certain UCITS)   10.1.1
89/298/EEC (Prospectus
    Directive)   4.4, 7.1, 7.2.1, 7.2.2,
                          7.3, 7.4.1, 7.7,
                          11.1.2, 11.1.4
  Art 1.1   7.2.2
  Art 1.2   7.4.2
  Art 2.2   7.4.2
  Art 3(e)   7.2.2
  Art 5   7.4.2
  Art 2.1   7.3
  Art 11   7.2.2
89/592/EEC (Insider Dealing
    Directive)   8.2, 11.1.2, 11.1.4
  Art 10   11.1.7
  Art 11   11.1.5, 11.1.7
89/646/EEC (Second Banking
    Directive)   1.1.1, 5.3.5
89/647/EEC (Solvency Ratio
    Directive)   6.7
90/211/EEC (mutual recognition
    of public offer prospectuses as
    stock exchange listing particulars)   7.2.3

91/308/EEC (counteracting
 money laundering) 5.6.10, 6.17, 10.3.5
93/6/EEC (Capital Adequacy
 Directive) 5.5.3.2, 6.7,
 11.1.2, 11.1.7
93/13/EEC (unfair terms in
 consumer contracts) 2.1.2, 2.1.4
93/22/EU (Investment Services
 Directive) 5.1.1, 5.2, 5.3.1,
 6.1, 6.2, 6.7, 6.15, 6.17,
 6.18, 6.19, 6.20, 11.1.2
 Art 3 6.4, 6.9
 Art 3(1) 6.3
 Art 3(3) 6.4
 Art 10 6.11, 6.14
 Art 11 6.16
 Annex 6.3, 6.10
94/18/EEC (co-ordinating the
 requirements for the drawing up,
 scrutiny and distribution of the
 listing particulars to be published
 for the admission of securities to
 official stock exchange listing, with
 regard to the obligation to publish
 listing particulars) 7.2.3
95/26/EC (amending Directives
 77/780/EEC and 89/646/EEC in
 the field of credit institutions,
 73/239/EEC and 92/49/EEC in
 the field of non-life insurance,
 79/267/EEC and 92/96/EEC in
 the field of life assurance, 93/22/EEC
 in the field of investment firms and
 85/611/EEC in the field of undertakings
 for collective investment in transferable
 securities, with a view to reinforcing
 prudential supervision) 11.1.2
97/9/EC (Investor Compensation
 Schemes Directive) 5.6.8, 11.1.2
98/31/EC (amending Directive
 93/6/EEC on the capital adequacy
 of investment firms and credit
 institutions) 11.1.2

00/12/EC (Codified Banking Directive) 1.1.1,
 1.3, 4.5
00/13/EC (E-Commerce Directive) 11.1.5
 Art 2(3) 11.1.5
 Art 3(1) 11.1.5
 Art 3(2) 11.1.5
 Art 3(3) 1.1.5
 Art 3(4) 11.1.5
 Art 11 11.1.5
01/34/EC (Securities Consolidation
 Directive) 11.1.2, 11.1.4
01/107/EC (Management
 Companies Directive) 10.10, 10.10.2
01/108/EC (Product Directive) 10.10, 10.10.1
02/65/EC (Distance Marketing
 of Financial Services
 Directive) 11.1.5, 11.1.6

Regulation

EC/1606/02 (application of
 international accounting standards) 11.1.4

England

Statute

Criminal Justice Act 1993 8.3
Partnership Act 1890 3.2.2.2

United States of America

Statutes

Securities Act 1933 7.8
 s 2(10) 7.8
 s 4(1) 7.8
Securities Exchange Act 1934 7.8
 s 4(a) 7.8
 s 21 7.8
 s 21A 7.8
 s 21B 7.8
 s 21C 7.8

CHAPTER 1

INTRODUCTION TO BANKING LAW

John Breslin

There are many facets to banking law. Banks perform a wide range of services, and in relation to ever more sophisticated types of financial instrument. The days are long gone when a bank merely took deposits and lent money, opening its doors in the late morning, and closing in the middle of the afternoon. Nowadays, a bank will offer – in some instances on a 24-hour basis through electronic banking media – such additional services as stock broking, securities custody, acting as insurance intermediary, small business adviser, and, depending on the sophistication and business needs of the customer, dealings in foreign exchange and financial derivatives. Accordingly, a bank increasingly no longer only acts as debtor and creditor and agent merely with regard to effecting and receipt of payments; it also acts as adviser, custodian, and other types of fiduciary agent.

In addition to this increased exposure to common law and contractual liabilities, banking business (along with other types of financial service provision) is a highly regulated industry. Accordingly, the range of statute law applicable to a bank and its activities has expanded exponentially in recent times.

There is, accordingly, a vast amount of case and statute law dealing with such issues as the regulation of banking activities, the treatment of payments within bank accounts, set-off of accounts, interest, and the general obligations of a bank to its customer. A full treatment of the law of banking is to be found in the standard texts. The purpose of this chapter and the next, however, is to give a comprehensive overview of two areas: first, the regulation of banks; and secondly, the law relating to the bank-customer relationship and payment mechanisms.

This chapter will deal with the following topics:

- The statutory regulation of banks.
- The use of EU 'passport' rights.
- Financial regulation and management systems.
- Regulatory powers and duties.
- The regulation of building societies and credit unions.
- Money laundering.
- Miscellaneous regulatory issues.

1.1 The statutory regulation of banks

Banks are regulated under the Central Bank Acts (the CBAs) 1942–98. There is a separate Act for trustee savings banks (Trustee Savings Bank 1989) and a separate Act in respect of the institution formerly known as the Agricultural Credit Corporation – ACC Bank plc. This is the ACC Bank Act 1992. However, this mirrors and incorporates the Central Bank legislative code, which applies to all other banks. At the time of writing, the scheme for the regulation of banks and other financial institutions in Ireland is in the process of undergoing wholesale amendment pursuant to what will be the Irish Financial Services Regulatory Authority Act, and anticipated ancillary legislation. Accordingly, the status quo will be summarised, together with anticipated reforms.

1.1.1 The status quo

The key Act underpinning the regulation of banks in Ireland is the Central Bank Act (CBA) 1971. It was substantially amended by the CBA 1989 and the CBA 1997. Broadly speaking, the CBA 1989 implements the First Banking Directive (77/780/EEC) which was the EC provision that harmonised the regulatory systems for banks across the European Community. Prior to the First Banking Directive, the respective schemes for the regulation of banks in Member States were varied, reflected local regulatory policies, and in general did not achieve equivalent levels of regulation. Accordingly, the harmonisation of those levels was seen as an essential pre-requisite to the establishment of a single market in banking. In addition, the existence of a variety of levels of regulation within the European Community was rightly seen as a recipe for forum shopping for those seeking to establish a bank.

Once an acceptable level of harmonisation was achieved by the First Banking Directive, there then followed, much later on, a Second Banking Directive (89/646/EEC), which was designed to ensure that a bank licensed in one Member State could easily start doing business in another Member State. (In 2000, a codifying directive was passed incorporating the Second Banking Directive and some of the financial supervision directives referred to below: Directive 00/12/EC (Codified Banking Directive).) Prior to the enactment of the Second Banking Directive, a bank which established or provided services in another Member State would have to seek a licence from the host State, and in many cases deposit with the host State regulator, a significant sum effectively by way of insurance in respect of its obligations incurred there. Such deposits were wasted capital and the requirement to obtain host State authorisation was an impediment to the development of a single market in financial services.

The Second Banking Directive was implemented by the European Communities (Licensing and Supervision of Credit Institutions) Regulations 1992 (SI 1992/395) (the 1992 Regulations). Broadly speaking, the thrust of the CBA 1971, CBA 1989 and the CBA 1997 (as supplemented by the 1992 Regulations) is to ensure that there is a rigorous licensing system in place for the carrying on of banking business, which is harmonised with systems in other EU States. This form of licensing is now referred to as 'authorisation'.

The CBA 1942 established the Central Bank of Ireland (CBI) as the agency entrusted with the control of monetary policy in Ireland. Since the establishment of the European Central Bank (ECB), which operates out of Frankfurt, and in anticipation of the introduction of the euro, that role was significantly diminished. The major scaling down of the CBI's powers was effected by the CBA 1998. The regulatory structure will again be fundamentally altered by the passing of the Irish Financial Services Authority of Ireland Bill 2001. This will establish the Irish Financial Services Authority as an overall regulatory body for all financial services, including banking, investment business and insurance. (The effect of this proposed legislation will be discussed in some more detail further below.)

Banking business, broadly speaking, means taking deposits from the public. There has, curiously enough, never been a statutory definition of banking business. However, the Second Banking Directive sets out a list of activities carried on by credit institutions. (In this regard it is important to note that, according to the lexicon of the Banking Directives, a bank is merely a subset of a general class – namely it is a type of credit institution: other types of credit institution include – so far as Irish law is concerned – building societies, credit unions and friendly societies.)

The core banking activities envisaged by the Second Banking Directive are taking funds from the public and granting credit. However, that Directive also provides a longer list of banking activities for the purposes of EU law – although it is important to recognise that not all such activities require a licence; indeed, the granting of credit does not necessarily require a licence under Irish law. The EU definition of banking activities is as follows:

(a) taking deposits;
(b) lending;
(c) financial leasing;
(d) money transmission services;
(e) issuing and administering means of payment;
(f) providing guarantees;
(g) trading in money market instruments, foreign exchange, financial futures and options, etc both on own account and as agent;
(h) participating in securities issues and providing ancillary services;
(i) corporate finance advice;
(j) money broking;
(k) portfolio management and advice;
(l) safekeeping and administration of securities;
(m) credit reference services; and
(n) safe custody services.

It will be seen from the above that not all such activities fall within one's traditional concept of what a high street bank does.

Under s 2(6)(h) of the Investment Intermediaries Act 1995 (the 1995 Act) (as amended by s 16(2) of the Insurance Act 2000), an authorised credit institution is exempted from the need to become authorised under that Act. This is convenient for many institutions, because as noted above, banks increasingly provide investment services (for example, stockbroking, advice on investments, etc). Accordingly, it means that a bank does not need to become authorised under the 1995 Act in addition to being authorised under the CBAs, when it provides investment services (as defined by the 1995 Act).

An application for a banking licence is made to the CBI. The precise current requirements for authorisation were set out in its 1995 Quarterly Bulletin, and in addition are to be found on the CBI's website. Broadly speaking, the applicant must have shareholder funds of at least €6.35 million; its owners and management must be fit and proper; it must be organised in a transparent manner; and any parent undertaking will be required to furnish a letter of comfort to the CBI in respect of any future liabilities of the bank once it becomes authorised; if its parent undertaking is not involved in financial services then the CBI must be satisfied that there is no risk of business contagion (that is, that the non-banking business will affect the solvency of the bank).

Because, however, of the breadth of the definition of taking deposits and other repayable funds from the public, a practical difficulty that can arise is when one has a company which is proposing to raise funds by way of debt, where the debt instruments (for example, bonds, loan notes, etc) are to be issued among a wide range of investors. The definition of 'banking business' for the purposes of domestic Irish law is contained in s 2 of the CBA 1971 (as substituted by s 70(b) of the CBA 1997). This provides that banking business includes:

(a) the business of accepting, on own account, sums of money from the public in the form of deposits *or other repayable funds* whether or not involving the issue of securities or other obligations, howsoever described, or

(b) the business aforesaid and any other business normally carried on by a bank, which may involve the granting of credits on own account.

The difficulty arises from the use of the phrase 'or other repayable funds'. When a company raises money in the debt market, it is of course repayable. However, by doing so the company could inadvertently find itself carrying on banking business, for example, by soliciting funds from a significant number of potential investors. There is nothing in the CBAs which states that one only needs a banking licence if one solicits funds from private investors. So a solicitation from a number of sophisticated large corporate investors could trigger the need for a banking licence. To an extent, CBI comes to the aid of the company through its Commercial Paper Exemption, 12 November 2002 (issued under s 8(2)(a) of the CBA 1971). In broad terms, the terms of the exemption depend on the size of the company issuing the debt instruments, the value of the securities, and the maturity of the debt being issued. In summary, the Commercial Paper Exemption provides as follows.

1.1.1.1 Securities with maturity date of less than one year

The exemption is available for three classes of person. The classes depend on whether the issuer is issuing securities with an original maturity of less than one year (referred to as 'commercial paper'), and whether or not the securities are 'asset-backed' (namely where the holder of the security can have recourse upon the issuer's default to specified assets). Irrespective of the class of person, however, the purchasers of such securities must be made aware that the securities do not have the status of bank deposit, are not within the scope of the Deposit Protection Scheme (see below), and the issuer is not regulated by the Central Bank.

The three classes of exemptee are as follows (in summary):

1. An issuer of commercial paper (other than asset-backed commercial paper) which has paid up share capital of €25 million (or the foreign currency equivalent), or whose obligations are guaranteed by its parent which has paid up share capital of €25 million (or the foreign currency equivalent), or which is an EU authorised bank, or OECD State. The security must be issued in minimum amounts of €125,000.

2. An issuer of asset-backed commercial paper where the asset cover is at least 100%, and where the paper is rated to at least investment grade by a recognised rating agency, and which is issued in minimum amounts of €300,000.

3. An issuer of securities with an original maturity date of more than one year so long as it complies with applicable corporate securities law of Ireland (or any other jurisdiction), or which is an OECD (Organisation for Economic Co-operation and Development) Member State.

1.1.2 The proposed new regime

As noted above, the Central Bank and Financial Services Authority of Ireland Bill 2002 (and anticipated ancillary draft legislation) envisages that the CBI will be reconstituted. It will have, as a constituent part, the Irish Financial Services and Regulatory Authority (IFSRA). This will be the body charged with the regulation of the whole of the financial services industry in Ireland. The IFSRA will have a consumer director, who will be charged with the protection and promotion of consumer interests. The IFSRA will have an innovative role – namely to educate and inform the investing public. The IRSRA will also have responsibility for the Deposit Protection Scheme (see below) and the Investor Compensation Scheme. There will be a Financial Services Ombudsman and the scheme for the processing of regulatory and supervisory enforcement actions will be radically overhauled and streamlined by the establishment of a Financial Services Tribunal.

Unfortunately, the new Act will not codify existing legislation. Instead, it operates to effect quite substantial amendments to the CBA 1971 (an Act which is itself heavily amended by the CBAs 1989, 1997, 1998, and the 1992 Regulations – see below). Accordingly, the statutory scheme will become more – not less – complex and cumbersome.

1.2 The 1992 Regulations

As noted above, before 1992, there were barriers in each EU Member State preventing or inhibiting banks from trading in jurisdictions other than that in which they were formed and obtained a licence. So if a bank established in, for example, Portugal, wanted to set up a branch in Ireland, it would have to seek a separate authorisation from the CBI notwithstanding that it had an authorisation from another Member State. This was not only inconvenient but also expensive, because it meant that the bank had to separately capitalise the local branch. Accordingly, it had to move capital to Ireland as a form of insurance deposit for the CBI. This was wasted capital, because the money did not earn any return – it merely sat in the CBI's coffers as cover for potential default by the Portuguese institution.

The single market project sought to establish a system whereby a bank or other credit institution authorised in one Member State could use its authorisation as a 'passport' with which it could do business freely in other Member States. This was the function of the Second Banking Directive. This Directive is implemented by the 1992 Regulations.

Under these Regulations (and their equivalent in other Member States), a bank incorporated in one Member State can now freely do business in other Member States without the need to obtain a separate authorisation there and without the need to dedicate capital to that other branch. The bank can also carry on business in another Member State by providing services into that State without establishing a branch there.

When a bank is using its passport to do business in another Member State, its business there is only supervised by the host State regulator in the interests of the 'common good' – namely consumer protection and customer treatment. The host State regulator has no role in carrying out the financial supervision of the bank. This is for the home State regulator alone.

Broadly speaking, if an Irish credit institution seeks to do business in another Member State, it must inform the CBI, which must immediately inform the regulator in the host State so that it can prepare for supervision in the host State not later than two months after the initial notification. The CBI cannot raise objections to the proposal, unless it has concerns as to the financial viability of the Irish bank.

If, however, the credit institution seeks to do business in the host State without establishing a branch there (for example, by way of direct marketing), then it must inform the CBI, and the host State regulator who has a month in which to prepare the supervision of the Irish bank's activities there. Once again, the basis on which the CBI can object to this is extremely limited.

It should also be noted that a wholly owned subsidiary (or at least 90% owned subsidiary – referred to as a 'financial institution') of a credit institution can 'piggy-back' on its parent's passport rights. However, it should be noted that a 'financial institution' cannot avail of these rights if the business it proposes to conduct in the host State includes the taking of deposits. In such a case, the 'financial institution' will have to obtain a banking authorisation in either its home or the host State. In all other cases, however, if X Ltd is a 95% owned subsidiary of an Irish authorised bank, X Ltd is permitted to establish in another Member State or provide services into another Member State without having to obtain an authorisation there. Various conditions must be satisfied before these 'piggy-back' rights can be availed of, for example, the parent must guarantee the obligations of the subsidiary, and the subsidiary must already be carrying on the relevant type of business in the home State.

It should also be noted that the 1992 Regulations not only provide for the passport procedure, but also impact on purely domestic regulation. For example, Reg 16 of the 1992 Regulations made it a criminal offence for a bank or other credit institution not to have in place proper administrative and control mechanisms appropriate for its business.

1.3 Financial regulation

Financial regulation is a highly complex area and is, in the main, the day to day issue of most concern to banks, their internal financial compliance experts, and their outside auditors. Financial regulation is effected by means of a number of CBI notices, which implement the many financial supervision directives issued by the EU (now mainly consolidated by the 2000 Codified Banking Directive referred to above). Broadly speaking, these requirements reflect the work conducted by the leading (G10) banking regulators, referred to as the 'Basle Committee'. In 1988, the first Basle Accord was agreed. This has become the template for financial regulation both at EU level, and throughout the OECD.

Very briefly, the components of a bank's regulatory capital are its 'own funds' – basically core capital such as equity share capital, topped up in certain permissible manners (for example, by way of subordinated loans), and its 'solvency ratio' – basically a financial cushion to cover certain market and borrower risks, and its liquidity requirements – which is the banker's art of predicting how much money will be required on a given day. Where the bank carries on investment business (namely, dealing in stocks, bonds, derivatives and other financial instruments), its regulatory capital must be supplemented to cover investment type risks under the Capital Adequacy Directive (93/6/EEC), for example, from adverse movements in share or index prices, and currency valuations. Furthermore, the scheme is also intended to operate to control the concentration on large exposures by a credit institution to (a) single borrowers, (b) single groups of connected borrowers, and (c) industry sectors. Risk on the investment side is also measured by an assessment of the possibility of the bank's counter-parties defaulting on their obligations to the bank (counter-party risk).

Clearly, banking is a complex business, and banks and other credit institutions are highly sophisticated forms of business operations. To this end, Reg 16 of the 1992 Regulations inserted a provision requiring a bank to have in place proper systems for the monitoring and management of its business. Although this is a criminal penalty and is not an indictable offence, it is clearly a highly important regulatory tool in the modern high-risk business environment banks operate in. Furthermore, its utility as a means of shareholder action should not be ruled out.

It is proposed that the existing scheme for regulation, which flowed from the 1988 Basle Accord, will be replaced in the next few years by 'Basle II'.

1.4 Regulatory powers and duties

The powers of the CBI as regulator for the Irish banking industry are very wide indeed. The principal regulatory tools available to the CBI include the ability to send inspectors into a bank, and ultimately the ability to revoke a bank's licence.

The CBI has the following important additional regulatory powers:

(a) monitoring through periodic and ad hoc demands for information and documentation (ss 17 and 18 of the CBA 1971 (as substituted by ss 36 and 37 of the CBA 1989));

(b) the issuing of directions to a credit institution under s 21 of the CBA 1971 (as substituted by s 38 of the CBA 1989);

(c) regulations to cover depleted assets and settle clearances (s 24 of the CBA 1971);

(d) application for injunction to prevent contravention of CBA (s 28A of the CBA 1971 (as inserted by s 44 of the CBA 1989));

(e) enforcement powers over 'passporting' institutions under the 1992 Regulations;

(f) powers of inspection under s 75 of the CBA 1997;

(g) control of deposit advertisements under s 27 of the CBA 1971 (as substituted by s 70(e) of the CBA 1997); and

(h) an injunction to restrain unauthorised banking business under s 74 of the CBA 1997.

1.5 Building societies and credit unions

As noted above, banks are a mere subset within the overall category of credit institutions. The most common form of non-bank credit institutions in Ireland are building societies and credit unions.

1.5.1 Building societies

Building societies are regulated by CBI under the Building Societies Act (BSA 1989). The powers of building societies to engage in financial activities other than their core business of deposit taking and lending on mortgages was expanded significantly by that Act in order to enable societies to compete more effectively with banks. However, such powers have to be specifically adopted by the society and, in some cases, approved by the CBI.

A building society enjoys 'passporting' rights under the 1992 Regulations (ie, the right to use its Irish authorisation to do business in other Member States).

1.5.2 Credit unions

Credit unions are an important force in the retail banking sector. They have their own legislative history and are regulated by the Registrar for Friendly Societies under the Credit Union Act (CUA) 1997. It is proposed that the IFSRA will take over this role in the future.

A credit union does not enjoy 'passporting' rights under the 1992 Regulations (ie, the right to use its Irish authorisation to do business in other Member States).

1.6 Money laundering

1.6.1 Criminal law

Money laundering is a significant threat to the stability and integrity of the financial system. To that end, the EU enacted a money laundering Directive the scheme of which is to place on the financial system the onus of spotting and preventing money laundering activities. The Directive was enacted in Ireland by the Criminal Justice Act (CJA) 1994 (as amended).

The thrust of the Act requires banks and other financial institutions to train themselves to spot potential money laundering offences. They must 'know their customer' (s 32 of the CJA 1994). Then they must report suspicious transactions to the police (s 57). A report by a bank under the 1994 Act of a suspicious transaction does not, however, amount to a breach of its duty of confidentiality owed to its customers (as to which see Chapter 2 below). In deciding whether or not to convict an institution for the offence of failing to notify a suspicious transaction, the court may take into account industry guidance on reporting. Industry guidance was drawn up by the CBI, in conjunction with the Revenue Commissioners and the banking industry. It is an offence to fail to report a suspicious transaction.

It is also an offence for a bank to 'tip off' a suspect that his activities have been reported to the police (s 58(2)).

However, crucially, the offence of secondary money laundering has recently been amended in an important manner (s 31 of the CJA 1994, as amended by s 21 of the Criminal Justice (Theft and Fraud Offences) Act (CJ(TFO)A) 2001). The new provision expands significantly on the potential liability for a bank or other credit institution, in that the mental state connected with the handling or assisting limb of the offence is broadened considerably.

Section 31 of the CJA 1994 (as amended by s 21 of the CJ(TFO)A 2001) now provides as follows:

> 31(1) A person is guilty of money laundering if, knowing or believing that property is or represents the proceeds of criminal conduct or being reckless as to whether it is or represents such proceeds, the person, without lawful authority or excuse (the proof of which shall lie on him or her) ...
> (c)   acquires, possesses or uses the property.

The significant change effected by this provision is that it is no longer necessary for the prosecution to prove that the bank had a criminal or dishonest intent. Under the section as originally enacted, broadly speaking, the bank would only be liable if it engaged in laundering (a) for the purpose of assisting the primary offender, or (b) dishonestly. Mere knowledge or belief that the money represented the proceeds of crime was not – of itself – sufficient to bring in a conviction. Indeed, this was entirely logical because such a state of mind triggers the reporting obligation under s 57 of the CJA 1994.

Under the provision as amended, the very state of mind required to trigger the reporting obligation could well constitute the state of mind required for the offence of acquisition, use and possession. Accordingly, at the very moment the bank comes under a legal obligation (enforceable by criminal sanction) to report a suspicious transaction, it automatically commits a criminal offence by reason of its use and possession of the assets. By making the report as required by the Act, the bank is, in effect, also signaling that one has the necessary state of mind to ground a conviction. To relieve against the rigours of this potential double jeopardy, a new s 31(8) of the CJA 1994 provides as follows:

> (8)   Where –
> (a)   a report is made by a person or body to the Garda Síochána under section 57 of this Act in relation to property referred to in this section, or
> (b)   a person or body (other than a person or body suspected of committing an offence under this section) is informed by the Garda Síochána that property in the possession of the person or body is property referred to in this section,

the person or body shall not commit an offence under this section or under section 58 [the anti-tipping off provision] of this Act if and so long as the person or body complies with the directions of the Garda Síochána in relation to the property.

Accordingly, the directions of the Garda Síochána become a vital element: without such directions, the bank commits the 'use and possession' offence automatically where circumstances arise in which it must make a report under s 57 of the CJA 1994.

It follows, therefore, that the legal protection afforded by the direction is only effective if such directions are issued immediately a report is made. If not, the bank will be operating in a 'limbo' period, where it is actually in breach of the criminal law merely by holding the deposit. The legal position resulting from the amendments made by the CJ(TFO)A 2001 are clearly unsatisfactory from a bank's point of view.

1.6.2 Civil liability

Civil liability for money laundering arises from the doctrine of constructive trusteeship. The doctrine of constructive trusteeship basically means that if a person is aggrieved by a wrongdoer's breach of trust, any third party (for example, a bank) intermeddling by rendering assistance to the wrongdoer, or by handling the proceeds of the wrong, can be made liable along with the wrongdoer. Where the wrongdoer is either beyond the reach of the law, or is not a good mark for damages, constructive trusteeship is a useful tool for plaintiffs who have suffered a breach of trust or other fiduciary duty. So the doctrine has been used by a company defrauded by its accounts manager (*Agip Africa v Jackson* [1990] Ch 265), by a government against a corrupt official who took bribes (*AG Hong Kong v Reid* [1994] 1 AC 324), and by regulatory authorities seeking to track down the proceeds of insider trading (*Nanus Asia Ltd v Standard Chartered Bank* [1990] 1 HKLR 396).

Civil liability has, accordingly, fallen into two distinct categories: first, knowing assisting or being accessory to a breach of trust; secondly, knowing receipt of the proceeds of a breach of trust. The key difficulty the courts faced was in deciding an appropriate test for liability so that a truly innocent and diligent third party would not face obligations – while at the same time holding some sort of sword of Damocles so that liability could be imposed in a proper case. It is an exceptionally difficult area on which to advise. Recently, also, the law with regard to knowing receipt has been updated by the English Court of Appeal in *BCCI v Akindele* [2000] Lloyd's Law Rep: Banking 292. In that case, it was held that in order to establish civil liability for knowing receipt, one must prove that the conscience of the recipient was affected by the receipt. In effect, one must prove at the very least a want to 'probity' – rather than mere negligence.

One of the practical issues which causes difficulty is to steer a course between compliance with the criminal law and civil law. It would be tempting for the bank, when it received funds which it knew were the proceeds of crime, to refuse to pay the moneys out to the account holder for fear of facing civil liability which might follow if it assisted in spiriting those funds away (thereby rendering the bank a constructive trustee for knowing assistance). However, while such an approach is attractive from the civil law point of view, the bank must also take into account the rigours of the criminal law (which entail not 'tipping off' the offender). This can be difficult and so ensuring that potential civil liability is reduced so far as possible (for example, from the victim of the crime or from the State in the form of the Criminal Assets Bureau) can be a delicate operation.

One must also factor into this the complication that can arise when it is only a mere suspicion which prompts the bank to make the report. For in such circumstances, the bank risks losing its customer if the suspicions turn out to be unfounded. A good example of how not to go about it is the case of *Re A Ltd* [2001] Lloyd's Law Rep: Banking 73–84. In that case, the bank sought the to freeze the customer's account (held by itself) without notice to the customer. It was suggested that this was conceptually impossible as effectively amounting to a party seeking *Mareva* relief against itself.

One useful approach is for the bank to proceed by way of interpleader summons (that is, an action brought by the bank against the two parties competing for title to the funds), or on a motion for directions as to how to deal with the funds based on its position as constructive trustee (*Finers v Miró* [1991] 1 WLR 35).

1.7 Miscellaneous regulatory issues

There are a number of regulatory provisions which should be mentioned for the sake of completeness:

(a) Deposit protection

There is a scheme for the protection of retail deposits should any credit institution go into insolvent liquidation. This is operated under the European Communities (Deposit Guarantee Schemes) Regulations 1995 (SI 195/168) (the EC(DGS)R 1995). Its operation is quite complex but can be summarised as follows. The scheme provides cover of 90% of one's deposit subject to a maximum of €20,000. As noted, only retail depositors can avail of the scheme, accordingly wholesale and interbank deposits are excluded.

(b) Control of charges

Bank service charges are subject to control by the Director of Consumer Affairs under Pt XII of the Consumer Credit Act (CCA) 1995.

(c) Control of financial transfers

The Financial Transfers Act (FTA) 1992 provides that the Minister for Finance may provide for the restriction of financial transfers between the State and any other countries. Compliance by credit institutions is obligatory. The Act has been used recently as a vehicle for 'smart sanctions' against particular individuals.

(d) Position of auditors

One of the features of the regulation of the Irish financial services industry is the imposition of onerous obligations on auditors of regulated entities. The auditor is no longer a watchdog: he must now be a bloodhound. There is an obligation on auditors under ss 46 and 47 of the CBA 1989 to notify the CBI of any matters going to the financial soundness of the institution being audited. The auditor must also report any deficiencies in the financial and accounting systems and controls within the institution.

(e) Restrictions on disclosure of information by CBI

Section 16 of the CBA 1989 imposes restrictions on the CBI passing on regulatory information to third parties. There are a number of 'safe harbours' whereby the CBI may share the information it has about regulated credit institutions, but these are, in the main, limited to disclosure to the court, to the police and to certain other regulatory agencies.

(f) Asset covered securities

An important part of the regulatory structure is the Asset Covered Securities Act (ACSA) 2001. This provides a statutory framework for trading in asset-backed securities. An asset-backed security is basically a receivable held by a bank, the benefit of which is converted into a bond and then issued to the market. The proceeds of the issue of the bonds then provides fresh capital for the bank to expand its loan book. The Act provides for special priority for holders of such bonds upon the insolvency of the issuer of the bond.

CHAPTER 2

RELATIONSHIP BETWEEN CREDIT INSTITUTIONS AND CUSTOMERS

John Breslin

This chapter will cover two general areas.

1. The bank/customer relationship.
2. Payment mechanisms.

The analysis of the bank/customer relationship will focus on the following issues:

- The bank's liability under the law of contract.
- The Unfair Terms in Consumer Contracts Regulations.
- The bank's liability under the law of torts.
- The banks' fiduciary duties.
- The banker's duty of confidentiality.
- The Central Bank codes of conduct.
- The Consumer Credit Act.
- The Statute of Limitations.
- The set-off of bank accounts.
- Dormant bank accounts.

The analysis of payment mechanisms will focus on the following issues:

- The law relating to cheques.
- Letters of credit.
- Interbank money transfers.
- The law relating to mistaken payments.

2.1 The bank/customer relationship

2.1.1 The bank's liability under contract law

The bank's primary duty to its customer is in the law of contract. Until recently, it was quite rare for banks to reduce to writing the respective obligations of the bank and the customer. However, various factors have driven many institutions to do so. One practical factor has been that the range of services provided by a bank has greatly expanded in recent times and accordingly this has contributed to a drive towards documenting the bank/customer relationship more assiduously than before. It should be noted that reducing the agreement to writing has legal consequences when dealing with consumers. Insofar as the customer is an individual acting outside the course of a trade, business or profession, and the contract is substantially in standard form, the agreement will be governed by the European Communities (Unfair Terms in Consumer Contracts Regulations) 1995 (SI 1995/27) (the UTCC Regulations 1995) – see further below.

Until the arrival of the technological advances that are now part of the everyday banking service, the banker's duty was merely to have its offices open during normal banking hours and to pay the customer his money depending on the terms upon which it was deposited (*Joachimson v Swiss Bank Corp* [1921] 3 KB 110; *Kinlan v Ulster Bank Ltd* [1928] IR 171). However, now the position is much more complex, with automated teller machines and internet services now becoming standard aspects of banking service, thereby enabling the bank effectively to provide a service all day long all year around.

One aspect of the old law between a bank and its customer remains, however, and that is the relationship of debtor and creditor (*Foley v Hill* (1848) 2 HL Cas 28). But when the bank pays or receives money pursuant to a cheque transaction, it is acting as agent for its customer. Indeed, this is so with regard to any payment made or received by the bank on its customer's behalf.

Specific performance is not available to compel a lender to lend money to a plaintiff (*Rogers v Challis* (1859) 27 Beav 175). Where a lender has failed to honour its contract to lend, the plaintiff's only remedy is in damages. In practical terms, this will often be the difference (if any) by which the interest rate charged by the defendant is lower than the interest actually paid by the plaintiff from whatever third party it has been able to secure funding from.

Where it is alleged that a lender has called in its loan in a breach of contract, then it is the express and implied terms, if any, of the loan contract which determine the matter. Where the lender has unconditionally agreed to maintain a credit facility for a defined period, it will be in breach of contract if it purports to call for repayment before that period has expired. Whether or not such a term exists is a matter of interpretation of any documents constituting a contractual agreement between the parties (*Williams & Glyn's Bank Ltd v Barnes* (English High Court, unreported, 26 March 1980, Gibson J)).

2.1.2 The Unfair Terms in Consumer Contracts Regulations

The UTCC Regulations 1995 implement the EC Council Directive on Unfair Terms in Consumer Contracts (93/13/EEC). The Directive can accordingly be called in aid in interpreting the UTCC Regulations 1995. The UTCC Regulations 1995 apply to any standard form contract between a consumer (being an individual acting outside the course of a trade, business or profession), and a business selling goods or supplying services to the consumer.

Some guidance is given in the Regulations as to what 'unfair' means. First, Reg 3(2) provides:

> For the purpose of these Regulations a contractual term shall be regarded as unfair if, contrary to the requirement of good faith, it causes a significant imbalance in the parties' rights and obligations under the contract to the detriment of the consumer, taking into account the nature of the goods or services for which the contract was concluded and all the circumstances attending the conclusion of the contract and all other terms of the contract or of another contract on which it is dependent.

Furthermore, Sched 3 to the Regulations contains an indicative and non-exhaustive list of generic terms which are deemed to be unfair. They include such things as terms which attempt to bind the consumer to terms before he has had the opportunity to become acquainted with it, or inappropriately binding the consumer to obligations where the supplier of goods or services is excused from its obligations.

The notion of 'good faith' is one which is, in general, alien to contract law in Ireland and in the UK (*Interfoto Picture Library Ltd v Stiletto Visual Programmes Ltd* [1989] QB 433). Mere inequality in bargaining power in itself creates no legal consequences in contract law, and the grounds for attacking contractual provisions in normal trading relationships as being unconscionable are severely limited. Accordingly, the Regulations introduce an important ground for attacking contractual provisions in standard form consumer contracts.

In determining whether a term satisfies the requirement of good faith, regard is to be had to matters set out in Sched 2 to the Regulations. These are (a) the strength of the parties' respective bargaining positions, (b) whether the consumer had an inducement to agree the term, (c) whether the goods or services were sold or supplied to the special order of the consumer, and (d) the extent to which the supplier has dealt fairly and equitably with the consumer (whose legitimate interests he has taken into account).

The Regulations apply to all the terms in a standard form contract other than what the UK Parliament has, in its equivalent of the Regulations, dubbed 'core terms'. Core terms are effectively terms which relate to the consideration or other basic commercial features of the contract. So Reg 4 provides that:

> A term shall not of itself be considered to be unfair by relation to the definition of the main subject matter of the contract or to the adequacy of the price and remuneration, as against the goods and services supplied, in so far as these terms are in plain, intelligible language.

Accordingly, the aim of the Directive was not the promotion of better trading standards or the control of price and quality.

The Regulations preserve the *contra proferentem* rule of construction and provide that any unfair term is deemed to be unenforceable against the consumer. Accordingly, while much of the content of the Regulations merely confirms judicially created mechanisms for correcting an imbalance as between contracting parties (such as the *contra proferentem* rule, and certain of the scheduled terms), the Regulations represent a fundamental realignment in contract law in these islands.

2.1.2.1 *First National Bank plc case – UK*

Significant assistance can be obtained by those advising consumers or businesses from the recent decision of the House of Lords in the *Director General of Fair Trading v First National Bank plc* [2000] 1 All ER 240. This is the first decision under the UK equivalent of the Regulations. (There has been an Irish case, however, but this is merely an order of the High Court without a written judgment and made in the context of an application brought under the UTCC Regulations 1995 with regard to certain standard terms in house building contracts.)

The facts of the *First National Bank* case were as follows. The plaintiff is the equivalent of the Director and is charged with the enforcement of the UK equivalent of the Regulations. The defendant (the bank) was a licensed credit provider who provided re-mortgaging facilities to consumers. The terms of the bank's standard form contract included the 'boiler plate' provision that interest on outstanding principal would accrue not only before any judgment obtained by the bank, but also after it. The term also provided that any interest accruing after judgment would not merge with the judgment. This provision arises from the phenomenon that occurs when judgment is granted upon a contract debt. The contract merges with the judgment and the principal becomes owed under the judgment and not the contract. Unless otherwise excluded by contract, any interest obligation also merges with the judgment such that interest accrues pursuant to the court's power to award interest – and not under the contract. If there is no merger of the contract with the judgment, then the interest meter continues to tick.

While the interest provision was somewhat technical, even arcane, it had significant implications for defaulting debtors against whom the bank obtained judgment. A judgment debtor could be given the right to repay the judgment debt by instalments, or over a period of time (referred to as a 'time order'). If the debtor complied with such an order, the effect of the 'no merger' provision in the loan agreement was that he none the less faced a bill for contractual interest accruing post-judgment. Depending on the rate of interest, and the duration of the instalments, the post-judgment interest could exceed the amount of the judgment. The judgment debtor could, in fact, avoid this happening by asking the court to write-off the interest; but few judgment debtors (or their advisers) appeared to be aware of this.

The Director General of Fair Trading brought proceedings to have the term declared unfair. As far as the Director General of Fair Trading was concerned, the issue was essentially one of transparency. Namely, the average consumer would not be aware of the effect of the clause if he defaulted on the loan, and repaid the amounts due pursuant to an instalment order made by the court.

2.1.2.2 First National Bank plc – first instance

At first instance, Evans-Lombe J dismissed the Director General's application and took the view that the provision with regard to post-judgment interest was not inherently unfair. He said:

> As a first step in answering the question whether the provisions of [the relevant term] are unfair, it seems to me appropriate to stand back, and without reference to statute or authority, consider whether, had a potential borrower had the effect of [the relevant term] drawn to his attention immediately before entering into a loan agreement containing that clause, he would immediately have replied to the question that they were unfair.

Evans-Lombe J then considered that because the effect of the provision was to require the agreed rate to be paid so long as the amounts owing where outstanding, it could not be viewed as inherently unfair.

As well as potential unfairness in substance, Evans-Lombe J considered whether there was any procedural unfairness. In other words, did the term deprive the consumer of an advantage he may reasonably be expected to receive? Evans-Lombe J held that the actual term complained of did not do so – although he strongly hinted that if there was procedural unfairness in this regard, it arose from consumers being unaware of their right to ask the court to reduce or extinguish altogether the rate of interest payable.

2.1.2.3 First National Bank plc – Court of Appeal

The Director General of Fair Trading appealed to the Court of Appeal, who reversed the decision of Evans-Lombe J. The Court of Appeal was swayed by the transparency issue. Peter Gibson LJ was unenthusiastic about the trial judge's approach – namely, to ascertain the fairness or otherwise of a term by reference to a hypothetical borrower. He said:

> The test of unfairness is not to be judged by personal concepts of inherent fairness apart from the requirements of the directive and the regulations, and we are far from convinced that a borrower would think it fair that when he is taken to court and an order for payment by instalments has been tailored to meet what he could afford and he complied with that order, he should then be told that he has to pay further sums by way of interest ...
>
> In our judgment the relevant term is unfair within the meaning of the regulations to the extent that it enables the bank to obtain judgment against a debtor under a regulated agreement and an instalment order ... without the court considering whether to make a time

order, or, if it does and makes a time order, whether also to make an order ... to reduce the contractual interest rate. The bank, with its strong bargaining position as against the relatively weak position of the consumer, has not adequately considered the consumer's interests in this respect. In our view the relevant term in that respect does create unfair surprise and so does not satisfy the test of good faith, it does cause a significant imbalance in the rights and obligations of the parties by allowing the bank to obtain interest after judgment in circumstances when it would not obtain interest under [the relevant courts legislation] and no specific benefit to compensate the consumer is provided, and it operates to the detriment of that consumer who has to pay interest ([2001] 2 All ER (Comm) 1000 at 1010).

These comments are interesting in that the court was prepared to contemplate unfairness arising from the actual operation of the clause in particular circumstances rather than by reason of inherent unfairness in the term itself.

2.1.2.4 *First National Bank plc – House of Lords*

The bank successfully appealed to the House of Lords. Like the trial judge, their Lordships were of the view that there was nothing inherently unfair in the bank bargaining for interest to be paid after judgment was entered against the borrower. Like Evans-Lombe J (but unlike Peter Gibson LJ), Lord Millett was of the view that the 'reasonable borrower' test was a useful one for evaluating whether the term was or was not fair. Their Lordships recognised that borrowers who defaulted on loans, had judgment entered against them and who were given time to repay the judgment debt would be legitimately aggrieved by the fact that contractual interest would continue to run, notwithstanding that the borrower made all his instalment payments. However, their Lordships were of the view that this phenomenon did not render the actual term unfair. Rather, this called for an amendment to the scheme for the granting of judgments in the county court, so that the court could factor into the judgment any contractual interest to be paid. From this it might be extrapolated that for a term to be unfair under the Regulations, it is not enough that in particular circumstances the consumer might be aggrieved by its operation. Something over and above this must be established.

There seemed to be a general consensus as to what this additional factor was. In Lord Bingham's words:

> A term falling within the scope of the regulations is unfair if it causes a significant imbalance in the parties' rights and obligations under the contract to the detriment of the consumer in a manner or to an extent which is contrary to the requirement of good faith. The requirement of significant imbalance is met if a term is so weighted in favour of the supplier as to tilt the parties' rights and obligations under the contract significantly in his favour. This may be by the granting to the supplier of a beneficial option or discretion or power, or by the imposing on the consumer of a disadvantageous burden or risk or duty ... The requirement of good faith in this context is one of fair and open dealing. Openness requires that the terms should be expressed fully, clearly and legibly, containing no concealed pitfalls or traps. Appropriate prominence should be given to terms which might operate disadvantageously to the consumer. Fair dealing requires that a supplier should not, whether deliberately or unconsciously, take advantage of the customer's necessity, indigence, lack of experience, unfamiliarity with the subject matter of the contract, weak bargaining position or any other factor listed in or analogous to those listed in Schedule 2 to the regulations.

Lord Millett put it this way:

> There can be no one single test ... It is obviously useful to stress the impact of an impugned term on the parties' rights and obligations by comparing the effect of the contract with the term and the effect it would have without it. But the inquiry cannot stop there. It may also

be necessary to consider the effect of the inclusion of the term on the substance or core of the transaction; whether if it were drawn to his attention the consumer would be likely to be surprised by it; whether the term is a standard term, not merely in similar non-negotiable consumer contracts, but in commercial contracts freely negotiated between parties acting on level terms and at arms' length; and whether, in such cases, the party adversely affected by the inclusion of the term or his lawyer might reasonably be expected to object to its inclusion and press for its deletion. The list is not necessarily exhaustive; other approaches may sometimes be more appropriate.

Lord Millett took the view that the hypothetical borrower would not be surprised by a term which meant that contractual interest would accrue after judgment until payment. He also pointed out that this is a standard term in commercial loan facilities. The unfairness arose not from the actual term, but from the fact that due to a quirk in the Rules of the County Court, the court's judgment would not necessarily encompass all of the borrower's contractual commitments.

The key difference between the approach taken by the Court of Appeal and the House of Lords, respectively, appears to be that the House of Lords was not prepared to hold that a term was unfair because it operated in a prejudicial manner in particular circumstances. The Court of Appeal, by way of contrast, was prepared so to hold; and in addition, the question of contractual transparency was an important issue. The contract should not contain hidden 'traps'.

2.1.2.5 *Core terms*

Whilst the judges at first instance and on appeal were divided as to whether the impugned term was unfair, they were unanimous in rejecting the bank's contention that the term was a 'core' term and therefore immune from attack pursuant to the Regulations. Lord Steyn said this about UK Reg 3(2) (the equivalent of Reg 4 which states that 'core' terms are outside scrutiny):

> ... reg 3(2) must be given a restrictive interpretation. Unless that is done reg 3(2)(a) will enable the main purpose of the scheme to be frustrated by endless formalistic arguments as to whether a provision is a definitional or an exclusionary provision. Similarly, reg 3(2)(b) must be given a restrictive interpretation. After all, in a broad sense all terms of the contract are in some way related to the price or remuneration. That is not what is intended. Even price escalation clauses have been treated by the Director as subject to the fairness provision ... It would be a gaping hole in the system if such clauses were not subject to the fairness requirement.

2.1.2.6 *Conclusions*

It is submitted that the following conclusions can be drawn from the House of Lords decision in the *First National Bank* case:

- the burden of proof is on the consumer or the Director of Consumer Affairs to satisfy the court that a particular term is unfair;
- the court will be astute to attempts to characterise the term as a 'core' term in an artificial or contrived manner thereby rendering it immune from challenge; and
- the term 'in order to be struck down' must be inherently unfair as it is not enough if it turns out to be unfair in particular circumstances or due to extraneous factors.

However, so far as Irish law is concerned, it may well be that the obligation impliedly imposed on service providers by Sched 2 to the Regulations to take into account the legitimate interests of the consumer may impel the court towards the approach adopted by the Court of Appeal, rather than the House of Lords because contractual transparency is, arguably, one of the consumer's legitimate interests.

2.1.3 The bank's liability under the law of torts

A bank is no different to any other kind of service provider and will be liable in damages to its customer if it performs its services in a negligent manner and the customer thereby suffers loss as a consequence. However, banks also face other aspects of liability in tort, for example, with regard to the law of defamation and to a lesser extent the law of deceit.

2.1.3.1 Negligence

A good example of a bank being liable for damages for negligence is *Towey v Ulster Bank Ltd* [1987] ILRM 142. In that case, the bank was tardy in receiving payments on behalf of its customer; in the meantime the payer became bankrupt. The bank was held to be liable in damages in the amount of unpaid cheques which would have been collected were it not for its negligence. Another interesting example is the 1996 English case of *Verity and Spindler v Lloyds Bank plc* [1996] Fam Law 213. In that case, the bank was held to have given negligent advice to the plaintiffs – a couple who embarked on a 'buy to let' business at the top of the UK property market in the late 1980s. When that market crashed the plaintiffs were faced with crippling interest payments. They sued the bank which had lent them the money and advised them. On the facts, the court held that the bank had transgressed beyond the role of mere lender and had in fact held itself out as being, and had become, a business adviser to the plaintiffs. Furthermore, having undertaken that role it performed it in a negligent manner, for example, by reason of inadequate advice on business projections. It should, however, be borne in mind that the bank is not a guarantor as to the profitability of the borrower's business: the temptation to over-apply the benefit of hindsight should be resisted (*McSweeney v Bourke and Investment Bank of Ireland* (High Court, 24 November 1980, unreported, Denham J)).

In normal circumstances, the mere fact that a lender has advanced funds does not necessarily entail the provision of advice. It is a question of fact in each case whether the lender has become an adviser thereby triggering a duty of care under the principles enunciated in *Hedley Byrne v Heller* [1964] AC 465.

2.1.3.2 Defamation

There is authority that when a bank wrongfully dishonours its customer's cheque, the words written on the back of the cheque (for example, return to drawer) are defamatory of the customer. The leading Irish authority is *Pyke v Hibernian Bank Ltd* [1950] IR 195. In that case, the Supreme Court were divided on the issue on whether words such as 'return to drawer – present again' were defamatory of the plaintiff. Maguire CJ held that the words were not defamatory. Black J held that there could be a variety of reasons of why the cheque was not honoured, not all of which involved an inference that the drawer of the cheque drew it knowing that he had not the funds or overdraft facility to meet it. However, Geoghegan and O'Byrne JJ held that the words were capable of having a defamatory meaning.

In the UK, the words 'refer to drawer' were held to have no defamatory meaning on the basis that the gist of the message was 'We are not paying; go back and ask the drawer why' (*Flach v London and South Western Bank Ltd* (1915) 31 TLR 334).

Conversely, in *Jayson v Midland Bank Ltd* [1967] 2 Lloyd's Rep 563; [1968] 1 Lloyd's Rep 409, the jury found that the words 'refer to drawer' were capable of lowering the plaintiff in the minds of right thinking people. More recently, in *Raafbye Corp Pty Ltd v Westpac Banking Corp Ltd* (Supreme Court of New South Wales, 21 October 1994, unreported, Levine J), it was held that the words 'refer to drawer' published on the back of a cheque were capable of conveying the imputation that the drawer is insolvent in the sense of being unable to pay the debt for which the cheque was issued. It was further held that no further inference was capable of being drawn from the words, for example, as to negligence or dishonesty. In the New Zealand case of *Baker v Australia and New Zealand Bank Ltd* [1958] NZLR 907, the words 'present again' were held to have a defamatory meaning.

In this context, however, even where a non-trader is defamed as to his credit rating he need not prove special damage; the plaintiff will be treated in the same manner as any trader because a person's 'employment and advancement' may well depend upon the person's credit (*Pyke v Hibernian Bank* [1950] IR 195 at 223, *per* Black J; *Kpohraror v Woolwich Building Society* [1996] 4 All ER 119).

2.1.3.3 Deceit

A bank is potentially liable in damages for deceit where it makes a fraudulent representation, which it knows to be untrue or is reckless as to its untruth, and the plaintiff relies on the statement to its detriment (*Forshall v Walsh* (High Court, 18 June 1997, unreported, Shanley J)). As the policy of the law is rigorous where the tort of deceit is concerned, a *novus actus interveniens* will not necessarily break the chain of causation between the defendant's deceit and the plaintiff's loss (*Smith New Court Securities Ltd v Scrimgeour Vickers (Asset Management) Ltd* [1994] 1 WLR 1271). In that case, the defendant induced the plaintiff to purchase shares in a company (Ferranti plc). This resulted in the plaintiff paying over the odds for the shares. However, a fraud occurred thereafter within Ferranti plc which caused the value of its shares to plummet on the stock market. The English Court of Appeal rejected the defendant's argument that it should not be liable for the extent of this loss. The Court held that the defendant, in the context of a tort such as deceit – which has a taint of fraud – could not rely on the fact that the fall in value of the shares was caused by a matter outside its control.

2.1.3.4 Relationship between contract and tort

From time to time the argument is made that damages in tort are not available where there is a contractual relationship between the parties (*Tai Hing Cotton Mill Ltd v Liu Chong Hing Bank Ltd* [1986] AC 80; *McCann v Brinks Allied Ltd* (Supreme Court, 4 November 1996, unreported)). It would seem that the better view is that the existence of a contract between the parties is not an automatic bar to the availability of a remedy in tort all things being equal (*Henderson v Merrett Syndicates Ltd* [1994] 3 WLR 761; *Kennedy v Allied Irish Banks plc* [1998] 2 IR 48).

2.1.4 A bank's fiduciary duties

Before the expansion in financial services now provided by banks, the rule used to be that a bank was either a creditor (where it lent money), or a debtor (where it took deposits), and only acted as agent in processing payments for customers by way of cheque and other means. However, because the services provided by banks are no longer limited merely to taking deposits and lending, the scope of legal duties has correspondingly expanded. As noted in Chapter 1, a high street bank might now find itself advising customers on buying stocks and shares, taking out life insurance, and (for business customers) making corporate finance and strategy decisions. These new areas of activity open up the scope to make profits but attract a form of liability as fiduciary.

Liability arises from conflicts of interest. The usual form of conflict of interest is between (a) the bank's own commercial interest and (b) the customer's interest. The other common form of conflict is where the interests of two separate customers conflict: how is the bank to resolve those conflicts fairly?

The law imposes a high duty of compliance on fiduciaries. A fiduciary is any person who takes upon himself the role of acting for another: for example, an adviser, property manager or other agent. The borderline between fiduciary liability and ordinary liability in tort for negligence is notoriously difficult to draw. Fiduciary actions are attractive from the plaintiff's point of view because not only will he be awarded damages if successful, he may also get an account of the defendant's profits.

The classic example of how it can arise is to be found in the old case of *Woods v Martins Bank Ltd* [1959] 1 QB 55. In that case, the plaintiff customer came into some money. He went to his bank for advice on how to invest it. The bank advised him to invest in a certain company. What the bank did not tell the plaintiff, however, was that the company was heavily indebted to the bank. The company went into insolvent liquidation. The plaintiff successfully sued the bank for failing to disclose the fact that it had a conflict of interest.

Conflicts of interest can arise in an infinite number of instances: for example, the bank acts for two parties in a take-over; the bank advises the customer to purchase stock which the bank's market makers wish to offload; a bank owes fiduciary duties to co-members of a syndicate; and the bank might advise pension fund trustees to invest in the bank's own shares. Conflicts abound in the financial services industry.

The methods available to a bank to limit and manage its conflict of interest include the following:

(a) provide for the informed consent of the beneficiary of the service in its contract: the effectiveness of such a term in the context of the provision of services to a consumer will depend on the compatibility of the term with the UTCC Regulations 1995;

(b) manage the conflict by hiving off services within the group; and

(c) manage the conflict by the erection of a Chinese Wall – that is, an internal organisational arrangement whereby the information within one division of the legal entity does not 'leak' to another division where possession of the information could potentially be abused (*KPMG v Prince Jefri Bolkiah* [1999] 2 AC 222).

2.1.5 The banker's duty of confidentiality

A bank owes an implied duty to keep obtained confidential information about the customer's finances (*Tournier v National Provincial Bank* [1924] 1 KB 461). There are exceptions to this duty:

(a) **Disclosure through legal compulsion**

The most common examples of this are, for example, pursuant to the Bankers' Books Evidence Act 1879 (as amended), s 57 of the Criminal Justice Act (CJA 1994), and revenue legislation.

(b) **Disclosure with the customer's implied or explicit consent**

It is unsafe to rely on the customer's implied consent (*Turner v Royal Bank of Scotland* (1999) 143 SJ LB 123).

(c) **Disclosure in the bank's own interests**

The most common form of this exception is where the bank is suing the customer and states the amount of the customer's loan or overdraft on the summons.

(d) A public duty to disclose

Examples of this are unusual.

One of the key difficulties with advising customers who are aggrieved by their bank's breach of duty in this regard is with regard to damages. Very often the customer suffers no contractual loss. Exemplary damages are not available for breach of contract. There is no authority as yet whereby the duty has been judicially framed as an aspect of tort law.

This area of the law merges into the law relating to the protection of confidences. In addition, the bank's duties as a data controller under the Data Protection Act (DPA) 1998 (as amended) are also relevant.

2.1.6 Codes of conduct

Under s 117 of the Central Bank Act (CBA) 1989, the Central Bank of Ireland (CBI) has promulgated codes of conduct to which credit institutions must adhere. These are quite extensive and are potentially of interest to plaintiffs seeking to establish, in a particular case, what best practice is. Copies are available on the CBI website (www.centralbank.ie).

A key question is whether or not the codes give rise to a right to damages. Section 117 of the CBA 1989 does not explicitly contemplate that an aggrieved customer of a bank should have a right to sue for a breach which causes him damage. This, therefore, strongly militates against a court holding that there is a right to sue for breach. However, in practical terms, it may well be that even if there is no express or implied right to sue, a plaintiff could bring an action for negligence and plead that the codes set out the appropriate standard of care. If this is breached then damages will follow. Equally, it could be argued that certain terms of the code may be implied terms.

2.1.7 The Consumer Credit Act 1995

The Consumer Credit Act (CCA) 1995 is an important and complex piece of legislation. Any issues arising under this Act should always to be considered in conjunction with the UTCC Regulations and the Contracts Negotiated Away from Business Premises Regulations 1989 (CNABP Regulations). The CCA 1995 applies to all forms of credit advanced to 'consumers', that is, individuals acting outside the course of a trade, business or profession.

The CCA 1995 contains detailed and complex provisions with regard to the manner in which consumer loans and other credit transactions should be documented, how the consumer should be treated during the course of the relationship, and what must be done if the credit provider seeks to enforce the terms of the agreement.

The practical consequences of the CCA 1995 are as follows:

(a) Before the credit agreement is entered into, the credit provider must have complied with the provisions of the CCA 1995 regulating the manner in which it marketed the services. Although there is no reported case law on the matter as at the time of writing, it is very likely that a credit agreement entered into in reliance upon a breach of the CCA's marketing requirements will be unenforceable.

(b) When the credit agreement is entered into, the credit provider must comply with the detailed documentary requirements set out in Pt III of the CCA 1995. In particular, copies of the agreement must be given to the consumer for signature, and the consumer must be given the right to a 14 day 'cooling off' period, in order to reflect on the commitments he is about to undertake. This right can only be waived in precise circumstances.

(c) During the course of the agreement the credit provider may only contact the consumer under very strict conditions. All correspondence must be sealed and marked private and must not be sent to the consumer's place of work. Equally, the consumer may only be contacted during office hours and not in the evenings or at weekends.

(d) If the consumer defaults on his obligations under the agreement, the credit provider cannot terminate the agreement or repossess the goods immediately. The credit provider must give the consumer a 'grace period' during which the consumer has the opportunity of remedying his breach. Only if the breach is not remedied can the credit provider enforce its agreement – whereupon a further warning must be given.

2.1.8 Statute of Limitations

As with any aspect of litigation, the Statute of Limitations 1957 (as amended) is an important factor to have in mind when taking instructions. The Statute is particularly important in the banking context because whether or not the Statute begins to run is often a complex issue.

The two most common issues which come up are as follows:

(a) overdrafts which are repayable on demand. Accordingly, the Statute does not run until the bank makes a demand of the customer; and

(b) guarantees which are usually repayable on demand. Accordingly, the Statute does not run until demand is made.

2.1.9 Set-off of bank accounts

Set-off can be a complex area. However, under Irish law all creditors and debtors have the right to set-off one balance due against any amount due by the other party. Banks enjoy this right also – although given the modern tendency to document the bank/customer relationship, this is now usually set out in the contract. However, it is important to bear in mind the limits of set-off.

(a) **Winding up**

Set-off is not permitted *after* the customer (being a company) has gone into winding up. In this regard the date of the winding up may relate back to the date of presentation of the winding-up petition to the court. Set-off is permitted (and perhaps is obligatory) as at the date of winding up. But no new set-off rights may be acquired by the solvent party after the date of winding up.

(b) **No set-off of contingent liabilities**

Unless permitted by contract, a contingent liability (for example, under a guarantee that has not yet been called) cannot be used to reduce a presently due and payable debt to the other party.

(c) **Special rules in EU insolvencies**

Where an Irish person has a right of set-off against a party which has become insolvent or gone into pre-insolvency administration (for example, examinership equivalent) in another EU Member State, the Irish party may only exercise its right of set-off if permitted by the law of that other EU Member State.

(d) Liquidated v unliquidated claims

Normally, unless the parties' contract so provides, it is not possible to set up an unliquidated claim (for example, for general damages in negligence) against a liquidated claim. However, the court has a jurisdiction in equity to permit such a set-off or a stay on enforcement of the liquidated claim where the claims are so closely related that it is just and equitable.

2.2 Payment systems

2.2.1 The law relating to cheques

The law relating to cheques is – perhaps – the most difficult aspect of banking law. The reason for this is because its foundation is firmly rooted in the law and practice of bills of exchange. Nowadays, most people are unfamiliar with the nature and operation of bills of exchange. So this causes conceptual difficulties – especially when one is forced back to first principles dealing with such issues as transfer, negotiability and holder in due course. However, many of these difficulties can be overcome if one bears in mind the following basic points of principle.

2.2.1.1 The nature of a cheque

- A cheque is a bill of exchange.
- A bill of exchange is merely an order by one person (usually a purchaser of goods or services) to his agent (usually his bank) to make a payment.
- The recipient of the payment (usually the seller of the goods or services) will usually instruct an agent (usually his bank) to receive the payment.
- The definition of a cheque is found in s 73 of the Bills of Exchange Act (BEA) 1882.

Some of us may have painful memories of having to understand the horrendous complexity of the law relating to situations where a cheque is stolen and perhaps indorsed to a third party in payment of goods, and consequent problems where the cheque is dishonoured. Unfortunately, such knotty problems can still arise but are on the wane for a number of reasons. The main reason is that cheques are seldom indorsed to a third party in payment of goods and services. Furthermore, as many cheques are nowadays made out in favour of a named payee, they cannot in effect be realised by any other person. So, it is worth bearing in mind the following basic points.

2.2.1.2 The cheque as property

- In the past, when a vendor received a bill of exchange as payment for goods or services, he would often 'sell' it to a third party. This enabled the third party to collect the proceeds. (The consideration provided by the third party was usually in the form of the face value of the bill discounted.)
- The method of transferring title to a bill of exchange depends on whether the bill is bearer or made out in favour of a named person. If bearer, it is transferred merely by delivery. If made out in favour of a named person, it is transferred by the transferor indorsing it (signing his name on the back) and delivering it to the transferee.
- Whether a cheque can be transferred depends on whether or not it is crossed 'account payee' or not. We will come back to this later.
- The transferee of the cheque, under the pre-BEA 1882 custom and practice (as subsequently codified in that Act) had the absolute right to be paid the full amount of the bill – so long as he paid value and had no notice of defects – for example, on the face of the bill. This is the concept of negotiability.

- The concept of negotiability must be distinguished from a mere transfer. A mere transferee of a thing in action takes the asset (that is, the face value of the payment) subject to any pre-existing equities as between the payer and payee of the asset. This does not occur where there is negotiability.
- It is, in summary, a useful rule of thumb that the transferee of a cheque should be entitled to receive the full amount of it subject to (a) acting in good faith and (b) there being no 'account payee' crossing.

At this stage it may be useful to say a few words about cheque crossings. A crossing on a cheque is simply an instruction by the drawer of the cheque. The addressee of the instruction depends on the nature of the instruction.

2.2.1.3 Crossings on a cheque

- A cheque without any crossing is fully transferable and negotiable.
- A cheque with a crossing must be collected by another bank. In other words, it cannot be directly encashed. To obtain cash for it one would normally expect to go to one's own branch who would then advance the face value pending collection by it of the proceeds. Technically speaking, the collecting bank is advancing the customer the proceeds pending collection by itself.
- Curiously, a cheque crossed and marked 'not negotiable' is capable of being transferred but not negotiated.
- At common law, crossing a cheque and marking it as payable to a particular person only did not necessarily mean that the cheque was incapable of transfer. This is the result of the rather strange case of *National Bank v Silke* [1891] 1 QB 435.
- Because of the *Silke* case the UK passed legislation to recognise the 'account payee' crossing. This was done so as to cut down instances of cheque fraud. A similar provision has not been passed in Ireland.
- However, it is now questionable whether such legislation is necessary. The *Silke* case is now open to question: a collecting bank crediting the proceeds to a person other than the named payee, or paying out cash to a person other than the named payee, could be held to be negligent: O'Connor, R, *The Law of Cheques and Analogous Instruments* (The Institute of Bankers, 1993, p 85). So all banks will – in practice – give effect to the 'account payee' crossing so that any person (other than the named payee) taking such a cheque in satisfaction of payment does so at his own risk.

This then brings us to the question of bank liability when dealing with cheques. In this context the bank, whether it is acting as paying bank or collecting bank, is acting as agent. Furthermore, the paying bank and the collecting bank may be different branches of the same bank – and (and just to add complication) even the same branch of the same bank. But for the purposes of the law, this is one of the few situations where different branches are treated as different legal entities.

To understand the bank's liability one must bear in mind the following principles.

2.2.1.4 The bank's liability in handling cheques

- At common law, if a collecting bank handles a cheque in a manner inconsistent with the rights of the true owner (for example, it has been stolen or fraudulently indorsed) its liability is in the tort of conversion.
- Because liability for the tort of conversion is more or less strict, the Cheques Act 1959 was passed to provide that the collecting bank would only be liable if it acted negligently or in bad faith. There is similar protection for the paying bank.

- Accordingly, whether or not the true owner of a cheque can make the paying or collecting bank liable turns on the question of whether or not the bank was negligent (or acted in bad faith – which is more difficult to prove).

2.2.1.5 Conclusions

Issues arising from disputes as to liability on a cheque can be complex and for in-depth treatment, see Rory O'Connor's book *The Law of Cheques and Analogous Instruments* which is recommended as an invaluable guide.

Briefly with regard to other payment mechanisms, a debit card (LASER card) is effectively a similar transaction to a cheque in that the customer directs its bank to make a payment to the retailer accepting the card. However, it is not a bill of exchange and so the question of the rights and liabilities of the parties is governed by the relevant contracts between the parties.

As regards a credit card, the situation is more or less the same as a debit card, except that the bank will make the payment by granting credit to the customer rather than debiting his bank account there and then. Once again, it is the relevant contract between the parties which governs.

Finally, travellers' cheques are not really a cheque in the BEA 1882 sense. Issues with regard to travellers' cheques must be dealt with in accordance with the contract between the issuing bank and the customer (for example, if the cheques are lost or stolen).

2.2.2 Letters of credit

A letter of credit is a form of payment mechanism. To this extent it is similar to a cheque. A letter of credit is an instruction by a purchaser of goods or services to its bank to make a specific payment upon presentation of specific documents to it: for example, bills of lading by the vendor or manufacturer.

The parties to the letter of credit are as follows:

(a) the purchaser of the goods;
(b) the purchaser's bank which issues the letter of credit – referred to as the issuing bank;
(c) the accepting bank – this may be a bank which undertakes to back the issuing bank's obligation to pay (for example, because the issuing bank has no status in the vendor's jurisdiction);
(d) the confirming bank – this is typically the bank in the vendor's jurisdiction which notifies the vendor that the credit has been opened and that he can ship the goods accordingly: this is usually the vendor's bank; and
(e) the vendor – referred to as the beneficiary.

A letter of credit cannot be dishonoured for insufficiency of funds. Before a bank issues the letter of credit it must take appropriate cover from its own customer (the purchaser of the goods or services). A letter of credit cannot be countermanded by the customer without the consent of the beneficiary of the credit (the vendor or manufacturer).

The bank is entitled to insist that the terms of the letter of credit are adhered to strictly by the beneficiary of the credit. So the document presented to it will be very carefully checked by the paying bank to ensure it complies with the form of document envisaged in the contract. For example, the quantity of goods, or their quality, will be specified in the contract and the document presented to it will be checked so as to ensure compliance with this. This is the doctrine of 'strict compliance'.

Subject to that, the only basis upon which a bank may refuse to pay out on a letter of credit is where there has been manifest fraud to the knowledge of the bank. It is a very serious matter for a bank not to pay a letter of credit on any other basis.

Letters of credit are typically governed by a code (called the UCP 500) which is incorporated into the contract by the parties.

There are different types of letter of credit. The most common form is where the bank merely makes a payment upon presentation of the required documents. This is a letter of credit payable 'at sight'. Others may have a 'time' element in that they might be payable on or before a specified date. Others may provide that they can be sold or discounted; these are 'negotiation' credits.

2.2.3   Interbank money transfers

Interbank money transfers is a complex area; however, problems can be tackled if one approaches it with a few basic pointers in mind.

There are two sides to each transaction: (a) the paying side and (b) the receiving side. On the paying side one has the actual purchaser who wishes to transfer the funds, the bank acting for it, and any agents acting for that bank – who are, effectively, sub-agents of the purchaser.

Conversely, on the other side one has the vendor who wants to get its money, together with its bank and any sub-agents acting for it.

The transfer is typically done by means of the paying bank (or its agents) debiting its customer's account with the payment and a corresponding credit by the recipient bank or banks. The payment is effected when there are funds available to be called upon by the vendor.

A payment cannot 'hang in the air' at the end of a business day. It has either happened or it has not. The earliest date or time in which it happens is when the paying bank puts in motion the payment mechanics. What this will be will depend on the facts.

There can be bilateral payments. Payments can also be effected through a central clearing system, for example, the US dollar clearing in New York. Another is the TARGET payment clearing system operated through member banks of the European System of Central Banks. This provides for real time gross settlements (ie, payment by electronic book entry, occurring with immediate effect and which is not netted off within a clearing system).

With regard to payments effected through a European Central Bank (ECB), such as the CBI, one must have regard to the European Communities (Finality of Settlement in Payment and Securities Settlement Systems) Regulations 1998 (SI 1998/539). These provide, broadly speaking, that a payment made by or to the ECB or to a Member State Central Bank will not be affected by the subsequent insolvency of the payer – provided that the parties do not have notice of the insolvency at the time of payment.

With regard to these, and any other centralised clearing system, one must also have regard to any rules or regulations governing the system. These may form implied terms of the contract or set a standard of service provision which may be a basis for deciding if there has been negligence or not.

2.2.4   The law relating to mistaken payments

When a person makes a mistaken payment to another, the payment is, subject to some limited exceptions, recoverable from the payee *at least* as an unsecured debt. The relevant principles for deciding this are found in the law of restitution. In the past the question fell to be decided according to the rather anachronous distinction based on whether the mistake was one of fact or law. This has gone. The question is now to ask whether the recipient has been unjustly enriched at the expense of the payer. In most cases of mistaken payment, the payee will have been so enriched. Accordingly, the payer will have a claim in restitution against the payee.

The only defence the payee has under the law of restitution is to show that he changed his position *in a bona fide manner* as a result of the payment. This is a difficult defence to establish. The payee must show that he was not aware of the mistaken payment. So, for example, if an Irish bank mistakenly transfers €10 million to X and X buys a chateau and vineyard in Provence, X can hardly claim that he was not aware of the payment.

In special circumstances, the payer's claim may be one where he can *trace* the payment into the assets of the payee and beyond. The significance of this is that this converts the claim from being merely unsecured (and worthless where the payee is bankrupt or insolvent) to one which is secured. So the payer may be able to steal a march on other claimants of the payee. However, the ability of a payer to set up such a tracing right is very limited, as he must show that the payee owed him a fiduciary duty in respect of the payment. This is very difficult in a normal commercial scenario.

So in normal commercial situations the court will not infer a fiduciary relationship between the parties so as to convert the payer's claim to a secured claim. The relevant authorities in this regard are *Chase Manhattan Bank NA v Israel-British Bank (London) Ltd* [1980] 2 WLR 202, *Re Irish Shipping Ltd* [1986] ILRM 518 and *Westdeutsche Landesbank Girozentrale v Islington London Borough Council* [1996] 2 All ER 961.

CHAPTER 3

FORMS OF SECURITY

Joseph Gavin and Tracy Gilvarry

3.1 Introduction

3.1.1 Why a creditor might wish to take security

There are essentially four reasons why a creditor might wish to take security:

1. In the event of a debtor becoming insolvent, it increases the prospects of the creditor being paid as secured creditors are paid out of the debtor's assets in priority to the debtor's general creditors.
2. If a creditor takes security over assets he may then be able to realise those assets through out-of-court enforcement procedures. This benefits the creditor in two respects. First, out-of-court enforcement procedures are less costly and less time consuming than court enforcement procedures. Secondly, the creditor may realise the assets at a time which he chooses. This may have the effect of optimising recoveries.
3. When taking security, the creditor only needs to measure the asset offered as security. Therefore, the need to conduct a credit inquiry into the debtor's business is disposed of.
4. In situations outside of insolvency, if a debtor defaults on payment he runs the risk of losing the assets which form the subject matter of the security. Such assets may be necessary to the carrying on of the debtor's business. Therefore, a debtor is more likely to pay a secured creditor in this situation (Gerard McCormack, Professor of Law, University of Manchester, has set out these reasons in his article 'The nature of securities over receivables' (2002) (23(3) The Company Lawyer 84.)

3.1.2 Why the law allows security

There are three main reasons why the law allows security. First, as the taking of security lowers the risk of non-repayment, the interest rates charged on a loan may be lower than those charged in a situation involving an unsecured loan. If security rights are available to the lender this will affect the assessment of the credit risk. This in turn could lead to a reduction in the amount of interest charged on the loan. McCormack states that this argument is a favourite of US law and economic theorists, Thomas Jackson and Robert Scott (Jackson and Scott, 'On the nature of bankruptcy: an essay on bankruptcy sharing and the creditors' bargain' (1989) 75 Virginia Law Review 155 at 161).

Jackson and Scott commented that 'Secured creditors, for example, would have paid for their priority position by accepting a lower rate of return and should therefore be allowed to retain the benefits of their initial bargain by receiving an equivalent value for their collateral in bankruptcy'.

However, this argument makes idealised assumptions about creditor behaviour that are not mirrored by real life experience. In reality, banks are in the business of making profits and will charge whatever rates of interest they think they will be able to get away with.

Secondly, a secured lender is protected, at least partially in the event of non-repayment by the debtor. Therefore, allowing security may encourage lenders to advance credit in situations where they may not otherwise do so.

The third reason why the law allows security is that the taking of security is seen as a fair exchange for the loan. The basis behind this reasoning is that the secured creditors and not the general creditors have bargained with the debtor for property rights over the assets secured under the loan agreement. (Gerard McCormack, 'The nature of securities over receivables' (2002) 23(3) The Company Lawyer 84.)

3.2 Legal issues for companies granting security

3.2.1 *Ultra vires*

The 'objects' of a company are the purposes for which a company has been formed. The importance of the objects clause is that it sets out the activities which the company may pursue. The company may not pursue activities which are unrelated to its objects. Such activities are described as being *ultra vires* the company's corporate capacity. Historically, if the transaction was *ultra vires* the company's corporate capacity, the transaction was deemed to be void and unenforceable at common law. This reasoning was based on the doctrine of constructive notice. Once a company's memorandum and articles of association are registered in the Companies Registration Office, they become public documents and therefore members of the public are fixed with constructive notice of the contents of the memorandum, including the objects clause.

With the exception of banks or other corporate entities whose main business it is to provide loans, a trading company may not have the power to borrow as part of its objects clause. A trading company may only borrow in the course of attaining the company's objects. However, most companies will have the express power to borrow. This power to borrow may only be exercised in the pursuit of the company's objects.

Companies have used a number of devices to make their power to borrow seem as if it is an object in itself. The courts have developed techniques to limit the legal efficacy of the devices. These devices are: first, companies have attempted to include dozens of different objects into the objects clause. Secondly, companies have inserted a *Cotman* clause in the memorandum stating that each object is a separate and independent object of the company. Thirdly, companies may insert a *Bell House* clause into the memorandum, which enables a company to pursue any business which the directors would believe to be advantageous to the company.

In response to these devices, the courts have developed the following techniques:

(a) **Main objects rule**

This rule was developed as a reaction to the draftsmen's inclusion of dozens of different objects into the objects clause. The main objects rule provides that where the objects clause provides for a multitude of different objects, the court will hold that many of them will not be exercisable in their own right but are only ancillary to the main object.

(b) **Independent objects clause/*Cotman* clause**

The draftsmen responded to the main objects rule by inserting an independent objects clause into the memorandum. This clause states that all paragraphs of the objects clause are to be construed independently of each other. The validity of the independent objects clause was recognised in the case of *Cotman v Brougham* [1918] AC 514.

(c) *Bell House* clause

The inclusion of a *Bell House* clause in a company's memorandum enables a company to pursue any business which the directors would believe to be advantageous to the company. This clause took its name from the case *Bell Houses Ltd v Citywall Properties Ltd* [1966] 2 All ER 674. The courts will uphold such a clause provided the following two caveats are satisfied:

- the clause must be compatible with the articles and memorandum of association of the company on their construction; and
- the directors must be acting *bona fide* at the time they entered the transaction in question.

3.2.1.1 Judicial interpretation

The decision in *Re Introductions* (*Introductions Ltd v National Provincial Bank Ltd*) [1968] 3 All ER 1221 demonstrated the limited effectiveness of these devices. In this case, the company had the object clause of providing tourist services. The company's constitutional documents contained both the *Cotman* and *Bell House* clauses. The company obtained a loan from a bank. The bank was aware that the proceeds of the loan were to be used for the pig rearing business. When the bank sought to recover the loan, the company claimed that the loan was *ultra vires* the company's objects. The bank argued that since the company's memorandum contained the *Cotman* clause, the act of borrowing was in effect an independent object of the company. The court dismissed this claim by stating that as far as a trading company is concerned, the borrowing of money could not be an object in itself. Such a company could only borrow money for the purpose of pursuing the company's objects. The court held that the bank could not rely on the *Bell House* clause by stating that the directors could not be regarded as acting *bona fide* where borrowing for the purposes of pig breeding. Furthermore, it would not be credible for the company to argue that pursuing the business of pig breeding was beneficial to the company's general business of providing tourist services.

Therefore, it is clear that the courts may cut down the scope of these clauses by placing limitations on their applicability. The Irish courts adopted a similar approach in the case of *Northern Bank Finance Corp Ltd v Quinn & Achates Investment Co* [1979] ILRM 221.

3.2.1.2 Enforcing an ultra vires *loan contract*

An issue of particular concern is what are the legal issues that arise when a company takes out an *ultra vires* loan with a bank and defaults on the repayment of the loan. Under normal circumstances, the bank would take legal action against the company for recovery of the monies based on the law of contract. However, the company never had the capacity to begin with to legally enter into the loan contract. Can the bank then ask the court to order the company to return the money, even though the company never had the authority to receive the money in the first place, that is, can a transaction *ultra vires* the company be enforced against the company?

There are a number of remedies available to the lender who enters into a loan which is *ultra vires* the borrowers objects.

(a) Section 8(1) of the Companies Act 1963

Section 8(1) of the Companies Act (CA) 1963 provides as follows:

> Any act or thing done by a company which, if the company had been empowered to do the same would have been lawfully and effectively done, shall, notwithstanding that the

company had no power to do such act or thing, be effective in favour of any person relying on such act or thing who is not shown to have been actually aware, at the time when he so relied thereon, that such act or thing was not within the powers of the company, but any director or officer of the company who was responsible for the doing by the company of such act or thing shall be liable to the company for any loss or damage suffered by the company in consequence thereof.

Therefore, where a loan is given to a company which is *ultra vires* the company's objects the lender may enforce the transaction provided he was not 'actually aware' at the time the transaction was entered into that the borrower was acting *ultra vires*. The courts looked at s 8(1) of the CA 1963 in the case of *Northern Bank Finance Co v Quinn & Achates Investment Co*. Keane J found that where the lender's solicitor had read the company's constitutional documents but misunderstood them, the lender is still deemed to be actually aware. On the basis of this decision, it would seem that the safest course of action would appear to be to refuse to inspect the memorandum and articles of the borrower before entering into a transaction. However, in practice, all banks will inspect the memorandum and articles and therefore lose the protection of s 8(1).

(b) **Regulation 6 of the European Communities (Companies) Regulations 1973 (SI 1973/163)**

Regulation 6 states that:

(i) In favour of a person dealing with a company in good faith, any transaction entered into by any organ of the company, being its board of directors or any person registered under these regulations as a person authorised to bind the company, shall be deemed to be within the capacity of the company and any limitation of the powers of that board or person, whether imposed by the memorandum or articles of association or otherwise, may not be relied upon as against any person dealing with the company.

(ii) Any such person shall be presumed to have acted in good faith unless the contrary is proven.

The following restrictions on the availability of Reg 6 should be noted. First, Reg 6 only applies to limited companies and, secondly, Reg 6 is only relevant where an outsider deals with the board of directors, or a person registered under the regulation as a person authorised to bind the company.

3.2.2 Transactions with directors

Part III of the Companies Act (CA) 1990 places extensive restrictions on transactions which could take place between a company and directors or connected persons. Part IX (ss 75–79) of the Company Law Enforcement Act (CLEA) 2001 introduced a range of amendments to Pt III of the CA 1990. The provisions of Pt IX of the CLEA 2001 are in force with effect from 1 October 2001. However, the primary prohibitions set out in s 31 of the CA 1990 still remain in force.

Section 31 of the CA 1990 provides that a company may not:

(a) make a loan or a quasi-loan to a director of the company or of its holding company or to any person connected with such a director;

(b) enter into credit transactions as creditor for such a director or person so connected; or

(c) enter into a guarantee or provide any security in connection with a loan, quasi-loan or credit transaction made by any other person for such a director or person so connected.

3.2.2.1 Credit transaction

A credit transaction is defined by s 25(3) of the CA 1990 as one in which:

> ... a creditor supplies any goods or sells any land, enters into a hire purchase agreement or conditional sale agreement, leases or licences the use of land, hires goods in return for periodical payments or otherwise disposes of land or supplies goods or services on the understanding that payment is to be deferred.

Section 75 of the CLEA 2001 amends s 25 of the CA 1990. The new section provides that the creation of a lease for a premium equal to the open market value of the relevant land and reserving a nominal annual rent of not more than €12.70 does not constitute a credit transaction. Two criteria must be met in this revised definition:

(a) the premium must be equal to the open market value of the land in question; and

(b) the annual rent must not exceed €12.70 *per annum*.

3.2.2.2 Connected persons

Section 26 of the CA 1990 sets out what is meant by the term 'connected person'. It states that:

> ... a person is connected with a director of a company if but only if he is that director's spouse, parent, brother, sister or child or person acting in his capacity as the trustee of any trust, the principal beneficiaries of which are the director, his spouse or any of his children or any body corporate which he controls, or a partner of that director.

A partner of the director is also a connected person, but no guidance is given as to whether this refers to a business partner, a personal partner or both. A body corporate is deemed to be connected with a director of a company if it is controlled by that director. Section 76 of the CLEA 2001 has amended s 26 of the CA 1990 in two respects. First, the reference to a 'partner' is now defined in the context of a partner within the meaning of the Partnership Act 1890. Secondly, a sole member of a single private member limited company is now presumed to be a connected person with the director of that company.

3.2.2.3 Exceptions to prohibitions in s 31

(a) **Minor transactions**

Section 32 of the CA 1990 establishes a *de minimis* rule permitting transactions otherwise *prima facie* falling foul of the prohibitions in s 31. Section 32 provides that if the aggregate value of all loans, quasi-loans and credit transactions entered into by a company with its directors or persons connected with those directors is less than 10% of its net assets or if there are no audited accounts 10% of the called up share capital, then s 31 prohibitions do not apply. The CLEA 2001 does not expand the range of transactions which can avail of s 32.

(b) **Group exemption**

Section 78 of the CLEA 2001 replaces s 34 of the CA 1990 and provides that any member of a group of companies can enter into the entire range of transactions prohibited by s 31, provided such transactions are in favour of another member of the group. Previously a distinction existed between group transactions by subsidiaries in favour of their holding companies and transactions entered into by any group member in favour of another group member. This distinction has now been removed. This group exemption will only apply provided that the authorisation procedure set out in s 34 of the CA 1990, as amended by s 78 of the CLEA 2001, is complied with. This procedure is known as the 'whitewash procedure'.

(c) Whitewash procedure

The 'whitewash procedure' only applies to the provision of a guarantee or security. It does not apply to the making of a loan, quasi-loan or credit transaction. The whitewash procedure is set out below:

- the directors of the company must meet to consider its affairs and the nature of the proposed guarantee or security;
- if the directors are satisfied that the company, after having entered into the guarantee or security, will be able to pay its debts as they fall due, they swear at the meeting a statutory declaration averring to the carrying out of a full enquiry into the affairs of the company and the forming of an opinion that having provided the guarantee or security, the company will be able to pay its debts as and when they fall due;
- an independent auditor of the company must prepare a report stating that the statutory declaration is reasonable;
- a copy of the declaration and the report and the notice convening an extraordinary general meeting (EGM) of the shareholders is sent to each shareholder of the company;
- an EGM must then be held at which the shareholders must approve the giving of the guarantee or security by way of a special resolution;
- an alternative to convening an EGM is for all the shareholders to sign a written copy of the resolution which has appended to it the statutory declaration and the report of the independent auditor; and
- the statutory declaration and report must then be filed in the Companies Registration Office within 21 days of the provision of the guarantee or security.

If all members of the company do not vote in favour of the special resolution, the company cannot enter into the guarantee or security for 30 days after the passing of the special resolution. This 30-day period is to enable the minority shareholders to apply to the court within 28 days of the passing of the special resolution to have the resolution cancelled. The company cannot provide the guarantee or security until the application is either confirmed by the court or disposed of.

(d) Holding company, subsidiary, or subsidiary of holding company

Section 35 of the CA 1990 as amended by s 79 of the CLEA 2001 provides that transactions entered into by a company with or for the benefit of its holding company, its subsidiary or a subsidiary of its holding company are not prohibited by s 31 of the CA 1990. This section applies to all types of transactions.

(e) Director's expenses

Section 36 of the CA 1990 provides that s 31 of the CA 1990 does not prohibit a company from doing anything in providing any of the directors with funds to meet vouched expenditure properly incurred, or to be incurred by him for the purpose of the company or for the purposes of enabling him to properly perform his duties as an officer of the company.

(f) Transactions in the ordinary course of business

Section 37 of the CA 1990 provides that transactions entered into in the ordinary course of business are not prohibited by s 31 of the CA 1990.

3.2.2.4 *Consequences of breach of section 31*

The CA 1990 sets out the consequences of a breach of s 31. These are as follows:

(a) s 38 provides the transaction is voidable at the instance of the company which includes the liquidator;

(b) ss 38(2) and 39 provides that the benefiting director or connected person, along with every director who approved the transaction is liable to the company for every gain made. They must also indemnify the company for any loss suffered by the company; and

(c) s 40 of the CA 1990 provides for criminal penalties for breach of s 31.

3.2.3 Financial assistance in connection with the purchases of and subscriptions for shares

Section 60 of the CA 1963 provides that it shall not be lawful for:

> ... a company to give, whether directly or indirectly, and whether by means of a loan, guarantee, the provision of security or otherwise, any financial assistance for the purpose of or in connection with a purchase or subscription made or to be made by any person of or for any shares in the company or, where the company is a subsidiary company, in its holding company.

Therefore, the giving of financial assistance in connection with the acquisition of shares in a company is prohibited. However, such an act may be lawful if it has been given under the authority of a special resolution of the members of the company passed within the previous 12 months. There must be attached to the resolution (in the case of a written resolution) or enclosed with the notice of the relevant general meeting, a copy of a statutory declaration of solvency of a majority of the directors. The declaration must be made at a meeting of the directors which is held not less than 24 days before the passing of the special resolution and must be made by either all of the directors or by a majority of them. According to s 60(4) of the CA 1963, the declaration must:

- state the form which the assistance is to take;
- the person to whom the assistance is to be given;
- the purpose for which the company intends those persons to use such assistance;
- that the declarants have made a full enquiry into the affairs of the company; and
- that having done so, they have formed the opinion that the company, having carried out the transaction whereby such assistance is to be given, will be able to pay its debts as they come due.

A director who makes the statutory declaration without having reasonable grounds for the opinion that the company will be able to pay its debts in full as they become due, is liable to imprisonment and/or a fine. If the company is wound up on the basis of insolvency within 12 months after the date of the declaration, it will be presumed that the directors did not have reasonable grounds for the opinion contained in the declaration. The directors will also be liable to account to the company if they have breached their fiduciary duty to the company.

Shareholders are notified of the transaction in advance and are given the opportunity to consider it. Notice of an EGM must be given to all shareholders. A copy of the statutory declaration of solvency must accompany the notice.

A copy of the director's declaration of solvency must be filed in the Companies Registration Office on the same day that the notice of the EGM is sent to the shareholders. If this requirement is not complied with, the validation procedure is not applicable.

Section 60 does not prohibit the following transactions:

- the payment of dividend properly declared by the company;
- the discharge of a liability lawfully incurred by the company;
- the lending by a company of money in the ordinary course of its lending business;
- the provision by a company of funding for an employee share scheme; and
- the making by a company of loans to employees other than directors to enable such employees to purchase or subscribe for shares in the company.

3.2.4 Registration of charges

The Registrar of Companies keeps a register of charges which are required to be registered under Pt IV of the CA 1963. Section 99(1) of the CA 1963 provides that:

> ... every charge created after the fixed date by a company, and being a charge to which this section applies, shall, so far as any security on the company's property or undertaking is conferred thereby, be void against the liquidator or any creditor of the company, unless the prescribed particulars of the charge, verified in the prescribed manner, are delivered to or received by the Registrar of Companies for registration in manner required by this Act within 21 days after the date of its creation, but without prejudice to any contract or obligation for repayment of the money thereby secured, and when a charge becomes void under this section, the money secured thereby shall immediately become payable.

Section 99(2) of the CA 1963 sets out the types of charges which must be registered. These are:

(a) a charge for the purpose of securing any issue of debentures;
(b) a charge on uncalled share capital of the company;
(c) a charge created or evidenced by an instrument which, if executed by an individual, would require registration as a bill of sale;
(d) a charge on land, wherever situate, or any interest therein, but not including a charge for any rent or any other periodical sum issuing out of land;
(e) a charge on book debts of the company;
(f) a floating charge on the undertaking or property of the company;
(g) a charge on calls made but not paid;
(h) a charge on a ship or aircraft or any share in a ship or aircraft; and
(i) a charge on goodwill, on a patent or a licence under a patent, on a trademark or on a copyright or a licence under a copyright.

There are two categories of registerable charges which may be relevant to the registerability of a security document. These are (e) and (f) above; charges over book debts of the pledgor and floating charges over the assets of the pledgor respectively.

Therefore, where a company executes a charge, the particulars of such a charge must be delivered to the Registrar of Companies within 21 days from the date of the creation of the charge. Failure to register the charge will render the charge void against the liquidator or any creditor of the company.

3.2.4.1 Registration process

Registration for an Irish company is undertaken by lodging a Form C1 with the Registrar of Companies. If a charge becomes void by virtue of non-registration, the whole sum secured by the charge is immediately payable on demand. The provision of s 288 of the CA 1963 must be borne in mind which provides that:

> ... where a company is being wound up, a floating charge on the undertaking or property of the company created within 12 months before the commencement of the winding up shall, unless it is proved that the company immediately after the creation of the charge was solvent, be invalid, except as to money actually advanced or paid, or the actual price or value of goods or services sold or supplied, to the company at the time of or subsequently to the creation of, and in consideration for, the charge, together with interest on that amount at the rate of 5% per annum.

3.2.4.2 Late registration of charges

If a company does not submit details of the charge for registration within the appropriate period, an application may be made to the court pursuant to s 106 of the CA 1963 for an order to either extend the time for registration or to rectify an error in the application. However, a court will only accept an application if it is satisfied that the omission to register the charge was accidental due to inadvertence or to some other sufficient cause, or is not of a nature to prejudice the position of the courts or shareholders of the company or that on other grounds, it is just and equitable to grant relief. Where a court is satisfied that one of the aforementioned grounds apply, it can exercise its discretion to extend the time limit. In the case of *Re Telford Motors Ltd* (27 January 1978, unreported), the court held that late registration will not be permitted where a winding up is being commenced.

3.2.4.3 Registration of charges on property in the State acquired by a company incorporated outside the State

Section 111 of the CA 1963 states that the provisions of s 99 of the CA 1963 shall also extend to charges over property in Ireland created by a company incorporated outside Ireland and which has an established place of business in Ireland. A record of these charges are put on a register in Ireland called the 'Slavenberg Register'. It is also standard practice for a company to make a precautionary filing where the pledgor is a company incorporated outside of Ireland which does not, at the time of creation of the security interest, have an established place of business in Ireland but the secured assets encompass Irish located assets.

Section 109 of the CA 1963 provides that copies of all charges required to be registered under ss 99 and 111 of the CA 1963 must be kept at the registered office of the chargeor if the chargeor is an Irish incorporated company, and/or at its principal place of business if the chargeor is a foreign incorporated company. Failure to comply with this provision will not affect the validity of the security interest.

3.2.5 Transactions in defraud of creditors

3.2.5.1 Fraudulent preferences

Section 286 of the CA 1963 (as amended by s 135 of the CA 1990) provides that:

> ... any conveyance, mortgage, delivery of goods, payment, execution or other act relating to property made or done by or against a company which is unable to pay its debts as they become due in favour of any creditor or of any person on trust for any creditor, with a view to giving such a creditor, or any surety or guarantor for the debt due to such creditor, a preference over the other creditors, shall, if a winding up of the company commences within 6 months of the making or doing the same and the company is at the time of the commencement of the winding up unable to pay its debts (taking into account contingent and

prospective liabilities), be deemed a fraudulent preference of his creditors and be invalid accordingly.

In the case of a voluntary winding up, the winding up is deemed to 'commence' on the date the relevant winding up resolution is passed. As regards a compulsory winding up, the 'commencement' is deemed to be the date the petition for winding up is presented.

Where the conveyance, mortgage, delivery of goods, payment, execution or other action is in favour of a 'connected person' the six-month time period is extended to two years. Any such act is deemed in the event of a company being wound up to be made with a view to giving such a person a preference over the other creditors, and to be a fraudulent preference.

Section 286(5) of the CA 1963 defines a 'connected' person as a person who, at the time the transaction was made was:

(a) a director of the company;
(b) a shadow director of the company;
(c) a director's spouse, parent, brother, sister or child;
(d) a related company;
(e) a trustee; or
(f) a surety or guarantor for the debt due to any person described in the foregoing sub-paragraphs.

The onus of proof lies on the liquidator to prove fraudulent preference. In the case of *Re Curran Construction Ltd v Bank of Ireland Finance Ltd* (8 September 1976, unreported), the court set out that in order to determine fraudulent preference, three principles must be determined. First, the act creating the conveyance, mortgage, etc must be a voluntary act of the company. Secondly, the company must go into liquidation within a six-month period of the act of creating the conveyance, mortgage, etc. Thirdly, the act of creating the conveyance, mortgage, etc must be done with the dominant intention of preferring one creditor over another.

3.2.5.2 Improperly transferred assets

Section 139 of the CA 1990 provides that:

> ... where on the application of a liquidator, creditor or contributory of a company which is being wound up it can be shown to the satisfaction of the court that any property of the company was disposed of either by way of conveyance, transfer, mortgage, security, loan or in any way whatsoever whether by act or omission, direct or indirect, and the effect of such a disposal was to perpetrate fraud on the company, its creditors or members, the court may if it deems it just and equitable to do so, order any person who appears to have the use, control or possession of such property or the proceeds of the sale or development thereof to deliver it or pay a sum in respect of it to the liquidator on such terms or conditions as the court sees fit.

When a court is deciding whether to make an order under s 139 of the CA 1990, the court must consider whether such an order would be just and equitable having regard to the rights of a *bona fide* purchaser for value of an interest in the property.

Therefore, if at the time a pledgor enters into a contract to provide collateral, he acts in good faith and there are reasonable grounds to believe that such an act would be for the benefit of, and conductive to his business, then there would not seem to be any grounds under which a court could make an order under s 139 of the CA 1990.

This section does not apply if s 286 of the CA 1963 applies and the transaction is shown to have been a fraudulent preference.

3.2.5.3 Conveyancing Act (Ireland) 1634

Section 10 of the Conveyancing Act (Ireland) 1634 applies to fraudulent conveyances, and was designed to ensure that a person who is about to go bankrupt does not alienate his property and thus defeat the claims of his creditors. This section is aimed at prohibiting bogus transactions.

Since more adequate remedies exist under more modern legislation, it is unlikely that the provisions of s 10 would be pleaded as a means of seeking to prevent the defeat of the interest of the creditor.

3.2.5.4 Avoidance of floating charges

Section 288 of the CA 1963 (as replaced by s 136 of the CA 1990) provides that a floating charge created by a company before the commencement of a winding up will be invalid if the company was insolvent when it created the charge. The charge will also be rendered invalid if the company was rendered insolvent as a result of creating the charge.

3.3   Security over land

A mortgage is a type of security whereby the lender takes an interest or claim in the property directly. Initially, mortgages were structured by way of an outright conveyance. A date was set when all of the monies had to be repaid. This date of repayment was called the legal date of redemption. If the mortgagor did not pay back all the money on the estate, then the title of the property was not returned. Equity however took a different view and deemed a mortgage a secured loan. Equity thought it unfair that the mortgagor would lose his property if the full amount of the loan were not repaid on the redemption date. Equity stated that a mortgagor had a right to redeem his mortgage by repaying the loan and any interest long after the legal date of redemption had passed. This gave rise to the equitable maxim 'there must be no clogs on the equity of redemption', which means that once the legal date of redemption has passed, a mortgagor on repayment of all the monies owed must be entitled to redeem that mortgage.

3.3.1   Creation of legal mortgages

(a)   **Creation of mortgage over registered land**

The method of creation of a mortgage depends on whether the land to become subject to the mortgage is registered or unregistered land. Registered land is governed by the Registration of Title Act 1964. In the case of registered land, once a mortgage document is executed, it is sent to the Land Registry and the mortgage is registered as a charge and the lender is issued with a charge certificate. The court in the case of *AIB v Glynn* [1973] IR 188 held that it was possible to create an equitable mortgage over registered land by depositing the original land certificate with the bank.

(b)   **Creation of mortgage over freehold unregistered land**

There are two methods of creating a mortgage over freehold unregistered land. The traditional method is by way of a conveyance of the fee simple subject to a proviso for redemption. The mortgagor conveys his land to the mortgage company. There is an outright conveyance. Once the money is paid off, the mortgage company is obliged to reconvey the property to the mortgagor. The second method is a more modern version of the first. It provides that the mortgagor retains the freehold title to the land but in reality grants a very long lease to the mortgage company, very often for 999 years. A provision is also included that the mortgagee is entitled to the freehold reversion.

(c) **Creation of mortgage over leasehold unregistered land**

Where the mortgagor is the holder of the leasehold interest in property he is not in a position to convey the land outright. A mortgage can be created over the property in two ways. The first is by assignment. The mortgagor signs over the entirety of his lease to the mortgagee, subject to the proviso of redemption. The second is a sub-demise. This method is more common than the first. The mortgage company is given a sublease over the land for a term slightly shorter than the term of the mortgagor's lease.

3.3.2 Creation of equitable mortgages

There are two methods of creating an equitable mortgage. The most popular is by way of an equitable deposit of title deeds. The deeds are held by the bank and no legal obligation is created. The second method is where there is an agreement or contract that a legal mortgage will be put in place. Equity will enforce that contract by specific performance.

3.3.3 Rights and duties of the mortgagee

(a) As a general principle, the mortgagee as part of its security is entitled to have the title documents relating to the land in his possession. No further securities can be created over the land without the mortgagee's prior notification. Once the charge document is registered, the mortgagee is given priority.

(b) Pursuant to s 19 of the Conveyancing Act (CVA) 1881 the mortgagee has a statutory power to insure the mortgaged property. In reality details relating to insuring the property is taken care of by the mortgage deed.

(c) The mortgagee has the right to enforce the security. There are a number of enforcement methods, which are as follows:

- court order for possession;
- sale of property outright without going to court.

    Section 19 of the CVA 1881 gives the mortgagee a power of sale on all mortgages created by deed. For this reason a court order for sale is not required when a mortgagee wishes to sell a property. However, if the mortgagor refuses to leave the property, the mortgagee may seek an order for possession from the court so that the property can be sold in vacant possession. The order for possession may be adjourned pursuant to s 7 of the Family Home Protection Act 1976. This section provides that the court has the power to adjourn possession proceedings if there has been non-payment of the mortgage by one of the spouses but it appears that the other spouse is capable of paying the mortgage. Section 20 of the CVA 1881 provides that the mortgagee's power of sale can only be exercised once proper notice has been given to the mortgagor;

- court order for sale.

    The mortgagee must apply to court for an order for sale where a legal mortgage has not been created over the property, that is, where a judgment or equitable mortgage is created over the property;

- mortgagee can take possession of the property.

  Where the mortgagee takes possession of the property, he can either take the rents from the property or may exercise his power of sale;
- appointment of receiver.

  The mortgagee may appoint a receiver to manage the property. Section 24 of the CVA 1881 expressly states that any receiver appointed is the agent of the mortgagee; and
- foreclosure.

  This method of enforcement is very rare in Ireland.

3.3.4 Rights and duties of the mortgagor

(a) The mortgagor has a right of sale, however this right is always subject to the mortgage.

(b) The mortgagor is entitled to pay off the mortgage at any time once the legal date of redemption has passed. Any clause in a mortgage deed preventing this right of redemption will not be enforced by a court.

(c) Section 16 of the CVA 1881 provides that the mortgagor is entitled to inspect and take copies of the title deed to the property.

3.3.5 Priorities in relation to mortgages

(a) **Priorities between legal interests**

The basic rules concerning priorities is as follows: if a legal interest has been validly created, then that interest is enforceable against all parties who subsequently acquire interest to the land. If there are two competing legal interests, the first in time prevails.

(b) **Priorities between equitable interests**

If there are two competing equitable interests, and if the equities are equal, the first in time will prevail.

(c) **Unregistered land**

Unregistered land is governed by the Registry of Deeds system. Prior to the Registry of Deeds (Ireland) Act 1707, the common law and equitable rules governed proprieties in relation to unregistered land. These rules were as follows:

- **The first legal, second legal**

  Successive legal mortgages are only possible if the first mortgage is created by demise or sub-demise. Legal interests take priority in the order of their creation. However, the first mortgagee will lose priority in the case of fraud, estoppel or gross negligence with respect to the title deeds.

- **The first legal, second equitable**

  The legal mortgage takes priority.

- **The first equitable, second legal**

  The legal interest will take priority if the legal mortgagee is *bona fide* and takes for value without notice of the earlier equitable interest.

- **The first equitable, second equitable**

  The first in time will prevail.

The above rules will not apply if the land has been registered in the Registry of Deeds. Where land has been so registered, the following rules in relation to priority will apply:

- **Registered v registered**
  Registered documents rank in the order in which Memorials of them are lodged for registration. Therefore, it is irrelevant whether the mortgages are legal or equitable for the purpose of determining priorities in this instance.
- **Registered v registerable but unregistered**
  Registered interest takes priority.
- **Registerable interest but unregistered v registered**
  Registered document takes priority even though it is later in time.

(d) **Registered land**

Priorities in relation to registered land is determined in accordance with the order of registration of the mortgage in the Land Registry and not the date of the creation of the mortgage.

3.4 Charges

3.4.1 Floating charges

A floating charge is a form of security created under the rules of equity in Ireland. Typically, a floating charge is a form of security that is created by a limited company over all of its assets. It is said that the charge floats in the sense that the assets of the company may be dealt with in the ordinary course of business by the company, notwithstanding the creation of the charge. Assets may be disposed of and new assets may be acquired, bringing them within the subject of the charge. The secured creditor has no right to be secured over any specific asset belonging to the debtor. If, however, the secured creditor becomes entitled to enforce its security, the charge ceases to float and it is said to crystallise. It then becomes a fixed charge on the assets of the debtor at that moment. Attachment of the security is created by means of a document described as a debenture.

3.4.2 Conduct of the business while the charge remains uncrystallised

The rationale for the creation of a floating charge is that the debtor is free to carry on its business unimpeded by the charge until the charge crystallises.

In the absence of restrictions contained in the debenture creating a floating charge, the debtor is free to carry on business in the ordinary way, dealing with property subject to the charge and acquiring property that will become subject to the charge. A company that has created a floating charge over its entire undertaking may sell property in the ordinary course of business. (It is useful to point out that if not prohibited by the terms of the debenture, the company may create a fixed charge in the ordinary course of business over property comprised in the floating charge, thereby giving priority to the holder of the fixed charge over the holder of the floating charge.)

The floating charge hovers over the charged property until the moment of crystallisation. At this point, the charge fastens onto the charged property and becomes in effect a fixed charge.

3.4.3 Fixed charges

A fixed charge is a form of security whereby a lender and borrower agree that in return for the lender advancing finance to the borrower, certain identifiable property will be present to satisfy the debt in the case of default by the borrower. One of the distinguishing features of a fixed charge is that the company is not free to deal with the charged property as it wishes.

3.4.4 Floating charges over book debts

The first case to deal specifically with book debts was *Re Yorkshire Woolcombers Association Ltd* [1903] 2 Ch 284 (also known as *Illingsworth v Holdsworth* [1904] AC 355 in the House of Lords, where the Court of Appeal was affirmed). A description of the floating charge was offered by Romer LJ in this case. He stated that if a charge has the following three characteristics, then it is a floating charge:

1   If it is a charge on a class of assets of a company present and future.
2   If that class is one which, in the ordinary course of business of the company, would be changing from time to time.
3   If you find that by the charge it is contemplated that, until some future step is taken by or on behalf of those interested in the charge, the company may carry on its business in the ordinary way as far as concerns the particular class of assets.

Romer LJ also expressly stated that he did not intend this definition to be exhaustive and charges that did not have these three characteristics may nonetheless be floating charges. Romer LJ held that the charge created in this case was a floating charge due to the lack of control of the charge-holder over the proceeds. The company remained free to collect the book debts and the proceeds were at its disposal for use in the ordinary course of business.

3.4.5 Fixed charges over book debts

Traditionally, it was considered impossible to take a fixed charge over present and future book debts. There are two reasons for this. First, imposing a fixed charge on book debts would starve the company of its everyday use of the proceeds of such book debts and could, in effect, paralyse the business. Secondly, book debts are fluctuating assets and it is a characteristic of floating charges that it is a charge on fluctuating assets, therefore it is not possible to impose a fixed charge on book debts.

The UK High Court in the case of *Siebe Gorman & Co Ltd v Barclays Bank Ltd* [1979] 2 Lloyd's Rep 142 overcame these difficulties and held that it was possible to create a fixed charge over book debts. In this case, the company was prohibited to deal with the uncollected debts but were free to collect the proceeds of the book debts and were required to pay them into an account in its name with the bank. Slade J stated that the distinguishing feature of whether a charge was fixed or floating was not the fluctuating character of the charged asset but rather the company's power to deal with the charged assets in the ordinary course of business. He held that since the company was not free to draw on the account without the consent of the bank, a fixed charge was created over the book debts.

In *Re Brightlife Ltd* [1987] Ch 200, the company purported to grant to the bank a fixed charge over its book debts. The company was free to collect the debts and pay them into its ordinary bank account, however it was not required to do so. Hoffman J held that the charge was a floating charge as the company was free to collect the proceeds of the book debts and to pay them into its bank account. Once the proceeds were in the account, they were then outside the charge over the debt.

Following these cases, it seemed that in order for a fixed charge to be created, the proceeds of the book debts needed to be paid into a bank account which the company maintained with the holder of the charge. Furthermore, the company could not withdraw from the account without the prior consent of the charge-holder. The draftsman of the charge in the case of *Re New Bullis Trading* [1994] 1 BCLC 485 sought to place a fixed charge on the proceeds of the book debts while at the same time allowing the company to deal with the proceeds of the book debts in the ordinary course of business. The debenture in this case purported to create two charges: a fixed charge over the uncollected book debts and a floating charge over their proceeds. The question the court addressed was whether the uncollected debts were subject to a fixed or floating charge at the time when the receivers were appointed.

The Court of Appeal looked at the true construction of the charge deed and held that the parties intended the book debts to be subject to a fixed charge while uncollected, and subject to a floating charge upon the payment of the proceeds into the bank account in the absence of any instruction being given concerning how the proceeds might be used. Therefore, the charge over the book debts was held to be a fixed charge until their proceeds were paid into a specified account.

The Privy Counsel decision of *Agnew and Another v Commissioner of Inland Revenue* [2001] 3 WLR 454 (also known as *Re Brumark Investments*) declared that *Re New Bullis Trading* was wrongly decided. In the *Re Brumark* case, a charge was created over the uncollected book debts of the company. The company was free to collect the proceeds and to use them in the ordinary course of business. The question for the court was whether the company's right to collect and deal with the proceeds free from the security meant that the charge on the uncollected debt, though described in the debenture as fixed was actually a floating charge until crystallised by the appointment of the receivers. Lord Millett stated that *Re New Bullis Trading* was wrongly decided and that the property and its proceeds were clearly different assets:

> ... whilst the debt and its proceeds are two separate assets, however, the latter are more traceable proceeds of the former and represent its entire value. A debt is a receivable; it is merely a right to receive payment from a debtor. Such a right cannot be enjoyed *in specie*; its value can be exploited only by exercising the right or by assigning it for value to a third party. An assignment or charge of a receivable which does not carry with it the right to the receipt has no value. It is worthless as a security. Any attempt in the present context to separate the ownership of the debts from the ownership of the proceeds (even if conceptually possible) makes no commercial sense.

Therefore, it is not possible to create a fixed charge over uncollected book debts and couple this in the same debenture with a floating charge over the proceeds of the debts. Lord Millett also pointed out that in order to create a fixed charge over book debts, it is sufficient to prevent the company from realising the debt itself. If the company seeks to do so, the charge-holder may refuse permission, or grant permission on terms or may direct the proceeds of the book debts. He stated that it is not necessary to go this far as it is not inconsistent with the nature of the fixed charge for the holder to appoint the company as agent and collect the book debts for its account on its behalf. However, the court made it clear that it is not enough to provide in the debenture that the account is a blocked account if it is not in fact operated as one. The court then held that since in the present case the company was left in control of the process by which the charged assets were extinguished and replaced by different assets, which were not the subject of a fixed charge and were at the free disposal of the company, a floating charge was created.

3.4.6 Irish position

In *Re Keenan Bros Ltd* [1986] BCLC 2542, the company purported to grant the bank a fixed charge over its present and future book debts. The debenture allowed the company to collect the book debts and to pay the proceeds into a designated account with the bank. The company was prohibited from making withdrawals from the account, disposing of the book debts or creating other charges over them without the consent of the bank. The Supreme Court held that a fixed charge had been created as the proceeds of the book debts were placed in a blocked account and were unusable by the company without the bank's consent.

The Irish Supreme Court revisited these issues again in the case of *Re Wogans Drogheda Ltd* [1993] 1 IR 154. In this case, the Supreme Court stated that in determining whether a charge is fixed or floating, the intention of the parties must be determined from the charge document and the conduct of the parties subsequent to the creation of the charge is not relevant for the purpose of determining the nature of the charge. Following this decision, the Irish position seems to be that if the terms of the debenture provides for a special restricted account to be designated by the lender, then in the absence of other terms indicating to the contrary, the charge may be a fixed charge even if the borrowing company remains in control of the proceeds.

The *Re Brumark* case has now set a new standard with regard to the distinction between fixed and floating charges by highlighting the point that 'labelling' and 'non-assignment' clauses in the debenture are insufficient to constitute a charge over book debts as a fixed charge. It is now not enough to provide in the debenture that the account is a blocked account if it is not operated as one. This case seems to be in conflict with the current Irish position set out by the Supreme Court in *Re Wogans Drogheda Ltd*. Should this issue be debated again in the Irish courts, it is likely that the Irish courts may be influenced by the *Re Brumark* decision.

3.5 Set-off and netting

Set-off is a procedure by which a creditor applies a debt due to him from a debtor against a debt owed by him to that debtor. Therefore, only a net balance remains payable. There are five categories of set-off in this jurisdiction.

1 Legal set-off.
2 Equitable set-off.
3 Bankruptcy set-off.
4 Banker's combination of accounts.
5 Contractual set-off.

Numbers 1–4 above will arise by operation of law. Contractual set-off extends the right to set-off beyond that arising by operation of law. Although contractual set-off fulfils a security function, it does not give any right over a creditor's asset, that is, debt, but merely an entitlement to set-off one personal obligation against another. An entitlement to set-off is not registerable as a security interest. Contractual set-off seeks to circumvent three principles of fundamental importance so far as rights of set-off arising by operation of law are concerned. These principles are:

(a) Mutuality of debts

The principle is based on the reasoning that obligations to set-off must arise between the same parties and in the same right. A difficulty may arise where deposits are made as security for the collateral obligations of third parties. There is no mutuality here as the debt owed by the bank is not owned by the third party. A way of overcoming this difficulty may be by obtaining a covenant or guarantee from the depositor agreeing to be liable for the third party's obligations.

(b) Contingencies

Contingent debts owed under a guarantee by a guarantor to a principal creditor may not be set-off in the event of the bankruptcy of the principal debtor unless the debts have been paid in full prior to the proof of the principal creditor in the insolvency.

(c) Permission to combine

Traditionally, banks have a right to combine or adjust customer accounts. However, in the case of *Bank of Ireland v Martin* [1937] IR 189 it was held that a bank may not combine a customer's deposit and loan accounts without assent from the customer. Contractual set-off will seek to circumvent this type of restriction.

3.5.1 Contractual set-off in insolvency

Where a debtor seeks to assert the contractual right of set-off in insolvency against the creditor's trustee in bankruptcy or against the liquidator, the issue arises as to whether this set-off on insolvency offends against the principle of *pari passu* distribution. This would result in a personal cross-claim diminishing an asset which would otherwise be available to the general body of creditors on insolvency.

The English and Irish courts seem to have different approaches in relation to contractual set-off in insolvency.

The English approach was set out in *British Eagle International Airlines Ltd v Compagnie Nationale Air France* [1975] 1 WLR 758. In this case, the House of Lords held that contractual set-off in insolvency is contrary to public policy as it circumvents the principle of *pari passu*. The only form of set-off available to the parties in this case was bankruptcy set-off. Bankruptcy set-off can only take place as between mutual debts in existence at the date of the insolvency.

The Irish approach to this matter was addressed in the case of *Dempsey v Bank of Ireland* (1963–93) Irish Company Law Reports 328. In this case, the depositor and bank agreed that in return for the bank acting as guarantor for the depositor, the depositor would indemnify the bank against its liabilities under the guarantee. Under the terms of the indemnity agreement, the bank was permitted to debit any of the depositor's accounts with any sums payable by the bank under the guarantee. At a date prior to the depositor's liquidation, the bank was called upon to pay under the guarantee. However, the bank only paid the amount under the guarantee some time after the commencement of the depositor's liquidation. The liquidator argued that the contractual right to set-off ceased on the date of the commencement of the liquidation as on that date, the entire assets of the depositor vested in him. Henchy J disagreed with the liquidator's argument and stated that when a liquidator takes over the assets of a company, he acquires only such title to the assets as the company had. Therefore, he takes the asset subject to any pre-existing enforceable right of a third party. The issue of contractual set-off in insolvency was revisited by the Irish courts in *Glow Heating Ltd v The Eastern Health Board* [1988] IR 110. In this case, the contract between a main contractor and a sub-contractor stated that in the event of default by the main contractor in paying the sub-contractor, the employer would pay the sub-contractor directly and deduct this amount from any sums due to the main contractor. Therefore, the contract permitted the employer to set-off a debt due by him to the sub-contractor against a debt due by him to the main contractor. The main contractor entered into liquidation. Some time later, the sub-contractor sought payment directly from the employer on foot of the contract. Costello J stated that the contract imposed a contingent liability, namely a liability to suffer a reduction in the event of default by the main contractor. Therefore, the court held that the liquidator took subject to this liability and that there was no breach of the *pari passu* principles.

Upon reflection of these cases, it now seems that the Irish courts will allow parties to operate contractual set-off in insolvency regardless of whether the debts to be set-off are mutual or contingent.

3.5.2 Flawed assets

A flawed asset is created when the depositor of the cash deposit agrees with the bank that the credit balance will not become payable until such time as the obligations of the depositor or some third party to the bank have been satisfied in full. A flawed asset does not purport to give the bank any right over the credit balance or to apply the credit balance against any debts due to it. Because of this, a flawed asset survives bankruptcy or insolvency of the depositor as it does not breach the *pari passu* rule. From an Irish bank's perspective, the flawed asset arrangement is of less importance than the provisions conferring rights of set-off, since the Irish courts allow parties to operate contractual set-off on insolvency. However, documents securing cash deposits should make a provision for flawed assets. First, because a flawed asset will continue as a form of security if the right of set-off is found to be ineffective and secondly, the flawed assets provisions will prevent the fund which is subject to the set-off from being depleted.

3.5.3 Netting

Section 1 of the Netting of Financial Contracts Act (NFCA) 1995 defines netting as:

> ... the termination of financial contracts, the determination of the termination values of those contracts and the set-off of the termination values so determined so as to arrive at a net amount due if any, by one party to the other where each such determination and set-off aforesaid is effected in accordance with the terms of a netting agreement between those parties.

A netting agreement is defined as an agreement between two parties only, in relation to present or future financial contracts between them providing, *inter alia*, for the termination of those contracts for the time being in existence, the determination of the termination values of those contracts and the set-off of the termination values so determined so as to arrive at a net amount due. Netting agreements may also provide for a guarantee to be given to one party on behalf of the other party solely to secure the obligation of either party in respect of the financial contracts concerned. It may also provide for the set-off of the net amount referred to above against the proceeds thereof and/or any money provided as security in respect of the financial contracts concerned.

Section 4 of the NFCA 1995 provides that:

> ... notwithstanding anything contained in any rule of law relating to bankruptcy, insolvency or receivership, or in the Companies Acts, or the Bankruptcy Act 1983, the provisions relating to netting, the set-off of money provided by way of security, the enforcement of a guarantee and the enforcement and realisation of collateral and the set-off of the proceeds thereof, as contained within a netting agreement or a guarantee provided for in such an agreement shall be legally enforceable against a party to the agreement and, where applicable, against a guarantor or other person providing security. The relevant provisions of the Netting Act will operate unless:
>
> (a) any enactment of rule of law would prevent the legal enforceability of the netting provisions of a netting agreement concerned on the grounds of fraud, misrepresentation or any similar ground and, in particular, by the reason of the application of:

(i) ss 57, 58 and 59 of the Bankruptcy Act 1988,
(ii) s 286 of the CA 1963, and
(iii) s 139 of the CA 1963;

(b) any provision of an agreement between the two parties concerned would make the netting, set-off, enforcement and realisation void whether because of fraud or misrepresentation or any similar grounds.

If parties enter into a valid netting agreement, and the circumstances set out in (a) and (b) above do not apply, then no provision of Irish law would prevent the secured party from either setting-off cash collateral or liquidating securities if the other party were to become subject to bankruptcy or other insolvency proceedings.

3.6 Registration of a security over intellectual property rights

There are primarily two ways in which to take security over intellectual property rights. The first method (and the most common) is to simply take a charge over the relevant intellectual property rights. The second method is taking an assignment of the rights while granting a right of redemption to the previous owner. This analysis deals with the first method.

Various pieces of legislation in Ireland, which follow, deal with intellectual property rights:

(a) **Registration requirements under the Patents Act 1992**

Section 85(1) of the Patents Act 1992 imposes a statutory obligation to record an interest in a patent or a *published* patent application. There is no obligation to register a security interest in a patent application which has *not* been published.

Failure to register the security interest with the Patents Office means that the document creating the charge will only be admitted in court as evidence of the security interest at the court's discretion.

While the 1992 Act does not expressly state any time limits in which to apply to register a security interest it is, however, strongly advisable that such application is made as soon as possible after the execution of the relevant debenture.

When making an application to register the security interest it is necessary to include a certified copy of the instrument creating the security interest. If the Controller is satisfied with the application he must register a notice of interest, including particulars of the instrument creating that interest.

As there is no particular form that such an application must take it appears that a letter should be directed to the Patents Office stating clearly the relevant patent numbers to which the security interest applies and attaching a certified copy of the debenture.

(b) **Registration requirements under the Trade Marks Act 1996**

The granting of a security interest (whether fixed or floating) over a registered trade mark or trade mark application or any right in or under it is a 'registerable transaction' within the meaning of s 29(2) of the Trade Marks Act (TMA) 1996 and, therefore, should be registered.

Section 29(3) of the TMA 1996 provides that until an application has been made for registration of the prescribed particulars of a registerable transaction, the transaction will be ineffective as against a person acquiring a conflicting interest in or under the registered trade mark in ignorance of it.

While the TMA 1996 does not expressly state any time limits within which to apply to register a security interest it is, however, strongly advisable that such application is made as soon as possible after the execution of the relevant debenture.

The form of application is not specified under the TMA 1996 or the Trade Marks Rules 1996 (SI 1996/199). However, the Trade Marks Office has prepared its own standard form of application.

An application to the Controller under s 29(1) of the TMA 1996 where the transaction is in relation to a security interest must be signed by or on behalf of the grantor of the right. The application must be accompanied by the prescribed fees and by a certified copy of the instrument or document upon which the name of the person, his title or interest is to be entered in the register is based. Finally, where a transaction is effected by an instrument chargeable with duty, the applicant must satisfy the Controller that the instrument has been duly stamped.

(c) **Registration requirements under the Copyright and Related Rights Act 2000**

In Ireland, it is not possible to register copyright. Therefore, there is no requirement to register a security interest over copyright pursuant to the Copyright and Related Rights Act 2000.

(d) **Registration requirements under the Industrial Designs Act 2001**

Where a person becomes entitled to a share in a design right as mortgagee, licensee or otherwise, he must apply to the Controller for the registration of notice of his or her interest in the Register. Any such application must be in writing, signed and be accompanied by a certified copy of the instrument upon which the claim of the person whose interest is to be entered in the Register is based.

Where an instrument creating such an interest is not registered, that instrument will not be entered in court as evidence of an interest to the design right in a design unless the court otherwise directs.

(e) **Registration requirements under the Companies Acts 1963–2001**

Section 99 of the CA 1963 as amended by s 122 of the CA 1990 requires that a company register charges with the Registrar of Companies, including a charge on goodwill, a trade mark and on a patent. The details of the charge created on the trade mark or patent should be registered within 21 days of the date of the debenture with the Companies Registration Office.

CHAPTER 4

STRUCTURED FINANCE – SECURITISATION

Tara Doyle

4.1 Introduction

Securitisation is a form of structured financing which has emerged in the past 20 years as a vital method of alternative financing for governments, financial institutions and corporates, as well as an important source of investment opportunities for pension funds, insurance companies and corporate treasury departments. This chapter will outline the taxation regime which has facilitated the development of the securitisation industry in Ireland and will examine the legal issues which have arisen in the context of this development.

While there is no generally accepted definition of the term 'securitisation', in essence securitisation is the issue of a security backed by a defined cash flow. A securitisation typically entails the establishment and management of a stand-alone bankruptcy remote special purpose company (SPV) for the purposes of acquiring assets that entitle their owner to future cash payments. A local or municipal government or government agency bank, building society, insurance company, trading company or other originator (Originator) generally originates the assets, which must have identifiable and reliable cash flows. The type of assets commonly securitised includes leases, loans, royalties, bonds, notes or other debt instruments or securities and receivables, derivatives and other financial assets. The acquisition is typically financed primarily through the issue of asset-backed securities in the form of bonds, notes or commercial paper (Notes) to investors (Noteholders) in the US or European capital markets.

The SPV generally authorises the Originator as 'servicer' to collect the receivables on behalf of the SPV which then uses the collection proceeds to pay principal and interest on the Notes and borrowings. In order to improve the credit risk profile, there will invariably be some form of credit-enhancement built into the structure in the form of over-collateralisation, a deferred purchase price mechanism, subordinated debt letter of credit, guarantee, surety bond, or reserve or collateral account. In addition, the SPV will typically enter into liquidity facility arrangements to ensure that timely payments of principal and interest are made to investors in the event of a delay in payment of the underlying receivables.

4.1.1 Originator perspective

The factors which drive a securitisation from an Originator's perspective are generally the following.

4.1.1.1 Capital raising

Securitisation involves funding based on the asset value and cash flow characteristics of an asset pool, rather than the liquidity or credit rating. The credit rating attaching to an Originator is an independent assessment of the likelihood of that Originator, whether corporate or government, being able to meet its debt obligations. Individual securities issued by the same company can be assigned different ratings. The highest rating that can be assigned to an Originator or a security is commonly known as 'Triple A'. There are currently three major rating agencies involved in the securitisation market of the Originator – Standard & Poor's Ratings Services, Moody's Investors Services Limited and Fitch Ratings Ltd. The agencies increase funding options for Originators and enables Originators with a poor credit rating to raise lower cost funding based on the credit quality of the relevant assets, as repackaged through a SPV with appropriate credit-enhancement techniques. This can enable Originators to obtain cheaper or longer term finance compared to the type of finance which could be raised by the Originator directly from the banks or the bond market. Moreover, an Originator may not have the credit rating for a successful Eurobond issue whereas Notes issued by a SPV and backed by an asset pool acquired from the Originator could have a much higher rating, hence diversifying the Originator's funding options.

A securitisation provides cash flow benefits in that the Originator has immediate access to the monies generated by the sale of the assets, rather than having to wait for them to be repaid in due course. This can release much needed cash to fund capital expenditure projects or expansion activities.

A securitisation programme can be structured so that the Originator can match its assets and liabilities, that is, use the receivables to repay the funding loan thereby reducing the risk of having to repay funding before receivables are paid.

A securitisation programme can allow an Originator to borrow at cheaper rates than its government. This is not the case with traditional funding sources available to non-sovereign borrowers. This ability to break through the rating ceiling has proven particularly attractive to Originators in emerging markets.

A securitisation enables an Originator to raise finance without having to constrain its business through the negative pledge covenants commonly found in bank loan agreements.

4.1.1.2 Improved balance sheet

An Originator can use a securitisation programme to strengthen its balance sheet by raising money without any borrowing appearing on its balance sheet while at the same time retaining the profits from the sold assets, net of programme costs. The Originator can use the sale proceeds to discharge outstanding liabilities and improve its debt to equity ratio and its return on capital, or to fund capital expenditure or expansion activities.

4.1.1.3 Capital adequacy advantages

Historically, a particular advantage of securitisations for banks, building societies and other financial institutions which are subject to capital adequacy regulations is that the Originator does not have to raise extra capital in order to support its assets. Usually an institution is faced with a choice of either raising extra capital to support its assets, selling its assets or restricting growth. In the case of a securitisation the Originator can sell its assets and still maintain its profits and, generally, its customer relationships. By taking assets off their balance sheets securitisations also allow Originators to free up capital which can then be put to use in more profitable activities.

The rapid growth in the collateralised loan obligation (CLO) market has been driven primarily by the desire of the financial institutions to reduce capital requirements held against low yielding assets, and thus free up cash for investment in assets or businesses with superior returns. In this regard, the CLO securitisation programmes provide an efficient and cost-effective capital management tool for such institutions.

The proposed new Basle Convention (Basle Committee on Banking Supervision, *New Basle Capital Accord*, January 2001) is expected to limit the importance going forward of this rationale for securitising assets.

4.1.2 Noteholder's perspective

The factors which drive securitisation from the Noteholder's perspective include the following.

4.1.2.1 Higher yield

Notes issued by a SPV in a securitisation programme generally involve a relatively higher return on investment than other investment grade fixed income securities of equivalent rating. The higher premium recognises the structured profile of the Notes and, in certain cases, the lower liquidity for the Notes. In the case of highly rated Notes which are traded as actively as any other bonds, the higher yield premium reflects the 'complexity spread', that is, the extra yield investors expect to compensate them for looking at anything complicated. However, as asset-backed securities become more common and their features more standardised, this complexity spread has tightened.

4.1.2.2 Standardised rating

The standardised rating of securitisation transactions provides a degree of security to investors and facilitates easy comparison between the different Note issues on offer to investors.

4.1.2.3 Tailored securities

Securitisation transactions are structured so that the risk associated with the underlying assets is transferred to investors willing to bear it for a price. The more risk-averse investors can subscribe for the senior, low-risk, low-yield, investment grade Notes and the more adventurous investors can opt for the junior, subordinated, high-risk, high-yield, speculative grade Notes. In addition, securitisation transactions enable investors to allocate their assets and risk across different industries and regions.

4.1.2.4 Direct asset claim

Investors in securitisation transactions usually have a security interest in the underlying assets, which can be enforced by a security trustee, appointed to act in that capacity on their behalf. The security trustee will have a direct claim against the underlying assets rather than an indirect claim through a corporate interest in the asset.

4.1.2.5 Insulation from corporate originator credit risk

Securitisations generally involve a true sale of the assets from the Originator directly, or through an intermediary vehicle, to the SPV. Accordingly, the insolvency of the Originator, or any intermediary vehicle, should not affect the SPV or the Noteholder, except as an administrative matter where the Originator is also acting as servicer. If the securitisation involves a revolving purchase of receivables, the Notes will generally provide for early amortisation on the insolvency of the Originator.

4.2 Taxation regime

In order for securitisation to be an effective form of funding for Originators, it is important that it does not result in any additional tax cost above that which would arise in the case of a more conventional form of funding, such as a bank loan or a corporate bond issue. It is important, therefore, that the SPV is structured so as to be 'tax neutral'. This means that the SPV's tax costs should be minimal and that Noteholders should not suffer any additional tax costs, such as withholding tax, as a result of the securitisation transaction.

In order to facilitate the growth of the securitisation industry in Ireland, the Department of Finance has introduced a number of legislative measures over the past 16 years. Section 31 of the Finance Act 1991 enabled the securitisation of domestic mortgages by Irish banks and building societies. In 1996, this was expanded to facilitate the securitisation of international assets through SPV's established in the International Financial Services Centre (IFSC) Dublin. In 1999, this was further expanded to facilitate the securitisation of a broader range of financial assets. Further changes were effected by the Finance Act 2003, which addressed various taxation issues that have arisen in the course of transactions, which have been carried out since 1999. The Finance Act 2003 has increased the nature and type of transactions which can take place and also provides for a deduction for all interest payable by an SPV irrespective of the normal interest recharacterisation rules. The current taxation regime for securitisations is set out in s 110 of the Taxes Consolidation Act (TCA) 1997.

Section 110 of the TCA 1997 facilitates securitisation by taxing SPVs as if they were trading companies. The importance of this 'deemed trading status' from a taxation perspective is that the SPV will get a deduction for the interest payments on its Notes, against the income it earns on the assets which it is securitising. Provided the transaction is structured so that the income earned matches the interest paid by the SPV, the SPV should make a minimal taxable profit. It is important that the SPV make a profit on each transaction from a corporate benefit perspective, but there is no set amount of profit which the SPV is required to make as a matter of Irish law. Generally, the profit earned by an SPV will be in the region of €1,000 per transaction, which would be taxed at 25% and result in a net tax cost of €250.

As noted above, it is important that the Noteholders do not suffer any additional tax as a result of the location of the SPV in Ireland. Noteholders should be subject to tax in the usual way in their home jurisdictions but should not be subject to tax in Ireland. In that regard, it is important that interest and principal payments to Noteholders be made 'gross', that is, free of withholding tax. Generally speaking, interest payments by an Irish SPV to a person or company outside of Ireland would be subject to withholding tax at the standard rate of income tax. However, if the interest is paid to a person located in an EU Member State (other than Ireland) or in a country with which Ireland has a double taxation treaty, interest can be paid gross. As the international capital markets generally demand that Notes be issued in bearer form, which means that ownership passes by delivery and is not determined by entry in a register, it is generally not possible for an SPV to determine whether the Noteholders meet this criteria. Accordingly, it is more common for SPVs to rely on the 'quoted eurobond' exemption which permits interest to be paid gross in circumstances where the Notes are in bearer form and are listed on a recognised stock exchange. The most common stock exchanges for this purpose are Luxembourg, London and, increasingly, Ireland. (See section 4.6 below for a discussion of the legal issues involved in listing Notes on the Irish Stock Exchange.)

4.3 Insolvency law issues

While the Department of Finance has introduced a number of legislative measures to facilitate the securitisation industry from a taxation perspective (as noted in section 4.2 above), there have unfortunately been no equivalent initiatives from an insolvency, securities and banking law perspective. Instead practitioners have been required to structure transactions and deliver opinions based on a legal regime which was never designed to deal with transactions of this nature. This paragraph will examine the insolvency law issues which have arisen and the manner in which practitioners have dealt with these issues.

As noted in section 4.1.2 above, one of the important features of a securitisation from a Noteholders perspective is that by investing in a security backed by cash flows from particular assets, the Noteholder is able to isolate its risk to the assets and is not required to take any risk on the Originator. This is achieved by transferring the assets to the SPV and by ensuring that the SPV is not related to the Originator for insolvency law purposes. This is commonly referred to as creating an 'off-balance sheet' SPV. While this has additional benefits for the Originator, as outlined in section 4.1.1.3 above, its primary purpose from the Noteholders' perspective is to ensure that on the insolvency of the Originator, the SPV's assets which fund the Notes cannot be accessed by the creditors of the Originator.

Section 140 of the Companies Act (CA) 1990 enables the High Court to order that the assets of a company which is related to an insolvent company be contributed to pay the debts of the insolvent company on its liquidation. Generally, companies will only be related for this purpose if they have common shareholdings or directors. It is therefore usual to structure SPVs so that their shares are owned by charitable trusts, or by nominee companies on trust for charitable purposes. This ensures that there is no common shareholding with the Originator. Generally, the board of directors of an SPV will consist of two Irish resident directors who are entirely independent of the Originator. While these features of the SPV will go a long way towards avoiding the application of s 140 of the CA 1990, companies will also be related to each other for these purposes if:

> ... the businesses of the companies have been so carried on that the separate business of each company, or a substantial part thereof, is not readily identifiable. (Section 140(5)(e) of the CA 1990.)

It is therefore important to ensure that the business of the SPV is carried on entirely independently of the Originator and it is not unusual for the transaction documentation to include separateness covenants which require the parties to a securitisation transaction to carry on separate businesses as a contractual matter.

In order to facilitate the development of the Irish securitisation industry it would be preferable if securitisation SPVs were removed from the ambit of s 140 of the CA 1990 entirely. However, pending any such legislative change it is important to bear these provisions in mind when structuring and opining on securitisation transactions.

In order to obtain the highest possible rating for the Notes, it is important that the SPV is bankruptcy remote and that the Notes are limited recourse obligations. This means that it should be impossible, or at least very unlikely, that the SPV be put into liquidation and also that the Noteholders should only be able to have recourse to the assets backing their Notes, rather than to the assets of the SPV as a whole. This second requirement is particularly important where the SPV is a 'multi-issuance vehicle', that is, where it enters into more than one securitisation transaction and issues different series of Notes backed by separate pools of assets.

In order to avoid the SPV being put into liquidation in the future, it is important to ensure that all of the creditors of the SPV agree not to petition to wind up the SPV. This structuring requirement presents two difficulties. First, it may not be possible to obtain the agreement of all creditors to the proposition and, secondly, the creditors' agreement in this regard may not be enforceable.

Generally, it will be possible to obtain the agreement of all parties to the securitisation transaction, who will usually be secured creditors of the SPV, to a clause requiring them not to petition to wind up the SPV, in circumstances where the debts due to them by the SPV have not been paid. Standard provisions to this effect will usually be included in the transaction documents. It is important to ensure that the pool of unsecured creditors, who are not party to the transaction documents, will be limited and that their debts are paid in priority to the secured creditors, so that they never have *locus standi* to present a petition to wind up the SPV. As the SPV will generally have no employees and will not rent premises the unsecured creditors are usually limited to professional advisers and the Revenue

Commissioners. (Please note that in some transactions, generally for foreign tax purposes, it is necessary for the SPV to have additional substance which generally involves it renting office space or hiring employees or secondees. Any such rental agreements will usually be entered into on a limited recourse basis with indemnities obtained from the Originator by the landlord if necessary. It is more difficult to limit recourses in an employment or secondment situation, so indemnities from the Originator are of greater importance.)

As noted in section 4.2 above, the SPV will usually be effectively tax neutral so that its annual tax bill will be relatively minor. When structuring the payment flows of the transaction, commonly referred to as the 'waterfall of payments', taxes due to the Revenue Commissioners as well as fees payable to professional advisers, will generally appear quite high in the waterfall so that they are paid in priority to the secured creditors.

The enforceability of clauses agreeing not to petition to wind up an SPV (non-petition clauses) has never been tested in the Irish courts (or indeed the English courts). However, as part of the Irish legal opinion which must be provided in relation to a securitisation transaction, the enforceability of non-petition clauses must be confirmed by the Irish legal advisers to the satisfaction of the relevant rating agencies. In opining on this question, it is necessary to consider the grounds on which such clauses would not be enforceable. The most likely reason that it would not be enforceable is on the grounds that any such non-petition clause might be contrary to public policy and therefore void. There are two main public policy considerations.

4.3.1 Protection of the rights of creditors

In general, when a company is in insolvent liquidation the unsecured creditors must be paid *pari passu*, that is they must be paid the same amount per euro owed to them. As noted above, there are no Irish or English cases which directly consider the enforceability of non-petition clauses. By way of analogy, however, we can consider cases on the enforceability of subordination agreements that are broadly similar in principle. In the case of a subordination agreement, a creditor agrees to contract out of its right to be paid *pari passu* and to allow other creditors to be paid in preference to it.

The leading English cases in the area of contracting-out of the insolvency rules are *British Eagle International Airlines v Compagnie Nationale Air France* [1975] 1 WLR 758 and *National Westminster Bank Ltd v Halesowen Presswork and Assemblies Ltd* [1972] AC 785. In the *Halesowen* case, the House of Lords decided that the statutory provisions with regards to set-off in insolvency were mandatory and therefore a creditor could not contract-out of them. In the *British Eagle* case, the House of Lords held that where the effect of an agreement is to provide that an asset would be distributed other than in accordance with the statutory rules in relation to the distribution of assets on a liquidation (that is, the *pari passu* rule), it would be contrary to public policy and therefore void. It had been suggested on the basis of the decisions in the *British Eagle* and *Halesowen* cases that subordination agreements might be contrary to public policy as an attempt to avoid the *pari passu* rule.

The *British Eagle* case was considered in Ireland in the case of *Re Glow Heating Ltd* [1988] IR 110. In the *Glow Heating* case, the Irish court interpreted the *British Eagle* case as authority for the proposition that:

> If a contract is one for the disposal of an asset belonging to the company then if the disposal is contrary to the *pari passu* provisions of s 275 the contract can be avoided as being contrary to public policy. But the phrase (contracting out of the Companies Act) is not to be interpreted as meaning that every contract is void by which a party to it obtains rights over the company's assets superior to those given to ordinary creditors under the section ...

The House of Lords decision [in the *British Eagle* case] in no way conflicts with the well established principle of insolvency law that a liquidator takes the company's property subject to the liabilities which affected it in the company's hands.

In the case of *Re Maxwell Communications Corp plc (No 2)* [1994] 1 BCLC 1, the English High Court upheld a subordination agreement by which the rights of a creditor were sought to be subordinated to the rights of other creditors in any insolvency proceedings. Vinelott J observed that the *pari passu* rule prevented a creditor from arranging that he would *obtain some advantage* in a winding up of a company to which insolvency principles did not entitle him, but subordination in no way undermined this principle. It was held therefore that there was no public policy consideration which rendered the subordination agreement invalid.

Under Irish law, s 275 of the Companies Act (CA) 1963 (as inserted by s 132 of the CA 1990) provides that the *pari passu* rule does not effect the enforceability of subordination agreements in the case of a voluntary liquidation. Even in the absence of this statutory provision it is doubtful whether there is any overriding public policy consideration which could prevent a subordination agreement from having effect post-liquidation. Accordingly, it is likely that the Irish courts would follow the *Maxwell* case if the matter of the enforceability of subordination agreements arose.

It is also worth noting in this context that in the early Irish case of *Deering v Hyndman* (1886) 18 LR (IR) 323 at 347, an agreement which purported to exclude the statutory right of set-off of mutual debits and credits under the bankruptcy legislation existing at that time was upheld by the court. This case is in contrast with *Halesowen* and suggests that the Irish courts may take a more lenient view of attempts to avoid the statutory rules on insolvency.

As non-petition clauses by Noteholders and other creditors in relation to securitisation transactions do not confer an advantage on the parties agreeing to such clauses against other creditors, they are arguably analogous to subordination provisions and therefore, on the basis of the *Maxwell* decision, should be enforceable. As noted in section 4.3.2 below, different considerations would apply to any covenant by a director.

4.3.2 Ousting the jurisdiction of the courts

Agreements which purport to oust the jurisdiction of the courts are considered void as contrary to public policy. It is possible that a court could construe a network of non-petition clauses as part of a scheme to prevent all of the Noteholders or other creditors petitioning to wind up the SPV and thereby oust the jurisdiction of the courts. If a creditor brought a petition before the court in breach of its agreement, the court might well refuse to enforce the non-petition clause and proceed to liquidate the company.

However, it is arguable that a non-petition clause does not constitute an agreement to oust the jurisdiction of the courts; it is merely an agreement by the creditor not to exercise a particular remedy. The court's jurisdiction over general disputes between the parties is not affected by the non-petition clause. Indeed, the court would have jurisdiction to hear any dispute in relation to the effectiveness of the non-petition clause itself. The agreement is therefore distinguishable from all of the cases on the question of ousting the jurisdiction of the courts as they concerned agreements to refer all disputes between the parties to arbitration tribunals or councils.

In addition, the jurisdiction of the court to liquidate the SPV would not be entirely ousted by the non-petition clause, as the rights of the shareholders, directors and possibly a limited class of creditors (such as the Revenue Commissioners) to petition to liquidate the

SPV would not be affected by the non-petition clauses affecting the Noteholders or other secured creditors.

In addition to the SPV's creditors, the rating agencies will be concerned about the possibility of the SPV's directors petitioning to wind up the SPV. Unfortunately, it is not possible to give the rating agencies much comfort in relation to the enforceability of an agreement by the directors not to place the SPV in liquidation. The directors owe fiduciary duties to the SPV and its shareholders which means they must always act in good faith in the interest of the SPV as a whole. There has also been recent case law in Ireland which has established that the directors may occupy a fiduciary position towards the creditors of the SPV in circumstances where the SPV is insolvent. Their duty in the case of an insolvent company is not to act contrary to the general interests of the creditors.

In addition to the common law duties, the directors of an Irish company are also subject to the provisions of the Companies Acts (CAs) 1963–2001 in relation to fraudulent and reckless trading. Under the CAs 1963–2001, where in the course of winding up a company or of examinership or receivership proceedings, it appears that any person was, while an officer of the company, knowingly a party to the conducting of company business in a reckless manner or was engaged in fraudulent trading, a court may declare any such officer personally responsible without limitation of liability for all or any part of the debts and liabilities of the company. The court has discretion to relieve the officer, wholly or partly, from such personal liability if it appears that the officer acted honestly and responsibly in relation to the company's affairs. Clearly, directors of a SPV would have to act responsibly in the event that the SPV became insolvent in order to avoid any common law or statutory liability.

For these reasons it is very likely that the Irish courts would refuse to uphold an agreement on the part of a director not to petition to wind up the SPV in circumstances where the company was insolvent and it would therefore be in breach of the common law and statutory duties of the director to enter into such an arrangement. Accordingly, because of the unenforceability of such agreements on the part of directors and the question marks over their enforceability in the context of secured creditors, it is important to ensure that the insolvency of the SPV is a remote possibility. The following paragraphs examine the techniques which are commonly used in this regard.

The first technique employed when structuring securitisation transactions in order to ensure that the SPV is bankruptcy remote is a conditional debt arrangement. Under a conditional debt arrangement the Notes are structured so that the debt owing to the Noteholders is equal to the lesser of:

(a) the agreed coupon (that is, interest) and principal repayment; and
(b) the capital value of the assets of the SPV which are supporting the particular Notes and the income generated therefrom.

The rationale behind the conditional debt arrangement is that the liability of the SPV to the Noteholders is characterised in terms of the relevant assets of the SPV. In this scenario, the amount of debt to the Noteholders effectively equals the value of the assets and income generated therefrom so that the assets always support the debt owing and accordingly no deficiency should arise. The intention of this arrangement is to ensure that the possibility of the SPV becoming technically insolvent is remote, as the debts due to the Noteholders effectively equal the value of the assets and income generated therefrom. The Noteholders would obviously have no incentive to petition to wind up the SPV since their debt could never be more than the amounts generated by the relevant pool of assets.

Any potential objections to this form of arrangement would be the same as those which arise in the context of a non-petition clause, namely that it is an attempt to avoid the *pari passu* rule. As with a non-petition clause and a subordination agreement, a conditional debt arrangement does not confer an advantage on the Noteholder against the other creditors and therefore should not be objectionable on public policy grounds.

The second technique that is commonly employed when structuring securitisation transactions, particularly where the SPV is a multi-issuance vehicle, is a limited recourse provision. 'Limited recourse' means that the recourse of the Noteholders is contractually limited to a particular pool of assets, which assets are secured in favour of those Noteholders. If effective limited recourse is achieved there should not be any incentive for the Noteholders to petition to wind up the SPV. (However, the unavailability of assets to meet the bondholder's claim is not a legal obstacle to obtaining an order to wind up the company.)

Section 216(1) of the CA 1963 provides as follows:

> [o]n hearing a winding-up petition ... the court shall not refuse to make a winding-up order on the ground only that the assets of the company have been mortgaged to an amount equal to or in excess of those assets, or that the company has not assets.

If their recourse were to a particular pool of assets over which they have effective security there would be little point in liquidating the SPV as a liquidation would not yield them any additional advantage.

While in theory the excess part of the debt due to a Noteholder over the amount realised by the sale of the security would be a debt due from the SPV to the Noteholder, the Noteholder would have no right of recourse against the assets of the SPV in general and so would have no incentive to petition to wind up the SPV.

In the case of *National Provincial Bank Ltd v Liddiard* [1941] 1 Ch 158, a limited recourse provision in the context of a guarantee was upheld, which would support the view that limited recourse clauses in Notes would be enforceable. By analogy with the *Maxwell* case, limited recourse clauses in respect of Notes should be enforceable as, like subordination agreements, they do not offend against the *pari passu* rule or confer any advantage on the Noteholder and so do not offend against any principle of public policy enunciated by the Irish courts in this area of law.

In addition to the insolvency issues discussed above, which are common to most securitisation transactions worldwide, when structuring a transaction involving an Irish SPV it is also important to advise clients on the examinership provisions of the Companies (Amendment) Act 1990. As you will be aware, the office of an examiner has no equivalent under English law and accordingly, it is very important that the consequences of examinership are discussed with clients and disclosed in the offering circular. From a securitisation perspective, the most important features of an examinership are the ability to suspend the rights of secured creditors during the examinership period and the possibility of the High Court ultimately approving a scheme of arrangement which compromises the rights of secured creditors.

Non-petition clauses in transaction documents involving Irish SPVs should also include reference to examiners so that the Noteholders and other secured parties agree not to petition to appoint an examiner to the SPV. The discussion above, in relation to the enforceability of such clauses in the context of a winding up of the SPV applies equally in the context of an examinership. In some cases a liquidity facility which would enable the Security Trustee to continue to make payments under the Notes during the examinership period may be built into the securitisation transaction.

4.4 Securities law issues

SPVs may be established as private companies or as public limited companies, depending on the nature of the Note offering. The law in relation to public offers of securities is discussed at length in Chapter 7 of this book and it is not intended to repeat those discussions in this chapter, other than to reiterate that if the Notes are to be offered to the public the SPV must be established as a public limited company (see s 33(1) of the CA 1963). Because of the difficulty of defining what constitutes a private placement for the purposes of the 1963 Act, most SPVs are set up as public limited companies. However, that does not mean that any offering circular issued in connection with a public offering of Notes constitutes a prospectus for the purposes of Pt III of the CA 1963.

Section 61(3) of the CA 1963 Act provides as follows:

> As respects [Notes] which, under the terms of issue must be repaid within five years of the date of issue, an offer for subscription or sale to a person whose ordinary business is to buy and sell shares or [Notes] (whether as principal or agent) shall not be deemed an offer to the public for the purposes of this Part.

As the application of s 61(3) is confined to Pt III of the CA 1963, it does not mean that an offering of Notes, with a maturity of five years or less to persons whose ordinary business is to buy and sell Notes, is a private placement and can therefore be carried out by a private limited company (s 33(1)(c) of the CA 1963 Act contained in Pt II of the CA 1963). However, it does result in the misapplication of the prospectus requirements of the CA 1963 which are contained in Pt III.

If the Notes are being offered to the public within the meaning of the CA 1963 and cannot avail of the exemption in s 61(3) of the CA 1963, the offering circular published in connection with the Note issue will constitute a prospectus for the purposes of Pt III of the CA 1963 and will have to comply with the requirements set out in that part. The principal requirements are summarised below:

(a) the offering circular must be dated, signed by each director and filed in the Companies Registration Office (CRO) on that date (s 47(1) of the CA 1963);

(b) copies of the material contracts (Material contracts are contracts entered into by the SPV in the previous five years other than contracts entered into in the ordinary course of its business) must be submitted to the CRO (s 47(1)(c) of the CA 1963);

(c) the offering circular must on its face specify the material contracts and refer to the fact that the offering circular and copies of the material contracts have been filed in the CRO (s 47(2) of the CA 1963);

(d) the Notes cannot be allotted until the fourth day after the offering circular is filed in the CRO (the four day rule) (s 56(1) of the CA 1963); and

(e) if the offering circular states that an application will be made to list the Notes on a stock exchange such permission must be applied for within three days of the date of the offering circular and if they are not listed within six weeks of the date of the offering circular, the Notes will be void (s 57(1) of the CA 1963).

The most problematic of these requirements is the four day rule as it impacts on the timing of a securitisation transaction. In effect it means that the offering circular must be finalised a week before the Notes are issued to investors. It is important that this timing requirement is brought to the attention of the other parties to the transaction at any early stage so that it can be factored into the overall timing of the transaction.

The offering circular must also comply with the contents requirements of Sched 3 to the CA 1963. These are outlined in greater detail in Chapter 7 of this book and apply equally to Note issues as they do to issues of share capital. The most problematic requirement from the perspective of a Note issuing SPV is the requirement to include an auditor report in relation to the profits and losses and assets and liabilities of the SPV for the period from incorporation. The auditors are required to consent in writing to the inclusion of their report in the offering circular (s 46 of the CA 1963) and an original letter of consent must also be filed in the CRO with the offering circular (s 47(1)(a) of the CA 1963).

In the context of a newly incorporated SPV, the preparation of an auditor report is not overly burdensome as it will generally confirm that the SPV has issued share capital of at least €38,100 (as required by s 19 of the CA 1963) and has not carried on any activities since incorporation other than those preliminary to the securitisation transaction. However, in the event that the SPV wishes to make a further or 'tap' issue of Notes, or if the SPV is a multi-issuance company which intends to engage in additional transactions and issue further series of Notes, this requirement can cause practical difficulties. While the CA 1963, and in particular Sched 3, was not designed with such transactions in mind, the need to produce an up-to-date auditors' report for every tap issue of Notes or issue of a further series of Notes can be avoided if the auditors' report, included in the initial offering circular, is prepared by reference to the first financial year end of the SPV. This will involve declaring a financial year end quite shortly after incorporation, but the advantage of this is that the SPV can then use the corresponding auditors' report for the purposes of all Notes which it issues until the end of the second financial year end. It is important for these purposes that the initial auditors' report appears in a general offering circular which is applicable to all Notes issued during the year, that is, any tap issues or further series of Notes are offered pursuant to a supplemental offering circular which supplements, and is read in conjunction with, the general offering circular.

In addition to the CA 1963, it may be necessary to consider the requirements of the European Communities (Transferable Securities and Stock Exchange) Regulations 1992 (SI 1992/202) (the 1992 Regulations) in the event that the Notes are offered to the public in Ireland. In the event that the 1992 Regulations, which implement the terms of the EU Prospectus Directive (89/298/EEC), apply, they are construed as one with the CA 1963. The 1992 Regulations will not apply in the following circumstances:

(a) the Notes are offered to persons in the context of their trades, professions, or occupations; and/or

(b) the Notes are offered to a restricted circle of persons; and/or

(c) the selling price of all the Notes offered does not exceed €40,000; and/or

(d) the Notes offered can be acquired only for a consideration of at least €40,000 per investor.

In practice, it is not difficult to meet at least one of these tests and thereby avoid the application of the 1992 Regulations, because Notes issued by Irish SPVs are for the most part marketed to institutional investors and are subject to high minimum subscription levels. However, if a retail offering were contemplated, the 1992 Regulations would need to be considered in greater detail.

4.5 Banking law

The Central Bank Acts (CBAs) 1971–97 define 'banking business' as:

> ... the business of accepting, on own account, sums of money from the public in the form of deposits or other repayable funds whether or not involving the issue of securities or other obligations, howsoever described. (Section 2 of the CBA 1971 (as amended).

In order to carry on banking business in Ireland, a person must be licensed to do so by the Central Bank of Ireland (CBI). There were concerns that the issuance of Notes by SPVs would constitute banking business and so fall to be licensed by the CBI. To address these concerns the CBI has issued a notice (the CP Notice) in relation to the circumstances in which the issuance of Notes can avail of an exemption from the requirement to obtain a banking licence. (Notice issued by the CBI of exemptions granted under s 8(2) of the Central Bank Act (CBA) 1971, as amended on 12 November 2002 (BSD C01/02).) The CP Notice creates two categories of Notes:

(a) Notes with a maturity of one year or more

If an SPV limits itself to issuing Notes with a maturity of one year or more it will not be required to hold a banking licence under the CBAs.

(b) Notes with a maturity of less than one year

If an SPV issues Notes with a maturity of less than one year, which are categorised by the CBI for the purposes of the CP Notice as 'commercial paper', it must comply with the requirements set out below in order to avoid having to obtain a banking licence:

- Commercial paper other than asset-backed commercial paper.
    - the SPV must have shareholders' funds (meaning paid-up share capital, capital reserves, revenue reserves and minority interests, as disclosed in the most recent audited accounts) of at least €25 million; or
    - the commercial paper must be guaranteed by a parent, other company or body corporate, or by a statutory body where the guarantor has shareholders' funds of at least €25 million; or
    - the commercial paper must be guaranteed by a credit institution (as defined by the Codified Banking Directive (00/12/EC) of 20 March 2000); or
    - the commercial paper must be guaranteed by an EU or Organisation for Economic Co-operation and Development (OECD) Member State; and
    - the commercial paper must be issued and transferable in minimum amounts of €125,000 or its foreign currency equivalent; and
    - the SPV must notify the CBI as soon as it commences activity.
- Asset-backed commercial paper.
    - at the time of issue the commercial paper must be backed by assets to at least 100% of the value of the commercial paper issued;
    - at the time of issue, the commercial paper must be rated at least investment grade (see the capital bank's implementation notice for credit institutions in relation to the EU Directive on the Capital Adequacy of Investment Firms and Credit Institutions of 30 June 2000 (BSD S2/00)) by one or more recognised rating agencies;
    - the commercial paper must be issued and transferable in minimum amounts of €300,000 or foreign currency equivalent; and
    - the SPV must notify the CBI as soon as it commences activity.
- General conditions for all commercial papers.
    - the commercial paper must carry the title 'commercial paper' and must identify the SPV as issuer by name;
    - it must be stated explicitly on the face of the commercial paper that it has been issued in accordance with an exemption granted by the CBI under s 8(2) of the CBA 1971;

- it must be stated explicitly on the face of the commercial paper that the investment does not have the status of a bank deposit, is not within the scope of the Deposit Protection Scheme operated by the Central Bank and that the SPV is not regulated by the CBI arising from the issue of the commercial paper; and
- any issue of commercial paper which is guaranteed must carry a statement to the effect that it is guaranteed and identify the guarantor by name.

4.6 Irish Stock Exchange listing

As noted in section 4.2 above, in order to avoid the imposition of withholding tax on payments to Noteholders, it is usually necessary to list the Notes on a recognised stock exchange. In addition to this tax benefit a stock exchange listing can also improve the marketability of the Notes as many investors are required by law, or by their own investment policies and restrictions to invest solely in listed securities. Historically Notes issued by Irish SPVs would generally be listed on the Luxembourg Stock Exchange or occasionally on the London Stock Exchange. However, in 1999 the Irish Stock Exchange (ISE) introduced special listing rules for specialist securities including asset-backed debt securities (the Listing Rules) which facilitated the listing of Notes issued by both Irish and non-Irish SPVs on the ISE. Since the inception of the Listing Rules, the ISE has gained a reputation for being a pro-active regulator and for providing a speedier turnaround of documentation than its counterparts in other EU jurisdictions. As a result, the listing of Notes on the ISE has become a regular feature of both Irish and non-Irish securitisation transactions. This paragraph examines the application of the Listing Rules and the European Communities (Stock Exchange) Regulations 1984 (SI 1984/282) (the 1984 Regulations).

The 1984 Regulations implemented the following EC Directives:

(a) the Admissions Directive (Directive (79/279/EEC) which governs the conditions for the admission of securities to official listing on a stock exchange situated or operating within an EU Member State;

(b) the Listing Particulars Directive (Directive (80/390/EEC) which is concerned with the requirements for drawing up, scrutiny and distribution of the listing particulars to be published in respect of securities admitted to official listing on a stock exchange situated or operating within the EU; and

(c) the Interim Reports Directive (Directive (82/121/EEC) which deals with the information which must be published on a regular basis by companies which have been admitted to official listing on a stock exchange situated or operating within an EU Member State.

The 1984 Regulations have since been amended by the European Communities (Stock Exchange) (Amendment) Regulations 1991 so as to implement the second Listing Particulars Directive. (This Directive deals with the mutual recognition of listing particulars where securities in a company are to be admitted to official listing on the stock exchange of more than one EU Member State.) The 1984 Regulations will apply in relation to any Notes which are listed on the ISE.

The 1984 Regulations permit the ISE to impose conditions for the admission of Notes to official listing and obligations on the issuers of Notes admitted to official listing which are more stringent or additional to the requirements of the directives. These additional requirements are set out in the Listing Rules, summarised below.

Pursuant to Reg 12 of the 1984 Regulations, where application has been made to the ISE for admission to official listing and the relevant listing particulars are approved by the ISE, they take the place of, and are deemed to be, a prospectus within the meaning of the CA 1963 Act and in any such case ss 43, 44(1), 45, 47, 361(2), 362 and 363 of the CA 1963 do not apply. Notable provisions of the 1963 Act which are superseded by the 1984 Regulations are ss 49 and 50 which provide that any untrue statement contained in a prospectus may attract civil and criminal liability.

In the context of a public offer, it is important to note that the four day rule (as discussed in section 4.4 above) regarding allotment of Notes is not superseded by the 1984 Regulations. Regulation 13 provides that on or before the date of publication of listing particulars in accordance with the directives, a copy of the listing particulars shall be delivered to the CRO for registration and any document which is published as, or containing, listing particulars shall, in a clear and conspicuous manner, state that a copy of those listing particulars has been delivered for registration. The four day rule will apply from the date that the listing particulars are registered with the CRO.

Given that the 1984 Regulations deem approved listing particulars to be the prospectus, within the meaning of the CA 1963, if the listing is contemporaneous with the proposed issue of the Notes then it is the 'listing particulars' that require registration in the CRO and not a 'prospectus' under the CA 1963, as the 'listing particulars' become the 'prospectus'.

In this regard although under the CA 1963 a prospectus is only required where there is an offer to the public, under the 1984 Regulations listing particulars are deemed to be a prospectus, notwithstanding that the issue in question is a private placement or is entitled to avail of the exemption contained in s 61(3) of the CA 1963 and discussed in section 4.4 above. This means that, when listing Notes that are offered on a private placement basis, the SPV must nonetheless deliver the listing particulars to the CRO for registration, even though a private placement usually does not involve delivering a prospectus to the CRO for registration.

As noted in section 4.4 above, the CA 1963 requires that a prospectus contain an auditors' report in relation to the profits and losses and assets and liabilities of the SPV for the period from incorporation. The Listing Rules do not require that such report and consent be included and as listing particulars become the prospectus under the 1984 Regulations, the need to include the report and consent in the offering circular does not apply.

Nevertheless, if the Notes are offered to the public and the listing takes place after the initial issue of Notes both the requirements of the CA 1963 and the 1984 Regulations need to be observed. Accordingly, if it is intended to list Notes it would be preferable to list them on issue if possible.

The Listing Rules contain detailed provisions in relation to the contents of the listing particulars, which it is not intended to discuss at length in this chapter (see Chapter 2 of the Listing Rules). The Listing Rules require an SPV to maintain a paying agent in Ireland until the date that the Notes are finally redeemed (see Rule 1.12 of the Listing Rules). The SPV is also required to appoint a listing agent although it is not necessary that the listing agent be an Irish entity. The listing agent must be registered with the ISE (see Rule 3.1 of the Listing Rules). The SPV will also be subject to the following ongoing obligations for so long as the Notes remain listed on the ISE:

(a) the SPV must ensure equality of treatment for all holders of listed Notes who are in the same position;

(b) any change in the rights attaching to listed Notes must be notified to the ISE without delay;

(c) the SPV must publish annual accounts as soon as possible after they have been approved and in any event within six months of the end of the financial period to which they relate, together with an annual report;

(d) a copy of all notices to Noteholders must be forwarded in final form to the ISE no later than the date of despatch. In addition, a copy, in draft form, of any proposed amendment to the memorandum and articles of association of the Issuer which would affect the rights of Noteholders must be submitted to the ISE for its prior approval;

(e) the SPV must ensure that adequate information is at all times available about the assets backing the Notes; and

(f) where the SPV intends to make a proposal to purchase any of its listed Notes, it must comply with the specific requirements set out in the Listing Rules.

All information which is notified to the ISE pursuant to the continuing obligations becomes a matter of public record, is reported through the ISE's information dissemination system and is carried by Reuters, Bloomberg and other services.

4.7 Conclusion

This chapter was designed to provide an introduction to the Irish legal issues in relation to securitisation transactions. It should be clear from the foregoing that advising in relation to securitisation transactions in Ireland has historically involved adapting existing statutory and common law principles to a rapidly evolving industry. It would greatly facilitate the future growth of the securitisation industry in Ireland if special legislation addressing the various legal uncertainties discussed above was introduced.

CHAPTER 5

INTRODUCTION TO FINANCIAL SERVICES

John Darby

5.1 Overview of the regulatory structure

In Ireland, financial services are regulated on a functional basis rather than on the basis of the identity of the persons providing such services. In general, any person that provides financial services must be authorised to do so by the Central Bank of Ireland (CBI).

5.1.1 The Investment Intermediaries Act 1995

Under Irish law, the activities of investment advisers are governed by the Investment Intermediaries Act (IIA) 1995, as amended by the Central Bank Act 1997, and rules and regulations made under the IIA 1995. The IIA 1995 implements European Union Council Directive 93/22/EU on investment services in the securities field (the Investment Services Directive), thereby including Ireland within the EU system of mutual recognition of authorisation and supervision systems in respect of investment advisers.

5.2 Role of the CBI

The CBI is the body which, pursuant to the IIA 1995, regulates and supervises investment advisers and it is the competent authority in Ireland for Investment Services Directive purposes. In addition to its traditional central banking functions, the CBI also regulates and supervises a broad range of other financial services businesses, including credit institutions, collective investment undertakings, companies licensed to conduct business in Dublin's International Financial Services Centre and the Irish Stock Exchange, and it members. Stockbrokers may carry on business as investment advisers and, in doing so, are subject to the Stock Exchange Act (SEA) 1995, which also implements the Investment Services Directive. The relevant provisions of the SEA 1995 are broadly similar to the corresponding provisions of the IIA 1995.

5.3 Authorisation requirements

5.3.1 Investment business firms

In general, it is the nature of the business carried on by a firm, rather than the type or class of the firm itself, which will determine whether that firm requires an authorisation under the IIA 1995. A number of specific firms or types of firms are exempted from the obligation to obtain such an authorisation.

An 'investment business firm' under the IIA 1995 means any firm carrying on either or both of (i) the provision of investment advice and (ii) the supply of one or more investment business services (including discretionary portfolio management), in each case to third parties on a professional basis. Subject to certain exceptions, authorisation under the IIA 1995 is required in order for a firm to act as, or claim or hold itself out to be, an investment business firm.

Unlike the Investment Services Directive, the IIA 1995 does not require or provide that in order for a firm to constitute an investment business firm, its regular occupation or business must be the provision of investment advice or investment business services. Therefore, even the incidental or infrequent provision of such advice or services by a firm may result in it being treated as an investment business firm for the purposes of the IIA 1995.

A firm which provides investment advice but supplies no investment business services would not constitute an 'investment firm' within the terms of the Investment Services Directive. However, it would be an investment business in Ireland within the meaning of the IIA 1995. Furthermore, a firm authorised under the Investment Services Directive in another EU Member State that wishes to provide investment advice in or from Ireland may find that its Investment Services Directive authorisation would not cover that business.

An authorisation under the IIA 1995 in respect of the provision of the investment business services will specify the classes of investment business services which may be provided by the firm.

An authorisation under the IIA 1995 will usually also specify ancillary or non-core services, which the authorised firm may provide. The CBI may amend an authorisation from time to time to vary the classes of investment business services or other non-core services, which it covers.

5.3.2 Investment instruments

Most investment advice and investment business services relate to a very broad category of investment instruments, described in the IIA 1995 as including:

(a) transferable securities;
(b) non-transferable securities creating or acknowledging indebtedness issued by or on behalf of a government, local authority or public authority;
(c) units or shares in collective investment undertakings;
(d) financial futures contracts;
(e) commodity futures contracts;
(f) forward interest rate agreements;
(g) agreements to exchange payments based on movements in interest rates, currency exchange rates, commodities, share indices and other investment instruments;
(h) sale and repurchase and reverse repurchase agreements involving transferable securities;
(i) agreements for the borrowing and lending of transferable securities;
(j) certificates or other instruments which confer all or any of the following rights:
- property rights in respect of any transferable securities;
- any right to acquire, dispose of, underwrite or convert an investment instrument, being a right to which the holder would be entitled if he or she held any such investment to which the certificate or instrument relates; or
- a contractual right (other than an option) to acquire any such investment instrument otherwise than by subscription;

(k) a rolling spot foreign exchange contract;
(l) options;
(m) a tracker bond or similar instrument; and
(n) hybrid instruments involving two or more investment instruments.

Investment instruments do not include the following instruments:

(a) any instrument acknowledging or creating indebtedness for, or for money borrowed to pay, the consideration payable under a contract for the supply of goods or services;
(b) a cheque or other similar bill of exchange, a banker's draft or a letter of credit; or
(c) a banknote, a statement showing a balance in a current, deposit or savings account or (by reason of any financial obligation contained in it) a lease or other disposition of property or an insurance policy.

5.3.3 Investment advice

For the purposes of the IIA 1995, the provision of investment advice comprises the giving, offering or agreeing to provide, to any person, advice on certain dealings in an investment instrument, on the making of a deposit or on the exercising of certain rights conferred by an investment instrument, or the giving, offering or agreeing to give, to any person, advice on the choice of a person providing investment business services.

Certain activities are not considered to be investment advice:

(a) advice given in a publication where the principal purpose of the publication taken as a whole is not to lead persons to invest in any particular investment instrument, to make a particular deposit or to deal with any particular provider of investment business services (with a non-relevant principal purpose);
(b) advice given in a lecture, seminar or similar event which has a non-relevant principal purpose and where persons engaged in the organisation or presentation of such event will earn no reward as a result of any particular decision by a person attending such event and arising out of such attendance in relation to investment instruments or deposits or in relation to the choice of a person providing investment business services;
(c) advice given in sound or television broadcasts which have a non-relevant principal purpose;
(d) advice to undertakings on capital structure, industrial strategy and related matters and advice relating to mergers and the purchase or sale of undertakings; and
(e) advice given by persons in the course of carrying on any profession or business not otherwise constituting the business of an investment business firm, where the giving of such advice arises from other advice or services given in the course of carrying on that profession or business, and where the giving of investment advice is not remunerated or rewarded separately from such other advice or services.

5.3.4 Investment business services

Investment business services, as defined in the IIA 1995, include managing portfolios of one or more investment instruments or deposits in accordance with mandates given by investors on a discretionary, client-by-client basis.

Investment business services also include, among other services, any or all of broking services, underwriting and custodian operations, in each case in respect of one or more investment instruments; and the administration of collective investment schemes and acting as a manager of a particular class of designated investment fund (a fund established under a tax scheme intended to promote investment in small and medium sized businesses and generally called 'business expansion scheme funds').

5.3.5 Excluded entities

The following bodies are among those expressly excluded from the definition of an investment business firm under the IIA 1995 (and accordingly no authorisation is required):

(a) a person who provides investment business services or investment advice only:
- to undertakings of which it is a subsidiary or which are its own subsidiaries or other subsidiaries of the same parent undertaking; and/or
- where those services consist exclusively of the administration of employee equity participation schemes;

(b) firms which provide investment business services consisting exclusively in dealing for their own account on futures or options markets or which deal for the account of other members of those markets or make prices for them and which are guaranteed by clearing members of the same exchange and where responsibility for ensuring the performance of contracts entered into by such firms is assumed by clearing members of the same market;

(c) insurance undertakings as defined in Art 1 of Council Directive 73/239/EEC (carrying on the activity of direct insurance other than life insurance) or Art 1 of Council Directive 79/267/EEC (carrying on the activity of direct life insurance) or undertakings carrying on re-insurance or retrocession activities described in Council Directive 64/225/EEC (Insurance Undertakings Directive);

(d) collective investment undertakings and the depositories and managers of such undertakings, insofar as their activities are already subject to regulation by the CBI (unit trusts in which the public may participate are regulated by the CBI under the Unit Trusts Act 1990; UCITS (undertakings for collective investments in transferable securities) within the meaning of Council Directive 85/611 are regulated by the CBI under the European Communities (Undertakings for Collective Investments in Transferable Securities) Regulations 1989 (SI 1989/78); fixed and variable capital investment companies are regulated by the Central Bank under Pt XIII of the Companies Act 1990; and limited partnerships are regulated by the CBI under the Investment Limited Partnerships Act 1994);

(e) persons whose main business is trading in commodities among themselves or with producers or professional users of such products and who provide investment business services only for such producers or professional users to the extent necessary for their main business;

(f) credit institutions which provide investment business services or investment advice within the terms of authorisations under the Council Directive 77/780/EEC (the First Banking Directive) as amended by Council Directive 89/646/EEC (the Second Banking Directive); and

(g) firms conducting investment business services which the CBI has exempted from authorisation because such services are provided only because they are necessary to the firm's main activities; and non-Irish collective investment undertakings approved by the CBI to market units in Ireland or authorised by another EU Member State.

Furthermore, a solicitor in respect of whom an Irish practising certificate is in force will not be considered to be an investment business firm by virtue of the provision by him in an incidental manner of investment business services or investment advice.

5.4 Application of authorisation requirements to affiliates

The IIA 1995 authorisation requirements do not apply to the affiliates of a firm which proposes to act as, or to claim or hold itself out to be, an investment business firm, unless such affiliates also propose to engage in such activities. However, before granting an authorisation to an investment business firm under the IIA 1995, the CBI must be satisfied that, where appropriate and practicable, the firm's associated or related undertakings are capable of being supervised adequately by the CBI.

'Undertakings' are defined in s 2(1) of the IIA 1995 as a corporate body, a partnership, an unincorporated body of persons or a sole trader, that is, any form of business organisation or economic unit.

Under Irish Regulations implementing the Investment Services Directive, the CBI may not grant an authorisation under the IIA 1995 to an investment business firm to provide investment business services where the CBI's effective exercise of its supervisory functions would be prevented by:

(a) the existence of close links between the firm and other persons;
(b) the laws, regulations or administrative provisions of a non-EU Member State governing person(s) with which the firm has close links; or
(c) difficulties involved in the enforcement of such laws, regulations or administrative provisions.

5.5 The authorisation process

5.5.1 How to obtain authorisation

5.5.1.1 *Application form*

In order to obtain authorisation under the IIA 1995, a firm must apply to the CBI and provide specified information on a standard application form.

5.5.1.2 *Authorisation fee*

Currently, no fee is chargeable in respect of an application for authorisation under the IIA 1995 and there is no annual or other charge levied on authorised firms in respect of their status as such. The Minister for Finance has the power under the IIA 1995 to prescribe such fees.

5.5.1.3 *How long does the authorisation process take?*

The processing of an application for authorisation usually takes approximately three to six months, but may take longer depending on the particular firm in question, the speed of response to inquiries and the nature and volume of such applications being considered by the CBI.

The IIA 1995 imposes a long-stop date on the authorisation process which reflects the provisions of the Investment Services Directive. An applicant must be informed of whether or not it has been authorised within:

(a) six months of the date of receipt of its application; or

(b) where additional information has been sought by the CBI in respect of an application, within the earlier to expire of a period of six months after receipt by the CBI of such information or 12 months after receipt of the application.

5.5.1.4 Are there different authorisation provisions for Irish and non-Irish applicants?

The application procedures for Irish and non-Irish applicants are the same. As a practical matter, however, inquiries made outside Ireland in connection with an application may in certain cases take somewhat longer to finalise than equivalent inquiries made within Ireland.

5.5.2 Information required

5.5.2.1 General information requirements

The IIA 1995 provides that an application must be in such form and contain such information as is specified by the CBI from time to time. The information currently required by the CBI includes the following details in respect of an applicant:

(a) details of its legal status, any registered number and address(es);

(b) details of current directors, including shadow directors (that is, persons in accordance with whose directions or instructions the directors of a company are accustomed to act unless the directors are accustomed so to act by reason only that they do so on advice given by such persons in a professional capacity) and of any directors with the previous three years; of persons who have or control (qualifying shareholders) a direct or indirect holding of shares or any other interest in the applicant which represents 10% or more of the capital or of the voting rights or any direct or indirect holding of less than 10% which, in the opinion of the CBI, makes it possible to control or exercise a significant influence over the management of the applicant (a qualifying holding); and of persons (other than employees, directors, qualifying shareholders, shareholders or disclosed professional advisers) who are in a position to exercise a significant influence over the management of the applicant firm;

(c) details of any group structure to which the applicant belongs;

(d) details of staff, including the number of employees, their distribution throughout the business, a copy of any code of conduct followed by employees, recruitment procedures followed by the applicant and staff training in relation to the provision of investment business services or advice;

(e) details of whether to the knowledge of the applicant, any of its shareholders, directors, partners or managerial staff have ever been convicted in Ireland or abroad of certain criminal offences, been declared bankrupt or been disqualified or restricted as a director of a company;

(f) a detailed description of the investment business services to be supplied by, and any other proposed activities of, the applicant;

(g) an analysis of the gross income of the applicant in the most recently completed financial year (or, if the applicant has not commenced trading, its projected income for the next 12 months) arising from the provision of each particular category of investment business service and details of any other income of the applicant;

(h) general business information, including details of any period in the applicant's history when it was dormant or engaged in any other activities and details of any insurance or investment business services provided by the applicant in the previous 10 years;

(i) the number of clients to which the applicant provides investment business services, an explanation of the circumstances where any client produces or is expected to produce more than 10% of the applicant's gross annual income, and details of the applicant's proposals for soliciting business;

(j) details of the applicant's bank or building society accounts and, if the applicant operates a client account or has custody of client assets, details of its arrangements in that regard;

(k) details of the procedures to be adopted for ensuring that complaints against the applicant will be investigated and resolved in an open and equitable manner and controls which are in place to ensure that only suitable investment products are sold to clients; and

(l) details of the applicant's professional indemnity insurance and any claims made under such policy during the previous three years.

5.5.2.2 Financial information

An application form for authorisation under the IIA 1995 must be accompanied by the audited annual accounts of the applicant for the previous three years, or, if the applicant has been in existence less than three years, since the establishment of its business, quarterly management accounts since the last audit or the last accounting year end date and a business plan detailing the applicant's expected activities over the next three years. The required audited accounts do not need to be conformed to Irish standard accounting practice if they were not prepared in accordance with such practice. The CBI may require the auditor of an applicant to furnish any information required under the IIA 1995 to be provided by the auditor of an authorised firm.

5.5.2.3 Individual questionnaires

Each director, manager and qualifying shareholder of an applicant and any person (other than named professional advisers) in a position to exercise significant influence over an applicant's management must complete an individual questionnaire.

The questionnaire includes details of the individual's position within the applicant, including:

(a) details of his or her responsibility;
(b) employment history (including any period of unemployment);
(c) relevant professional business qualifications;
(d) memberships in any professional bodies, exchanges or associations;
(e) any other relevant training;
(f) other business interests (current and over the previous 10 years);
(g) personal bank details;
(h) references (to be supplied where applicable by persons by whom the individual was engaged or employed in the conduct of investment business during the previous five years); and
(i) a wide range of queries relevant to the individual's good reputation and character. These queries include whether the individual has been:
  - convicted of any offence in Ireland or elsewhere (except minor motoring offences) or been subject to penalties for tax evasion;

- declared bankrupt or is the subject of bankruptcy proceedings;
- refused or had withdrawn any authorisation to carry on an investment, banking or insurance business in Ireland or elsewhere;
- publicly censured or disciplined by a regulatory body in Ireland or elsewhere because of his business activities or is undergoing any investigation or disciplinary procedure (or the individual's employer, to his knowledge, has been so censured or disciplined or is undergoing any such procedure);
- refused entry to any profession or been dismissed or requested to resign from any office or employment or fiduciary office; or
- within the last 10 years, been the director of a company in Ireland or elsewhere which has gone into liquidation, receivership or examinership while he was a director or within three years of his ceasing to be a director.

The questionnaire also includes an undertaking by the relevant individual to comply with the IIA 1995 and an authority from the individual to the CBI to make inquiries (including inquiries with the Gardaí) regarding the information contained in the form and to disclose that information, in the course of carrying out the bank's statutory functions. Any person who it is subsequently proposed would take up an office or role such as those described above must also complete an individual questionnaire.

5.5.3 Substantive review of applicants

5.5.3.1 *Specific grounds for refusal of authorisation*

The CBI may not grant authorisation under the IIA 1995 unless the applicant satisfies certain requirements set out in s 10 of that Act:

(i) the applicant is a company incorporated in or outside Ireland or an unincorporated body which is subject to a partnership agreement or an industrial and prudential society (co-operative) or a sole trader, provided in all cases that the applicant has made arrangements to ensure that its activities will be carried out in such manner as would ensure that the requirements of the Investment Services Directive are satisfied; and

(ii) the applicant satisfies the CBI:

    (a) that, where applicable, its memorandum and articles of association will enable it to operate in accordance with the IIA 1995 and any condition or requirement imposed under that Act;

    (b) that it has the minimum level of capital specified by the CBI;

    (c) as to the probity and competence of each of its directors and managers;

    (d) as to the suitability of each of its qualifying shareholders;

    (e) as to its organisational structure and management skills and that adequate levels of staff and expertise will be employed to carry out its proposed activities;

    (f) that it has and will follow established procedures to enable the CBI to be supplied with all necessary information and to enable the public to be supplied with such information as the CBI specified; and

    (g) that the organisation of its business structure is such that it and any of its associated or related undertakings, where appropriate and practicable, are capable of being supervised adequately by the CBI.

The foregoing requirements apply equally to Irish and non-Irish applicants.

5.5.3.2 Capital requirements

The initial capital requirements which the CBI applies to firms for the purposes of authorisation under the IIA 1995 implement EU Council Directive 93/6 on capital adequacy of investment firms and credit institutions (the Capital Adequacy Directive).

5.5.3.3 Qualifications of directors

The individual questionnaire is intended to elicit information that will enable the CBI to determine whether or not it can be satisfied with the probity and competence of the directors and managers of an applicant. The CBI will also meet with certain representatives of the applicant. The CBI does not require a proposed director or manager of an investment business firm to have any particular formal qualifications or be a member of any particular profession or other business organisation. However, the CBI does require that such a person have sufficient experience or expertise to carry out his intended functions.

The IIA 1995 imposes no requirements as to the number of Irish citizens or residents who must serve as directors, managers or employees of an authorised investment business firm. However, practical business requirements of operating such a firm in Ireland would usually necessitate at least some of its directors, managers and employees being based in Ireland.

5.5.4 Appeal of refusal of authorisation

If the CBI refuses to grant an authorisation, it must serve notice on the applicant of its decision to do so stating its reasons for the refusal. Within 21 days of receipt of such notice, the applicant may appeal the CBI's decision to the High Court. The CBI must publish notice of a refusal of authorisation in *Iris Oifigúil* and in at least one national newspaper within 28 days of the decision to refuse.

5.6 Overview of substantive regulation

5.6.1 Mandatory regulation

In accordance with the requirements of the Investment Services Directive, certain obligations are imposed on authorised firms.

Some of these obligations are contained or set out in the provisions of s 10 of the IIA 1995 itself (for example, obligations with regard to qualifying holdings), or statutory instruments made under its terms (for example, obligations in respect of bonding), while others are contained in documents or notices issued by the CBI. An authorised firm will therefore be bound directly by any obligations set out in the IIA 1995 (or statutory instruments made under its terms) to the extent that they are expressed as applicable to such a firm. The firm's authorisation will also be granted subject to certain stated conditions and requirements, including a requirement that the firm comply with any CBI notice relevant to it, as well as any other conditions and requirements specific to that firm which the CBI may impose.

The CBI has broad power to impose conditions and requirements under the IIA 1995. Conditions and requirements may be imposed by it in respect of all or any authorised firms (including in respect of matters in an associated or a related undertaking), either at the time authorisation is granted or thereafter. An authorised firm may appeal to the High Court against imposition of any condition or requirement by the CBI. The High Court has the power to confirm, vary or rescind such condition or requirement.

The CBI also has the power to give directions to investment business firms (including authorised and formerly authorised firms) in relation to any matter related to the operation of an investment business firm or to an acquiring transaction.

5.6.2 Code of conduct

The CBI currently requires all authorised firms (except certified persons) and all persons operating in Ireland under an Investment Services Directive passport to comply with the code of conduct drawn up by the CBI. A separate code of conduct for investment managers has been drawn up which contains, in addition to provisions almost identical to those contained in the general code of conduct, certain requirements regarding the issuing of contract notes by investment managers.

Both codes of conduct (together referred to as the Code) require that firms comply with certain general standards set out in the IIA 1995. The Code also imposes certain specific requirements which give effect to these general requirements, including provisions that a firm will comply with the following.

5.6.2.1 Anti-fraud

The firm must:

(a) not recklessly, negligently or deliberately mislead a client to any perceived advantages or disadvantages of a transaction;

(b) not engage in conduct which creates a false or misleading impression as to the market in any investment instrument (any such firm will also be subject to the general requirements of Irish law in respect of insider trading); and

(c) comply with the provisions of Irish legislation relating to the offence of money laundering.

5.6.2.2 Conflicts

The firm must:

(a) take reasonable steps to ensure that neither the firm nor any of its employees or agents give or take inducements likely to conflict with the recipient's duties;

(b) ensure that effective Chinese Walls (ie, artificial divisions preventing the sharing of information within the firm so as to ensure that no conflict takes place) are in place between different areas of business of the firm and between the firm and its connected parties and that all procedures relating to the maintenance of Chinese Walls are in writing and are notified to all employees of the firm; and

(c) take reasonable care in executing transactions with or for its clients to ensure that it deals to the best advantage of its clients and will comply with the requirements of the Code in respect of the order in which transactions for clients, employees and for the firm's own account must be dealt with.

5.6.2.3 Client disclosure and consent requirements

The firm must:

(a) provide to the client a copy of the firm's terms of business or (in the case of an investment manager) investment management agreement (which must include, among other things, details of the client's investment objectives and restrictions and the firm's charges and an outline of the firm's policies in relation to conflicts of interest) and copies of records relating exclusively to the client on request;

(b) procure in advance from any private (non-professional) client to or for who, the firm recommends or undertakes any transaction in derivatives a signed statement acknowledging the risks resulting from such transactions, provided that an investment manger may employ certain techniques and instruments for efficient portfolio management and to provide protection against exchange risks;

(c) not recommend transactions to a non-discretionary client or effect transactions with or for a discretionary client unless the firm has taken all reasonable steps to ensure that the client understands the risks involved;

(d) in the case of investment managers:

- unless otherwise specified in the investment management agreement, issue to the client periodic information stating the value of the portfolio at the beginning and end of period, its composition at the end, and, in the case of a discretionary portfolio, changes in its composition between those dates and certain other information set out in the Code; and

- send to the client a contract note in respect of every purchase or sale of an investment instrument which is entered into for or with a client containing the information specified in the Code and not later than the business day following the date of execution of the transaction; and

(e) in the case of firms other than investment managers, issue periodic information to any client for whom the firm acts on a discretionary or advisory basis or in respect of any derivatives and derivatives related cash balances. Such a client must sign the firm's terms of business.

5.6.2.4 *Professional and private assessment*

The firm must:

(a) assess whether a client is a professional client within the terms of the Code and make a written record of such assessment (for these purposes, 'professional clients' comprise persons who would be institutional clients or professional clients for the purposes of the bonding requirements imposed under the IIA 1995 together with large companies, that is, corporate bodies which are not permitted to draw up an abridged balance sheet); and

(b) before entering into a relationship with a private client, take reasonable steps to obtain from the client details of his investment objectives, investment experience and other facts about his financial position.

5.6.2.5 *Soft commission arrangements*

The firm must comply with the restrictions imposed by the Code on dealing for a client (or advising a client to deal) through any party pursuant to an agreement under which the firm would receive goods or services in return for an assurance that not less than a certain amount of business would be put through or in the way of another person (a soft commission agreement) unless:

(a) the only benefits to be provided under the agreement are goods and services which can reasonably be expected to assist in the provision of services to the firm's clients as outlined in the Code and which are in fact so used;

(b) the other party agrees to deal to the best advantage of the client;

(c) the firm is satisfied on reasonable grounds that the terms of business and methods by which the relevant dealing services will be supplied do not involve any risk of comparative price disadvantage to the client; and

(d) adequate prior written disclosure of the agreement is made to the client. The firm must write to clients affected by such an agreement outlining why a soft commission arrangement is in their best interests. Clients affected by such an arrangement must also be informed annually of the percentage of total commission paid by the firm under the relevant arrangements, the nature of goods and services received by the firm under those arrangements, and where practical, the value of such goods and/or services as a percentage of total commission on a cost basis.

5.6.2.6 Books and records

The firm must:

(a) keep for a period of at least six years a record of all transactions entered into by the firm and a copy of each agreement entered into with discretionary clients;

(b) keep a written record of all written complaints received against the firm from its clients and have in place an adequate written procedure for the effective consideration and proper handling of such complaints; and

(c) have an effective written procedure for the recording, monitoring and approval of personal account transactions of the firm's employees, associates and connected persons.

5.6.3 Insider dealing

Irish insider dealing legislation is contained in Pt V of the Companies Act (CA) 1990. The CA 1990 imposes certain restrictions on dealings in securities of a company comprising of shares or debt securities for which dealing facilities are, or are to be, provided by the Irish Stock Exchange; or rights, options or obligations in respect of such shares or debt securities or any index relating in such shares or debt securities (listed securities). These restrictions are imposed on dealings by, among others, persons who are, or have in the preceding six months been, connected with the company in question and, as a result, are in possession of unpublished price-sensitive information relating to those securities.

Restrictions also apply to dealings in listed securities of a company by persons connected with another company where the unpublished price-sensitive information relates to a transaction involving the two companies.

A person is connected with a company if, 'being a natural person':

(a) he is an officer of or shareholder in that company or a related company; or

(b) he or she occupies a position (including a public office) that might reasonably be expected to give him access to certain information by virtue of any professional, business or other relationship between himself (or his employer or a company of which he is an officer) and that company or related company or by virtue of being an officer of substantial shareholder in that company or a related company.

The CA 1990 also provides that, subject to certain exceptions, it will not be lawful for a company to deal in any listed securities at any time when an officer of that company is precluded from dealing in those securities as aforesaid. A company will not be so precluded by reason only of information in the possession of an officer of that company if:

(a) the decision to enter into the transaction was taken on its behalf by a person other than the officer;

(b) it had in operation at that time written arrangements to ensure that the information was not communicated to that person and that no advice in relation to the transaction was given to that person by a person in possession of the information; and

(c) the information was not so communicated and such advice was not so given.

Breaches of these provisions of the CA 1990 have both civil and criminal consequences.

5.6.4 Financial resources

The CBI's capital adequacy requirements, which implement the Capital Adequacy Directive, provide that a firm's capital may not fall below either the relevant level of initial capital required or one-quarter of its preceding year's fixed overheads, determined by reference to its most recent audited accounts.

5.6.5 Prior approval of appointments

The CBI will usually require that an appointment as a director, chief executive, manager, etc of an authorised firm be subject to the prior written consent of the CBI, which would have to be satisfied as to the probity and competence of the proposed appointee.

5.6.6 Qualifying holdings

5.6.6.1 *Consideration of transactions*

Under the IIA 1995, the CBI must consider notification of a proposed acquiring transaction within three months of the date of receipt of notification or, where within one month of such date the CBI requests further information, the date of receipt of that information. An acquiring transaction may not proceed unless the CBI has approved it in writing or the foregoing period has elapsed without the CBI having refused to approve the transaction.

An acquiring transaction will be valid only if it is entered into within 12 months of the CBI's written approval (unless the CBI has set a different timetable for the transaction) or, if applicable, the end of the three-month period referred to above. Otherwise, title to any shares or other interest shall not pass by virtue of the terms of the transaction and any consequential purported exercise of powers relating to such shares or other interest (including voting rights) will be invalid.

5.6.6.2 *Disapproval of transactions*

The CBI must refuse to approve an acquiring transaction where it is not satisfied as to the suitability of the person proposing to make the acquisition or the transaction is likely to be prejudicial to the sound prudent management and/or the proper and orderly regulation and supervision of an authorised firm.

5.6.6.3 *Appeal*

Where the CBI refuses to approve an acquiring transaction or makes its approval subject to conditions or requirements, the proposed acquirer may appeal such refusal (or the imposition of such conditions or requirements as the case may be) to the High Court. Such an appeal must be brought within one month of communication of the refusal or conditional approval. If the High Court decides in favour of the appeal, the CBI must make a new decision reversing its earlier decision within three months of the date of the High Court's determination.

5.6.6.4 *Prejudicial influence*

The CBI may impose conditions or requirements on an authorised firm or give a direction to such a firm and/or its directors. It may also seek to have the authorisation of the firm revoked if a person with a qualifying holding exercises its influence in a manner likely to be prejudicial to the prudent and sound management of the activities of the investment firm.

5.6.7 Prudential rules

The IIA 1995 (and certain requirements of the CBI imposed under that Act) contains prudential rules which must be observed by authorised firms.

5.6.7.1 *Administration matters; record-keeping*

As part of the authorisation requirements under the IIA 1995, the applicant must satisfy the CBI as to its organisational structure and management skills and that adequate levels of staff and expertise will be employed to carry out its proposed activities. These include administrative and accounting matters.

The auditor of an authorised firm, when preparing an audit or any other report which the CBI requests the auditor to make, must carry out such investigations that will enable the auditor to form an opinion as to whether the firm has kept proper accounting records and maintained satisfactory systems of control of its business and records and systems of inspection. If the auditor forms the opinion that the firm has failed in respect of any of the foregoing, the auditor's report must so state. The auditor must inform the CBI, as soon as possible after an audit, whether in the course of the audit any breaches of the IIA 1995 were identified. The auditor must also report to the CBI if at any time he has reason to believe, among other things, that there are material defects in the accounting records or systems of control of the business and records of the firm. The auditor may also be asked by the CBI to report on such matters.

An authorised firm organised as an unincorporated body of persons or a sole trader (other than a certified person or a person who does not provide investment business services) is required to appoint an auditor to audit and report on its accounts on an annual basis. The CBI may set out requirements for the accounts and audit of such a firm.

The code of conduct imposed by the CBI on all authorised firms (excluding certified persons) and firms operating in Ireland under the Investment Services Directive passport includes certain relevant requirements regarding the recording of transactions, documentation to be sent to clients, records and procedures for recording, monitoring and approving personal account transactions with employees and other related parties.

The CBI may also require an investment business firm to keep at their offices in Ireland such books and records and other documents as the CBI specifies.

5.6.7.2 *Safeguarding client assets*

The CBI has issued requirements with regard to the safekeeping of client money and investment instruments by authorised firms (excluding certified persons). These requirements do not apply to firms, which are authorised under the Investment Services Directive in another EU Member State.

Such requirements include the following:

(a) all monies and investment instruments received by the firm from or on behalf of a client must be treated as client money or investment instruments unless, in the case of money it is due and payable to the firm in accordance with the requirements;

(b) client monies must be held in a client account with certain eligible credit institutions (principally, banks authorised under the First Banking Directive). Where such a credit institution is in the same group as the firm, this must be disclosed to the client, the client monies must be designated as such in the accounts of the credit institution holding them and such accounts must include the word 'client' in their title. Any credit institution holding such accounts must acknowledge that it is not entitled to combine such an account with any other account or exercise any right of set-off or counterclaim against money in that account in respect of any sum owed to it by the firm;

(c) client monies must be paid into a client account as soon as possible after (and by no later than the next business day) or paid out in accordance with the requirements;

(d) additional requirements (notification to clients or obtaining client consent) apply where it is proposed to hold client money in a client account outside the European Economic Area (EEA);

(e) certain calculations must be made on each business day and reconditions must be performed every month to ensure that the correct amount is held in client accounts;

(f) a firm which holds clients' investment instruments must keep safe, or arrange for the safekeeping of, any documents of title in respect of such investment instruments, ensure that any registerable investments are properly registered in the name of the client, or, with the client's consent, in the name of an eligible nominee as described in the requirements and ensure, where an electronic record of title is maintained, that the client entitlements are separately identifiable from those of the firm;

(g) a firm must not use a client's investment instruments for its own account unless it has obtained the client's prior written consent to do so;

(h) a firm must notify the client of the firm's obligations to the client in respect of the client's investment instruments and must procure from any custodian holding such investments suitable acknowledgements safeguarding the position of the client; and

(i) a firm holding clients' investment instruments must perform certain reconciliations in respect of its books and records at least every six months and provide each client at least once a year with a statement listing all property owned by the client for which the firm is accountable.

A firm must also ensure that an auditor examines its books and records in respect of client money or investment instruments at such intervals as may be specified by the CBI. Such auditors must report to the CBI on whether the bank's requirements have been complied with.

5.6.8 Investor compensation

Under the IIA 1995, an authorised firm providing investment business services must hold a bond.

The bond must provide that, in the event of the inability or failure of an authorised firm to meet its financial obligations in relation to money received by it from or on behalf of clients, certain money will become available to a person approved by the CBI. The money will be applied for the benefit of any client of the firm who has incurred loss or liability because of the inability or failure of the firm to meet such financial obligations.

Certain types of authorised firm are exempted from the requirement to hold a bond, including an authorised firm:

(a) which has a certificate from the Minister for Finance entitling it to the benefit of a reduced corporation tax rate on profits yielded by certain activities carried on in the International Financial Services Centre in Dublin (principally, the provision of financial services to non-resident persons);

(b) which is already a member of a compensation scheme of a prescribed standard; and

(c) which provides investment business services only to certain professional investors and institutional investors.

Bonding requirements are not required to be met by any authorised firm in respect of the types of activity described in item (c) above.

A bond must be obtained from an insurance company or be given by the authorised firm together with a guarantee from a credit institution (in each case, the insurance company or credit institution must be authorised as prescribed in the bonding requirements). The period of validity of a bond must be 12 months. A copy of a firm's bond must be displayed prominently in all premises at which the firm carries on business as an authorised firm. A firm's sales literature and notepaper relating to its business as an authorised firm must mention the fact that the bond is in existence.

The European Parliament Council Directive 97/9/EC on Investor Compensation Schemes has been implemented in Ireland by the Investor Competition Act 1998.

5.6.9 Advertising

Any firm which is not entitled to provide investment business services or investment advice under the IIA 1995 may not advertise, supply or offer to supply or make any other solicitation in respect of investment business services or investment advice or hold itself out to be an investment business firm.

The CBI may, if it considers it expedient to do so in the interest of proper and orderly regulation and supervision of investment business firms or the protection of investors, give a direction to an investment business in relation to:

(a) a content or form of any advertisement or other means of soliciting client money or investment instruments or business; or

(b) any advertisement relating to any service provided or business undertaken by business; or

(c) any advertisement relating to any service provided or business undertaken by the firm; or

(d) for the withdrawal of an advertisement or to cease advertising.

If, in contravention of the IIA 1995 or a direction given by the CBI as described above, a person (the advertiser) advertises inviting persons to enter, or offers to enter, into an investment or inviting persons to exercise any rights conferred by an investment or in either case containing information calculated to lead directly or indirectly to persons so doing, then:

(a) the advertiser shall not be entitled to enforce any agreement to which the advertisement related and which was entered into after the issue of the advertisement or to enforce any obligation to which a person is subject as a result of any exercise by him or her after the issue of the advertisement of any rights to which the advertisement related; and

(b) the other party or the person who has exercised rights (the counter-party) shall be entitled to recover any money or other property or investment instruments paid or transferred by him under the agreement or any such obligation together with compensation for any loss sustained (in the case of a person entering into an investment agreement as a result of having paid money or transferred property or investment instruments under that agreement).

The compensation described above will be such as the parties agree to or as is determined by the High Court on the application of either party.

In effect, therefore, an agreement or an exercise of rights made on foot of an advertisement issued in contravention of the IIA 1995 (or of a direction as described above) is voidable at the instance of the counter-party. The High Court may allow such an agreement or obligation to be enforced or money or property or investment instruments paid or transferred on foot of such agreement or obligation to be retained, under certain conditions.

The CBI may give various directions in connection with advertisements which are in contravention of the provisions of the IIA 1995 or which are misleading.

The CBI has also imposed more specific requirements in relation to advertising by authorised firms (other than certified persons), including any person operating under an Investment Services Directive passport, as follows:

(a) Advertisements should be fair and not misleading, and their purpose should be clear and not disguised in any way.

(b) A firm should not seek to take improper advantages of any characteristics or circumstances that may make its clients or potential clients vulnerable, for example by exploiting their credulity or lack of experience or knowledge in a manner detrimental to the interests of its clients or potential clients.

(c) An advertisement should always be so designed or presented that anyone who looks at it can see immediately that it is an advertisement.

(d) An investment business firm must not exert undue pressure or influence on a client in order to induce them to purchase, sell or retain an investment or to exercise or refrain from exercising any right conferred by an investment.

(e) Any commendation quoted must be complete or a fair representation, accurate and not misleading at the time of issue and relevant to the investment, investment business service or investment advice advertised. It must not be used without the consent of the author and, if the author is an associated or related entity or an employee of the investment business firm, the advertisement must state that fact.

(f) Any comparisons or contrasts used in an advertisement must be based either on facts verified by the investment business firm or on assumptions stated within the advertisement, must not mislead, must be presented in a fair and balanced way and must not omit anything material to the comparison or contrast.

(g) Any information in any advertisement about the past performance of an investment or of a firm must be relevant to the performance of the investment or firm advertised, and be a complete record of, or a fair and not misleading representation of, the past performance of the investment or firm. It must not be selected as to exaggerate the success of or disguise the lack of success of the investment or firm and be based on the actual performance and not on simulated figures. Furthermore, it must contain a warning that neither past experience nor the current situation is necessarily a guide to future performance.

(h) Where an advertisement contains any forecast or projections, whether of a specific growth rate or of a specific return, or rate of return, it should make clear the basis upon which that forecast or projection is made. It must explain, for instance, whether reinvestment of income is assumed, whether account has been taken of the incidence of any taxes or duties, and if so how, and whether the forecast or projected rate of return will be subject to any deduction either upon premature realisation or otherwise.

(i) Advertisements should comply with the CBI's specific requirements in respect of:
- guarantees;
- commendations;
- comparisons;
- related investments;
- past performance;
- taxation;
- unusual risks;
- fluctuations;
- investment income;
- foreign currency;
- investments which are not readily realisable;
- investments carrying contingent liability;
- front-end loading (where deductions for charges and expenses are spread unevenly throughout the investment period and concentrated in the early part of that period);
- redemption charges;
- cancellation;
- property funds;
- forecasts or projections;
- direct offers; and
- unsolicited calls.

5.6.10 Money laundering

The Criminal Justice Act (CJA) 1994 implements EU Directive 91/308/EEC on money laundering. The CJA 1994 makes it an offence to conceal, disguise, convert, transfer or remove from Ireland any property which is or represents the proceeds of drug-trafficking or other criminal activity for the purposes of avoiding prosecution or the making or enforcement of a confiscation order. It is also an offence:

(a) to take any of the foregoing steps for the purpose of assisting any person in avoiding prosecution or confiscation; and

(b) to handle property knowing or believing it to be the proceeds of drug-trafficking or other criminal activity.

The CJA 1994 obliges a defined category of financial institutions and other bodies which would include most investment business firms (designated bodies) to take certain measures to assist in the prevention and detection of money laundering. These include:

(a) taking reasonable measures to establish the identity of certain customers or third parties for whom the designated body has reason to believe the customer is acting; and

(b) retaining copies for at least five years of documents used to establish identity and records of transactions.

The CJA 1994 does not specify what would constitute reasonable measures for these purposes but the CBI's Guidance Notes, while not legally binding, set out best practices in this regard.

Designated bodies and their directors, officers and employees are obliged to report to the gardí where they know or suspect that an offence in respect of money laundering or in respect of prevention and detection measures has been committed.

5.6.11 Use of the internet

There is currently no specific Irish regulation regarding the use of the internet by investment advisers, although the same general principles outlined in this chapter would apply equally to the use of the internet for the provision of advice as to any other media.

5.7 Enforcement

5.7.1 Penalties

A range of penalties or other consequences may flow from a breach of the IIA 1995, or obligations imposed pursuant to that Act.

5.7.1.1 Criminal proceedings

Under the IIA 1995, it is a criminal offence, among other things, to:

(a) fail to be authorised under the IIA 1995, if required to be;

(b) apply for authorisation under the IIA 1995 knowingly or recklessly using false or misleading information or making false or misleading statements;

(c) fail to maintain such books and records as the CBI may require;

(d) advertise investment business services or investment advice if not entitled to provide such service or advice under the IIA 1995 or to fail to comply with directions given by the CBI in connection with advertising; and

(e) contravene certain provisions of the IIA 1995 in respect of the maintenance of client accounts.

The CBI or the Director of the Public Prosecutions (DPP) may prosecute such an offence summarily. Only the DPP may prosecute on indictment.

Any officer, employee or person purporting to act on behalf of a firm may be guilty of an offence where the firm has committed an offence with his consent or connivance or which is attributable to him or has been facilitated by his neglect. Such offence will not be sentenced to imprisonment unless the offence was committed wilfully. There are also provisions in the IIA 1995 for penalties for continuing offences.

A breach of the IIA 1995 may also be prohibited by civil proceedings. On application of the CBI to the High Court in a summary manner, if the High Court is of the opinion that there has occurred or is occurring a breach of the IIA 1995 or a failure to comply with a condition or requirement imposed in relation to an authorisation of an investment business firm or with a direction of the CBI, the High court may make an order prohibiting the continuance of the breach or failure.

5.7.1.2 Revocation of an authorisation

The CBI has the power itself to revoke an authorisation granted to a firm under the IIA 1995 if requested by the firm or if the firm has failed to operate as an investment business firm within 12 months of the date of its authorisation or for a period of more than six months or is being wound up.

The CBI has a further power to apply to the High Court for an order revoking the authorisation of a firm in various circumstances, including where:

(a) it is expedient to do so in the interest of the proper and orderly regulation and supervision of investment business firms and/or in order to protect investors;

(b) the firm has been convicted on indictment of any offence under the IIA 1995 or any act under which the CBI exercises statutory functions or any offence involving fraud, dishonesty or breach of trust;

(c) circumstances have materially changed since the grant of authorisation, such that a difference decision would be taken in relation to an application for authorisation by the firm has systematically failed to comply or has failed to comply to a material degree with a condition or requirement of the IIA 1995;

(d) the firm has systematically failed to comply or has failed to comply to a material degree with a condition or requirement of the IIA 1995;

(e) the firm no longer fulfils any or all of the conditions or requirements imposed by the CBI;

(f) the firm has infringed to a material degree upon the code of conduct;

(g) a director, manager or qualifying shareholder of the firm is no longer deemed by the CBI to fulfil the conditions imposed by the IIA 1995 to hold that position; and/or

(h) the firm has so organised its structure that it and/or its related or associated undertakings are no longer capable of being supervised to the satisfaction that might be made as described in item (g) above.

The CBI must serve notice on a firm of its intention to apply to the High Court for a revocation of its authorisation. It is specifically obliged under the IIA 1995 to give the firm an opportunity to deal with the concerns of the CBI in respect of any director, manager or qualifying shareholder in connection with which such an application might be made as described in item (g) above.

5.7.1.3 Winding up

The CBI may apply to the High Court to have an authorised or formerly authorised firm wound up (or dissolved or put in bankruptcy as appropriate) on a number of bases, including:

(a) that the CBI considers it to be in the interest of the proper and orderly regulation and supervision of investment business firms; or

(b) that it is necessary for the protection of investors that the firm be wound up; or

(c) that the firm has failed to comply with any direction given by the CBI under the IIA 1995.

5.7.1.4 *Directions and confirmation of directions*

The CBI has broad powers to issue directions:

(a) to investment business firms (whether proposed for authorisation, authorised, formerly authorised or unauthorised);

(b) to directors of any such firms; and

(c) to any person purporting to act or whom the CBI reasonably believes is acting as, or on behalf of, an investment business firm.

Where the CBI gives a direction it may, or, where it is of the opinion that such direction is not being complied with, shall, apply to the High Court in a summary manner for an order confirming the direction. The High Court may treat a breach of its order as contempt of court, for which a person may be imprisoned until the contempt is purged.

5.7.1.5 *Determination of breach of condition or requirement*

Where it appears on the basis of information provided by an authorised officer or an inspector appointed by the CBI that there has been a breach by an investment business firm or a professional body of a condition or requirement imposed by the CBI, under certain sections of the IIA 1995 the CBI may apply to the High Court in a summary manner for a determination that there has been a breach of such condition or requirement. The High Court may issue a reprimand to the relevant firm or direct that is must pay to the CBI a specified sum in respect of such a breach, or dismiss the application and/or make any other order it considers appropriate.

Alternatively, the CBI may notify the firm or body in question, giving reasons for the notification and stating that the CBI will apply to the High Court as described above unless the firm or body elects to have the question of its non-compliance determined by a committee. The committee will be appointed by the CBI from a panel established by the Minister for Finance. Such a committee would have the same powers as the High Court described above, but the firm or body in question could appeal to the High Court against a determination of the committee.

5.7.1.6 *Probity and competence of employed persons*

The CBI may apply to the High Court for a direction that an authorised firm have one of its officers or employees removed or dismissed if the CBI considers that the person's probity is liable to render him unsuitable to act as an officer or employee of an authorised firm, or that he is not competent in respect of matters of the kind with which he would be concerned. (In the latter case, the direction may be to suspend the officer or employee for a specified period of time, or in the case of an employee, to remove him from a particular area of employment.) The word 'employee' is broadly defined in the IIA 1995 and would be deemed to include a person employed under a contract for service (for example, a consultant).

Any such application will be made having given notice to the firm and officer or employee concerned, and any direction made on foot of it would be served on that officer or employee, who may apply to the High Court for the revocation of such direction.

Any person subject to such a direction may not, without the written consent of the CBI, be employed in any capacity in connection with an authorised firm or any other entity which the CBI supervises or regulates. If the CBI refuses its consent, the person subject to the direction may appeal its decision to the High Court. Any person who accepts or continues in any employment in contravention of such a direction will be guilty of an offence.

Any authorised firm or any entity supervised by the CBI must take reasonable care not to employ or continue to employ a person in contravention of such a direction.

5.7.1.7 Personal liability of officers

If (i) a firm is being wound up, (ii) is unable to pay all of its debts, and (iii) has contravened the requirements of the IIA 1995 to keep such books and records as are required by the CBI or to designate client accounts appropriately in its financial records, the High Court may, on application by certain parties including the CBI, if it thinks proper, declare one or more of (i) the officers, (ii) beneficial owners, (iii) former officers, or (iv) former beneficial owners of the firm in default to be personally liable for all or such part of the debts of the firm as the High Court thinks fit. Such a declaration could be made only if the contravention described above contributed to the inability of the firm to pay its debts or resulted in substantial uncertainty as to the (i) amount, (ii) location, (iii) ownership or otherwise of the assets and liabilities of the firm or of the monies or investment instruments of clients of the firm or has substantially impeded its orderly winding up.

The High Court would also not make such a declaration if it considered that:

(a) the officer took all reasonable steps to secure compliance by the firm with the relevant requirements of the IIA 1995; or
(b) the officer has reasonable ground for believing, and did believe, that a competent and reliable person, acting under the supervision or control of a director who had been formally allocated such responsibility was charged with the duty of ensuring such compliance and was in a position to discharge such duty.

5.7.1.8 Civil liability

The IIA 1995 does not contain specific provisions for the imposing of civil liability on investment business firms for contraventions of its provisions or obligations imposed under such provisions, save to the limited extent that compensation may become payable to clients. Whether any such liability would arise would depend on the general law of contract and tort.

5.7.2 Mechanisms of enforcement

The IIA 1995 provides in considerable detail for the mechanisms whereby the CBI may obtain the information which it requires to supervise investment business firms and to enforce the provisions of the IIA 1995.

5.7.2.1 Authorised officers

Persons authorised by the CBI have broad powers exercisable in respect of investment business firms, professional bodies, persons who the CBI has reasonable grounds to believe have provided or are providing investment business services or investment advice and associated or related undertakings, including:

(a) certain powers to enter and search premises and to inspect books, records or other documents on the premises;
(b) the power to take copies of or extracts from books, records and other documents found in the course of such an inspection; and
(c) the power to require any person who carries on investment business services or gives investment advice and any person employed in connection with those activities to give the authorised officer information containing the investment business services or investment advice or the persons carrying on or employed in connection with such activities and other related information.

In each case such powers being subject to the detailed provisions of the IIA 1995. The CBI may also require certain returns to be made to it by an investment business firm or approved professional body or associated or related undertakings. Any such requirements may be imposed on a person outside Ireland.

In the event of a failure by an officer, employee, shareholder or agent to co-operate with an authorised officer, if required under the IIA 1995, the authorised officer may certify the refusal to the High Court, which may inquire into the case and make any order or direction it thinks fit.

5.7.2.2 High Court-appointed and Central Bank-appointed inspectors

The CBI may, where it is of the opinion that it is in the interest of the proper and orderly regulation and supervision of investment business firms or the protection of investors, apply to the High Court for the appointment of one or more inspectors to investigate the affairs of an investment business firm and, where necessary, any subsidiary or associated or related undertaking, and to report on such inspection as the High Court may direct.

Such an inspector has broad powers to seek the production of books, accounts, records and other documents of, or relating to the business of, the firm being investigated. The inspector may also examine on oath or by written interrogatories on oath the officers, employees, shareholders and agents of that firm.

Having considered the inspector's report, the High Court may also make such order as it thinks fit, including an order for the wind up, dissolution or bankruptcy of the firm.

The High Court may direct that any person dealt with in the inspector's report would be liable to such extent as the High Court may direct, on the application of the CBI, to repay to the CBI the fees and expenses of the investigation.

The CBI may itself appoint an inspector to investigate:

(a) the affairs and conduct of the business of an authorised firm or its associated or related undertakings;

(b) compliance of the authorised firm with the IIA 1995 and the obligations imposed under the Act; and

(c) any other matters the CBI may consider appropriate if it is of the opinion that it is necessary for the effective administration of the law relating to investment business firms or the effective discharge of the CBI's functions under the IIA 1995.

Such an inspector would have broadly similar powers to those of a High Court-appointed inspector.

5.7.2.3 Warrants

The IIA 1995 sets out the procedure for a District Court judge to issue warrants to enter and search premises for books, records or other documents.

5.8 Extra-territorial application

5.8.1 Application of the IIA 1995

The IIA 1995 (and the requirement for authorisation under that Act, or as appropriate, the Investment Services Directive) applies to activities carried on inside or outside Ireland.

Accordingly, an investment business firm operating in Ireland and having its registered office in a non-EU Member State, and which is authorised under the Investment Service Directive in such Member State, could carry on in Ireland the activities so authorised under the Investment Services Directive passport.

CHAPTER 6

THE REGULATION OF INVESTMENT BUSINESS SERVICES

John Darby

6.1 Introduction

The legislation governing the regulation of investment business services in Ireland is the Investment Intermediaries Act (IIA) 1995 and the Stock Exchange Act (SEA) 1995. Both these pieces of legislation transpose into Irish law the Investment Services Directive 93/22/EU of 10 May 1993 (the ISD).

6.2 The types of investment firms or services regulated under Irish law as a result of the implementation of the ISD

6.2.1 Types of investment firms or services regulated under Irish law as a result of the implementation of the ISD

(a) Investment business firms regulated by the IIA 1995. These are firms other than stockbroking firms that provide one or more 'investment business services' or 'investment advice' to third parties on a professional basis. 'Investment business services' for the purposes of the IIA 1995 are as follows:

   (i) the reception and transmission, on behalf of investors, of orders in relation to one or more investment instrument (as defined below);

   (ii) the execution of orders in relation to one or more investment instrument other than for own account;

   (iii) dealing in one or more investment instrument for own account;

   (iv) managing portfolios of investments in accordance with mandates given by investors on a discretionary client by client basis where such portfolios include one or more investment instrument;

   (v) underwriting in respect of issues of one or more investment instrument or the placing of such issues or both;

   (vi) acting as a deposit agent or deposit broker;

   (vii) the administration of collective investment schemes, including the performance of valuation services or fund accounting services or acting as transfer agents or registration agents for such funds;

   (viii) custodial operations involving the safekeeping and administration of investment instruments; and

   (ix) acting as a manager of a designated investment fund within the meaning of the Designated Investment Funds Act 1985.

'Investment advice' is defined as:

> ... the giving or offering or agreeing to give to any person advice on the purchasing, selling, subscribing for or underwriting of an investment instrument or on the making of a deposit or on the exercise of any right conferred by an investment instrument to acquire, dispose of, underwrite or convert an investment instrument or deposit or the giving or offering or agreeing to give to any person advice on choice of a person providing investment business services.

Certain types of advice are excluded from this definition such as advice given in a newspaper, magazine or television broadcasts which are not calculated to lead persons to invest in particular investment instruments or advice given in lectures or seminars.

(b) Member firms of the Irish Stock Exchange authorised under the SEA 1995. These are firms whose regular occupation is the provision of investment services on or off the floor of a stock exchange on a professional basis. Investment services for the purposes of the SEA 1995 are (i)–(iv) of the list of investment business services referred to above.

6.2.2 Investment instruments for the purposes of s 2 of the IIA 1995

(a) Transferable securities including shares, warrants, debentures including debenture stock, loan stock, bonds, certificates of deposits and other instruments creating or acknowledging indebtedness issued by or on behalf of any body corporate or mutual body, government and public securities, including loan stock, bonds and other instruments creating or acknowledging indebtedness issued by or on behalf of a government, local authority or public authority, bonds or other instruments creating or acknowledging indebtedness or certificates representing securities.

(b) Non-transferable securities creating or acknowledging indebtedness issued by or on behalf of a government, local authority or public authority.

(c) Units or shares in undertakings for collective investments in transferable securities within the meaning of the European Communities (Undertakings for Collective Investments in Transferable Securities) Regulations 1989 (SI 1989/78) (the 1989 Regulations), and any subsequent amendments thereto, units in a unit trust, shares in an investment company, capital contributions to an investment limited partnership.

(d) Financial futures contracts, including currency futures, interest rate futures, bond futures, share index futures and comparable contracts.

(e) Commodity futures contracts.

(f) Forward interest rate agreements.

(g) Agreements to exchange payments based on movements in interest rates, currency exchange rates, commodities, share indices and other financial instruments.

(h) Sale and repurchase and reverse repurchase agreements involving transferable securities.

(i) Agreements for the borrowing and lending of transferable securities.

(j) Certificates or other instruments which confer all or any of the following rights, namely:

- property rights in respect of any investment instrument referred to in sub-paragraph (a) of this paragraph; or

- any right to acquire, dispose of, underwrite or convert an investment instrument, being a right to which the holder would be entitled if he held any such investment to which the certificate or instrument relates; or
- a contractual right (other than an option) to acquire any such investment instrument otherwise than by subscription;

(k) Options including:
- options in any instrument in sub-paragraphs (a)–(j) of this paragraph; or
- currency, interest rate, commodity and stock options including index option contracts.

(l) Hybrid instruments involving two or more investment instruments, and includes any investment instrument in dematerialised form.

6.2.3 Investment instruments for the purposes of s 3(1) of the SEA 1995

(a) Transferable securities, units or shares in undertakings for collective investments in transferable securities within the meaning of the 1989 Regulations, financial futures contracts including index futures contracts, commodity futures contracts, future or forward interest rate agreements, interest rate swaps, exchange rate swaps, warrants or other instruments entitling the holder to subscribe for investment instruments, borrowing and lending of transferable securities, repurchase agreements, units in a unit trust, shares in an investment variable capital or fixed capital company, capital contributions to an investment limited partnership, debentures, including debenture stock, loan stock, bonds, certificates of deposit, other instruments creating or acknowledging indebtedness, government and public security, including loan stock, bonds and other instruments creating indebtedness issued by or on behalf of a government, local authority or public authority, bonds and other instruments creating or acknowledging indebtedness issued by or on behalf of any body corporate or mutual body, and certificates representing securities.

(b) Certificates or other instruments which confer:
- property rights in respect of any investment instrument referred to in paragraph (a) of this definition; or
- any right to acquire, dispose of, underwrite or convert an investment instrument, being a right to which the holder would be entitled if he held any such investment to which the certificate or instrument relates; or
- a contractual right (other than an option) to acquire any such investment instrument otherwise than by subscription.

(c) Options in any instrument referred to in paragraph (a) of this definition.

(d) Any investment instrument in dematerialised form.

(e) Any instrument similar to investment instruments defined in sub-paragraphs (a), (b), (c) or (d) of this paragraph.

6.2.4 The supervisory authority for most investment business firms and for stockbroking firms is the Central Bank of Ireland

The supervisory authority for investment business firms (who only provide investment business services relating to units or shares in undertakings for collective investments in transferable securities, units in a unit trust, other collective investment scheme instruments, acting as a deposit agent or deposit broker or the transmission of orders for shares in a company listed on a stock exchange, or bonds so listed, or for prize bonds) is the Irish Minister for Enterprise, Trade and Employment.

Investment product intermediaries are also regulated by Pt IV of the IIA 1995. These are defined as an investment business firm or a solicitor who acts as a deposit agent or a deposit broker or provides a service of the reception and transmission of orders to a product producer in certain instruments listed in the IIA 1995 or shares in a company which are listed on a stock exchange or bonds so listed or prize bonds. Certain types of investment product intermediaries who engage only in restricted activities are deemed authorised as an investment business firm under the IIA 1995.

6.3 Distinct authorisation for each type of investment firm (or service)

Although the Irish legislation implementing the ISD does not provide for a distinct authorisation for each type of investment firm organised under Irish law, both the IIA 1995 (s 10(10)) and the SEA 1995 (s 18(11)) provide that an authorisation to act as an investment business firm or a stockbroking firm must specify the classes of investment services which may be provided by the particular investment business firm or stockbroking firm. These provisions reflect Art 3(1) of the ISD. The authorisation may also specify additional services which an investment business firm or stockbroking firm may provide, including those set out in Sched C of the Annex to the ISD.

The appropriate supervisory authority may amend or vary the classes of investment business services or other services which an investment business firm or stockbroking firm is authorised to provide. An investment business firm or stockbroking firm may only provide the classes of investment business services or other services which are specified in its authorisation.

The grant of an authorisation may be given unconditionally or it may be given subject to such conditions or requirements, or both as the supervisory authority considers fit.

6.4 The rules of the two-men management

Article 3(3) of the ISD refers to the 'two-men management rule' which states that the direction of a firm's business must be decided by at least two persons meeting the conditions set out in Art 3, but allowing authorisation to be granted to natural persons if appropriate arrangements are made. The IIA 1995 does allow an authorisation to act as an investment business firm to be granted to natural persons acting as partners or to an individual (referred to as a sole trader) to act as investment business firms. The SEA 1995 also permits the authorisation of stockbroking firms as partnerships of natural persons but not a firm consisting of one individual. The IIA 1995 states that an investment business firm which is a sole trader will not be authorised unless it has made arrangements to ensure that its activities will be carried out so as to ensure that the requirements of Art 3(3) of the ISD are complied with (s 10(5)(a) of the IIA 1995). In addition, the appropriate supervisory authority may impose conditions or requirements or both on an investment business firm which is an unincorporated body of persons or a sole trader so as to achieve an equivalent level of supervision as for a firm which is a body corporate.

There is extensive verification of the reputation and experience of the persons who effectively direct the business of an investment firm. All directors and shareholders of an investment business firm which is a body corporate, all members of an investment business firm which is a partnership and any individual who applies as a sole trader must fill out a detailed individual questionnaire when the firm is applying for authorisation. The questionnaire requires details of the relevant experience of the person to be given, their professional business qualifications, detailed questions as to their reputation and character, other business interests and personal bank details. In addition, the names of at least two referees who are familiar with that person's investment business activities must be given and permission given to the appropriate supervisory authority to take up the references.

These requirements reflect the provisions of the IIA 1995 (s 10(5)(c)), whereby an investment business firm must satisfy the appropriate supervisory authority as to the probity and competence of each of its directors and managers.

Section 18(5)(d) of the SEA 1995 also states that a stockbroking firm must satisfy the Central Bank of Ireland (CBI) as to the probity and competence of each of its directors and managers. An individual questionnaire in similar terms to that which must be completed by directors and managers of investment business firms must also be completed by directors and managers of stockbroking firms.

6.5 Investment firms covered by the ISD that are natural persons and that provide services involving the holding of third party assets

The specific provisions contained in the Irish legislation implementing the ISD dealing with sole traders are set out at section 6.4 above.

If the investment business firm or stockbroking firm is an unincorporated body of natural persons, that is, a partnership, the date of commencement of the partnership must be returned to the appropriate supervisory authority as well as the names and status of the partners. In addition, each partner of an investment business firm must complete the individual questionnaire referred to at section 6.4 above. Details of any shareholdings by the partners of 10% or more in any company must be included. Details must be given of any person in a position to exercise a significant influence over the management of the partnership. Where the firm is an unincorporated body of persons, if such an agreement does not already exist, the firm must draw up a partnership agreement.

Where the investment business firm is a sole trader, he must give details of any person in a position to exercise a significant influence over the management of the business. The Irish legislation implementing the ISD allows for specific requirements to be imposed on all investment business firms and stockbroking firms in relation to the holding of monies and investment instruments for clients. The appropriate supervisory authority may impose requirements on firms or impose requirements, or approve of rules in the rules of a professional body which has been approved by the appropriate supervisory authority regulating the holding of monies and investment instruments by firms on behalf of clients.

All investment business firms and stockbroking firms must keep at an office or offices in Ireland such books and records (including books of account), in respect of client money and client investment instruments as may be specified from time to time by the appropriate supervisory authority and ensure that such books and records are examined at specified intervals by an auditor who is to report on whether the requirements imposed by the appropriate supervisory authority have been complied with (s 52 of the IIA 1995 and s 52 of the SEA 1995). Such requirements have been drawn up by the CBI for stockbroking firms. These set out detailed provisions relating to the holding of client monies including measures on the types of credit institutions to be used, segregation of funds, interest, records and reconciliations. There are also measures to ensure the safeguarding of investment instruments held for clients. Requirements for investment business firms regulated by the IIA 1995 are currently being drawn up by the CBI and the Minister for Enterprise, Trade and Employment.

6.6 Conditions set with regard to the shareholders or members of an investment firm covered by the ISD which applies for an authorisation to do business

The IIA 1995 provides that an investment business firm authorised under the IIA 1995 must satisfy the appropriate supervisory authority as to the suitability of each of its 'qualifying shareholders'. Qualifying shareholders mean the holders of shares in an investment business firm or any other person who has or controls 10% or more of the capital or of the voting rights of an investment business firm or any person who has a holding of less than 10% but is in a position to exercise a significant influence over the management of the firm. The details required in the individual questionnaire referred to at section 6.4 above, must be completed by qualifying shareholders or persons who propose to become qualifying shareholders. The appropriate supervisory authority can assess the suitability of the shareholders or other persons on the basis of the information received. The information must also be returned by the members of an unincorporated body of persons and by sole traders.

Section 18(5)(e) of the SEA 1995 likewise requires the CBI to be satisfied as to the suitability of the qualifying shareholders of a stockbroking firm. Included with the information to be returned when applying for authorisation as a stockbroking firm under the SEA 1995, there must be a detailed analysis of the shareholder or partnership structure of the firm, and details of any person or persons having control or ownership of the firm including any person whose shareholding or other commercial relationship with the firm might influence the firm to a material degree. Where the shareholder is a corporate or partnership, the most recent audited accounts must be provided and in the case of an individual shareholder a detailed curriculum vitae is required. Qualifying shareholders who are also individuals must complete the individual questionnaire which is in similar terms to the individual questionnaire which must be completed by the qualifying shareholders of investment business firms regulated by the IIA 1995.

6.7 Capital requirements

Section 10(5) of the IIA 1995 states that an investment business firm shall not be authorised under the IIA 1995 unless it has the minimum level of capital specified by the appropriate supervisory authority. In addition, there are continuing capital requirements. Section 10(7) of the IIA 1995 states that the supervisory authority may impose conditions or requirements from time to time in respect of the level of capital to be maintained by investment business firms, having regard to the ISD and the Capital Adequacy Directive (Directive 93/6/EEC of 15 March 1993) (CAD).

The capital requirements for investment business firms regulated by the CBI have been set out in a notice by the CBI dated 29 December 1995, as amended by a notice dated 28 June 1996 (the CAD implementation notice) implementing the CAD. The CAD implementation notice provides for a continuing capital requirement that a firm's capital must never be less than one quarter of their preceding year's fixed overheads.

Firms must also provide their own funds and financial resources which are equal to or in excess of:

(a) capital requirements in respect of position risk, underwriting, settlement and counter-party risk and large exposures for their trading book business in accordance with the CAD implementation notice;

(b) the capital requirements in respect of foreign exchange risk in accordance with the CAD implementation notice for all business. of investment firms;

(c) the capital requirements imposed by the Solvency Ratio Directive (Directive 89/647/EEC of 18 December 1989) for all business (excluding trading book business and illiquid assets which have been deducted in arriving at financial resources); and

(d) the capital requirements which may be imposed by the CBI to cover risks arising in connection with business outside the scope of the CAD or Solvency Ratio Directive.

6.8 Appeal against refusal to grant the authorisation

A proposed investment business firm which is applying for authorisation pursuant to the IIA 1995 may appeal to the High Court of Ireland within 21 days of receipt of a notice from the appropriate supervisory authority that authorisation has been refused against such refusal (s 10(3) of the IIA 1995).

A stockbroking firm which is applying for authorisation under the SEA 1995 also has 21 days from receipt of a notice from the CBI that authorisation has been refused, to appeal to the High Court against such refusal (s 18(3) of the SEA 1995).

6.9 Conditions additional to or stricter than those contained in the ISD for granting an authorisation to do business

Section 10 of the IIA 1995 largely follows the criteria as set out in Art 3 of the ISD relating to the conditions for authorisation, although the IIA 1995 sets them out in more detail. The following conditions set out in s 10 are an addition to those set out in the ISD:

(i) the investment business firm, if it is an unincorporated body of persons, must draw up a partnership agreement if such agreement does not already exist;

(ii) the appropriate supervisory authority must be satisfied that, where applicable, the memorandum and articles of association of a proposed investment business firm contain sufficient provisions to enable it to operate in accordance with the IIA 1995;

(iii) the proposed investment business firm must satisfy the appropriate supervisory authority that it has and will follow established procedures to enable the appropriate supervisory authority to be supplied with all information necessary and to enable the public to be supplied with any information which the supervisory authority may specify;

(iv) the appropriate supervisory authority may set out conditions or requirements or both to monitor the solvency of an investment business firm which is a partnership or a natural person including monitoring the solvency of its proprietors;

(v) the appropriate supervisory authority may direct the investment business firm to alter its memorandum or articles of association in the interests of the proper and orderly regulation and supervision of investment business firms and the protection of investors or both;

(vi) investment business firms may also be subject to such conditions or requirements or both as may be imposed by the supervisory authority in the interest of any or all of the following:
- the proper and orderly regulation and supervision of an investment business firm; or
- the protection of investors or clients or both;

(vii) the appropriate supervisory authority may impose requirements on an investment business firm to organise its business or corporate structure or control of any associated undertaking or related undertaking not supervised by the appropriate supervisory authority so that the firm, and where appropriate and practical, the business of an associated or related undertaking, either collectively or individually, are capable of being supervised under the IIA 1995; and

(viii) conditions or requirements may be imposed on an investment business firm which is a partnership or individual so as to achieve an equivalent level of supervision to that of a firm which is a body corporate.

Similar additional requirements apply to stockbroking firms with the exception of (viii) above.

Both the SEA 1995 and the IIA 1995 allow additional conditions or requirements relating to the proper and orderly regulation of investment business firms or stockbroking firms to be imposed.

6.10 Application to investment firms other than those covered by the ISD of any of the conditions and rules regarding the authorisation to do business laid down in the ISD

The IIA 1995 has potential application to investment business firms other than those covered by the ISD. The definition of 'investment business firm' is by reference to providers of investment business services or investment advice. Investment business services for the purposes of the IIA 1995 are listed at section 6.2.1 above. In addition to those listed in the Annex to the ISD, the following additional investment business services are also covered by the IIA 1995:

(a) acting as a deposit agent or deposit broker;
(b) the administration of collective investment schemes, including the performance of valuation services or fund accounting services or acting as transfer agents or registration agents for such funds;
(c) custodial operations involving the safekeeping and administration of investment instruments; and
(d) acting as a manager of a designated investment fund within the meaning of the Designated Investment Funds Act 1985.

The definition of 'investment instruments' in the IIA 1995 is also wider than those listed in Sched B of the Annex to the ISD. Investment instruments for the purposes of the IIA 1995 are listed at section 6.2.2 above. The following investment instruments are listed in the IIA 1995, in addition to those set out in Sched B of the Annex to the ISD:

(a) non-transferable securities creating or acknowledging indebtedness issued by or on behalf of a government, local authority or public authority;

CHAPTER 6: THE REGULATION OF INVESTMENT BUSINESS SERVICES

(b) commodity futures contracts;

(c) sale and repurchase and reverse repurchase agreements involving transferable securities;

(d) agreements for the borrowing and lending of transferable securities;

(e) certificates or other instruments which confer all or any of the following rights, namely:
   (i) property rights in respect of any investment instruments referred to in the definition of transferable securities; or
   (ii) any right to acquire, dispose of, underwrite or convert an investment instrument being a right to which the holder would be entitled if he held any such investment to which the certificate or instrument relates; or
   (iii) a contractual right (other than an option) to acquire any such investment instrument otherwise than by subscription;

(f) hybrid instruments involving two or more investment instruments.

Therefore, investment business firms which deal in investment business services or investment instruments (which are not listed in Scheds A or B of the Annex to the ISD but which are listed in the IIA 1995), are subject to the authorisation and regulatory regime set out in the IIA 1995 even though they might not be covered by the ISD.

The definition of 'investment instruments' in the SEA 1995 is set out at section 6.2.3 above. Also included in the definition of 'investment instruments' are certificates or other instruments which confer:

(a) property rights in respect of any investment instrument; or

(b) any right to acquire, dispose of, underwrite or convert an investment instrument being a right to which the holder would be entitled if he held any such investment to which the certificate or instrument relates; or

(c) a contractual right (other than an option) to acquire any such investment instrument other than by subscription.

The definition of 'investment services' in the SEA 1995 does not go beyond those listed in Sched A of the Annex to the ISD. However, stockbroking firms which deal in investment instruments which are not listed in Sched B of the Annex to the ISD but are listed in the SEA 1995 are subject to the authorisation and regulatory regime set out in the SEA 1995 even though they might not be covered by the ISD

6.11 The prudential rules drawn up in compliance with Art 10 of the ISD

The IIA 1995 and the SEA 1995 contain various prudential rules with which investment business firms or stockbroking firms must comply. These rules deal with the various headings set out in Art 10 of the ISD.

Both the IIA 1995 and the SEA 1995 set out conditions with which investment business firms or stockbroking firms are obliged to comply with before authorisation will be granted. Authorisation can be revoked if the firm no longer complies with such conditions. These conditions include the firm satisfying the appropriate supervisory authority as to:

(a) its organisational structure and management skills and that adequate levels of staff and expertise will be employed to carry out its proposed activities;

(b) that it has and will follow established procedures to enable the appropriate supervisory authority to be supplied with all information necessary for the supervisory authority and to enable the public to be supplied with any information the supervisory authority may specify; and

(c) that the organisation of its business structure is such that it and any of its associated or related undertakings where appropriate and practical are capable of being supervised adequately by the supervisory authority.

The rules of conduct for investment business firms drawn up pursuant to s 37 of the IIA 1995 and the conduct of business rules drawn up for stockbroking firms under s 38 of the SEA 1995, provide that firms must have effective written procedures for the recording, monitoring and approving of personal account transactions of employees, associates and connected persons and all employees must, as part of their contract of employment, sign an undertaking relating to Irish legislation on insider dealing.

6.12 Member States shall make adequate arrangements for instruments belonging to investors with a view to safeguarding the latter's ownership rights

Section 52 of the IIA 1995 and s 52 of the SEA 1995 are relevant in this regard. These provisions are summarised in section 6.5 above and allow the appropriate supervisory authority to impose requirements on investment business firms or stockbroking firms regarding the holding of money or investment instruments or both for clients. These requirements or rules relating to various matters, may include:

(a) the rights, duties and responsibilities of an investment business firm or stockbroking firm in relation to investment instruments including the lodgment to and withdrawal from a client account of client investment instruments;

(b) the acknowledgements or statements to be issued by an investment business firm or stockbroking firm in respect of client investment instruments received, held, controlled or paid by it arising from its business as an investment business firm or a stockbroking firm; and

(c) the safekeeping of client investment instruments and documents of title relating to such investment instruments.

Requirements have been drawn up by the CBI in respect of stockbroking firms. These provide for:

(a) the proper safeguarding by stockbroking firms of investment instruments held for clients;

(b) for clients to be notified of the obligations which the firm has in relation to investment instruments;

(c) the proper registration of registerable safe custody investments;

(d) the segregation of instruments;

(e) measures relating to the holding of safe custody investments with an eligible custodian in an eligible account; and

(f) the reconciliation of books and records.

The legislation also provides for books and records to be kept in respect of client money and client investment instruments as may be specified from time to time by the appropriate supervisory authority. It also ensures that any such books and records are examined at such intervals, as may be specified by the appropriate supervisory authority, by an auditor who shall state whether the provisions of the legislation are being complied with. Non-compliance with the requirements of the legislation relating to books and records is an offence. It is also an offence for a director, officer or employee of an investment business firm or stockbroking firm to misappropriate fraudulently any money or investment instruments held, controlled or paid on behalf of a client by that investment business firm or stockbroking firm.

6.13 Investment firms are to be structured and organised so as to minimise the risk of conflicts of interest

The codes of conduct which were drawn up under s 37 of the IIA 1995 in respect of investment business firms provide that firms must ensure that effective 'Chinese Walls' are in place between the different business areas of the firm and between the firm and its connected parties. All procedures relating to the maintenance of Chinese Walls are to be in writing and notified to all employees of the firm. Chinese Walls are defined as an arrangement within an organisation or firm or between it and any associate which requires information obtained by the firm or an associate in the course of carrying on one part of its business of any kind to be withheld in certain circumstances from persons with whom it deals in the course of carrying on another part of its business.

The codes of conduct also state that an investment business firm must make reasonable efforts to avoid conflicts of interest and where they cannot be avoided ensure that its clients are fairly treated.

These provisions are designed to reflect s 37(1)(f) of the IIA 1995 which provides that the codes of conduct shall include provisions to seek to ensure that an investment business firm makes a reasonable effort to avoid conflicts of interest and when they cannot be avoided, to ensure that its clients are fairly treated.

The terms of business which investment business firms and stockbroking firms are obliged by the codes of conduct to send to their clients must contain an outline of the firm's policies in relation to conflicts of interest.

Section 37(1)(f) of the IIA 1995 is replicated in s 38(1)(f) of the SEA 1995 for stockbroking firms and the rules of conduct for stockbroking firms contain similar requirements regarding conflicts of interest and Chinese Walls.

6.14 Prudential rules additional to, or stricter than, those laid down in the ISD

As set out in section 6.11 above, both the IIA 1995 and the SEA 1995, together with the codes of conduct or conduct of business rules made thereunder for investment business firms and stockbroking firms, set out various prudential rules which largely cover the criteria set out in Art 10 of the ISD. Other prudential rules set out in the Irish legislation, which may be noted, are as follows:

(a) the memorandum and articles of association of an investment business firm or stockbroking firm must be approved by the appropriate supervisory authority who may require that any proposed amendment shall not be made without the prior consent in writing of the appropriate supervisory authority (s 15 of the IIA 1995 and s 23 of the SEA 1995);

(b) the appropriate supervisory authority has power to impose a requirement on an investment business firm or stockbroking firm to keep a proportion of their assets in the form of liquid assets so as to enable the firm to meet its liabilities as they arise. The firm can also be required to maintain a certain ratio between its assets and its liabilities (s 18 of the IIA 1995 and s 26 of the SEA 1995);

(c) investment business firms or stockbroking firms must ensure the probity and competence of employed persons and the appropriate supervisory authority has power to apply to the High Court to have an officer or employee of a firm dismissed if their probity is liable to render them unsuitable to act as an officer or employee of such a firm. If an employee or officer is not competent in respect of matters with which he is concerned in his position, the appropriate supervisory authority may apply to court to have him removed or suspended or moved from a particular area of employment.

The rules of the Irish Stock Exchange contain various prudential rules with which stockbroking firms must comply. These include matters relating to the following:

(a) the suitability of stockbroking firms;
(b) compliance by employees of stockbroking firms with the rules of the Irish Stock Exchange and to the provision of information to the Irish Stock Exchange on employees;
(c) the maintenance of personnel records;
(d) the provision of information on controllers of the firm;
(e) notifying the Stock Exchange of changes in the holding company of the firm;
(f) notifying the Stock Exchange of changes in directors and senior officers;
(g) the provisions of governing dealing in investment instruments listed on the Irish Stock Exchange or for which a dealing facility exists on the Exchange and the reporting of such transactions to the Exchange;
(h) the measures to ensure compliance by stockbroking firms with the rules of the Irish Stock Exchange and setting out disciplinary procedures against stockbroking firms; and
(i) the measures governing the settlement of transactions and specific provisions relating to inter-dealer brokers and primary dealers using their services.

6.15 The prudential rules applicable to any other investment firm not covered by the ISD

As noted in section 6.10 above, the legislation implementing the ISD in Ireland is potentially applicable to investment firms additional to those covered by the ISD. The prudential rules would be applicable to all investment business firms or stockbroking firms who are regulated by the IIA 1995 or the SEA 1995.

6.16 Rules of conduct drawn up by your country in compliance with Art 11 of the ISD

A code of conduct has been drawn up for investment business firms regulated by the CBI under the IIA 1995 pursuant to s 37. A code of conduct is currently being drawn up for firms regulated by the Minister for Enterprise, Trade and Employment. Section 37(1) of the IIA 1995 allows conditions or requirements to be imposed on any class of investment business firm. A specific code of conduct has been drawn up in respect of investment managers which is quite similar in terms to the code of conduct for investment business firms. Conduct of business rules have also been drawn up for stockbroking firms pursuant to s 38 of the SEA 1995.

Reference has been made throughout these responses to specific provisions of the codes of conduct. In general, they provide that firms are to:

(a) act honestly and fairly in conducting their business and with due skill, care and diligence;

(b) employ effectively the resources and procedures necessary for the proper performance of their business activities;

(c) seek from their clients information regarding their financial situations, investment experience and objectives as regards services requested;

(d) make adequate disclosure of relevant material and information including commissions in their dealing with clients;

(e) make reasonable efforts to avoid conflicts of interest and, when they cannot be avoided, ensure that clients are fairly treated; and

(f) comply with all regulatory requirements applicable to the conduct of their business activities so as to promote the best interests of their clients and the integrity of the market.

The code provides that a copy of the firm's terms of business must be provided to clients not later than the time of providing the first service to the client. Such terms of business must include outlines of the services to be provided, charges and the firm's policies in relation to conflicts of interest. Firms must inform clients of whether or not there is a compensation fund or comparable protection in existence and the nature and level of protection available from such fund. A firm or its employees must not exert undue pressure or undue influence on clients.

Investment business firms must ensure that advice to or discretionary transactions with a client are suitable for that client and that if a firm is managing a portfolio for a client on a discretionary basis that the portfolio remains suitable.

Investment business firms must also take reasonable care in executing transactions with or for their clients to ensure that it deals to the best advantage of its clients. The circumstances which must be considered in determining whether a firm has taken reasonable care are set out in the code of conduct.

The code of conduct contains provisions setting out circumstances in which a firm may calculate a weighted average price for a series of transactions.

The priority in which a firm must deal with transactions from its clients, employees and for its own account are also set out.

There are prohibitions on firms engaging in conduct which creates a false or misleading impression as to the market in or the price or value of any investment instrument. Investment business firms must also ensure that transactions are promptly allocated to the appropriate account once they have been executed. Clients may grant discretion to operate their account only to a firm and not to particular employees though they can restrict who may be responsible for the operation of the discretionary account within the firm.

The code of conduct also sets out the periodic information that a firm, which acts on a discretionary or advisory basis for a client, must send to the client and the frequency with which such information must be given.

There are prohibitions on firms dealing for any client or advising a client to deal with a frequency or an amount so great that such dealings might be deemed to be excessive. This is unless the firm has been instructed so to deal after informing the client, that in the firm's opinion, the dealings are excessive.

The code of conduct also contains provisions as to the keeping of records of transactions and to complaints made against them from their clients. Personal account transactions of employees, associates and connected persons of an investment business firm must be recorded, monitored and approved and the firm must have effective written procedures for doing this. There are also measures to deal with insider trading by employees.

An investment business firm must take reasonable steps to ensure that neither it nor its employees or agents offers, gives or accepts inducements which would be likely to significantly conflict with any duties of the recipient or the recipient's employers.

There must be effective 'Chinese Walls' in place.

The code of conduct contains restrictions on investment business firms dealing for a client through any other party pursuant to a soft commission agreement.

Investment business firms are to ensure compliance with the provisions of Irish law dealing with money laundering.

Similar provisions are contained in the code of conduct for investment managers. The firm's investment management agreement must be given to each client at the outset of the client relationship. The provisions relating to compensation schemes and exerting undue pressure or influence on a client are not contained in the code of conduct for investment managers. The code of conduct for investment managers contains specific provisions providing for such firms to issue a contract note in respect of every purchase or sale of an investment instrument that is entered into for or with a client and sets out the details required to be contained in the contract notes. Specific details must be contained in respect of a contract note in respect of a sale or purchase of a derivative. Specific details are also required for future transactions which close out an option position or when an option has been exercised by or against a client.

Conducts of business rules in similar terms have also been drawn up by the Irish Stock Exchange for stockbroking firms. There are specific measures on the responsibilities of a stockbroking firm to its clients. There are also specific measures on contract notes and specific disclosure requirements for stockbroking firms. In the case of recommendations or analysis which a stockbroking firm has which might materially affect the price of an investment instrument, a firm must not deal in such investment instruments for its own account until clients to whom such material is provided have had a reasonable time to react to it.

There are also detailed provisions in the IIA 1995 and the SEA 1995 on advertising by investment business firms and stockbroking firms. Advertising requirements have been drawn up the CBI pursuant to the IIA 1995 and the SEA 1995. They deal with matters such as:

(a) the format of the advertisement;
(b) not taking improper advantage of any characteristic or circumstances which may make the clients or potential clients of a firm vulnerable;
(c) not to exert undue pressure or undue influence on a client; and
(d) the statements which must be included in advertisements must relate to the various types of investment.

There are also provisions regulating forecasts or projections in advertisements, direct offers and unsolicited calls. Article 13 of the ISD allows Member States to adopt rules governing the form and content of advertising by investment firms in the interest of the general good.

6.17 Rules of conduct additional to or stricter than the rules of conduct laid down by the ISD

The Criminal Justice Act (CJA) 1994 is the Irish legislation on money laundering and the codes of conduct for investment business firms drawn up under the IIA 1995 and SEA 1995 provide specifically that stockbroking firms and investment business firms must comply with this legislation. Investment business firms and stockbroking firms are required to demonstrate that the provisions of the money laundering legislation have been notified to all relevant staff, appropriate training has taken place and that they are also bound to comply with the provisions of any guidelines issued or adopted by the CBI relating to money laundering. The CJA 1994 implements the EC Directive 91/308/EEC on money laundering. The CJA 1994 makes it an offence to conceal or disguise any property representing the proceeds of drug trafficking, or other criminal activity or converting or transferring such property or removing it from Ireland for the purpose of avoiding prosecution. Certain measures designed to prevent money laundering must be taken by listed categories of undertakings and by credit and financial institutions involved in certain activities, for example, safe custody services and credit reference services. Those designated bodies are required to take 'reasonable measures to establish the identity of any person for whom it proposes' to provide one or more of the listed services and measures must also be taken to identify any third party for whom such a person is acting.

The Irish law relating to bank secrecy applies only to banks. There are no specific provisions in the Irish legislation implementing the ISD in dealing with confidentiality in relation to investment business firms or stockbroking firms.

6.18 Applicability to investment firms other than those covered by the ISD of any of the rules of conduct applicable as a result of the implementation of the ISD

As noted in section 6.10 above, the legislation implementing the ISD in Ireland is potentially applicable to investment firms additional to those covered by the ISD. The codes of conduct are potentially applicable to all investment business firms or stockbroking firms who are regulated by the IIA 1995 or the SEA 1995.

6.19 Obligation to take account of the professional nature of the person for whom the service is provided. Clear distinction between professional and non-professional investors

Section 37 of the IIA 1995 and s 38 of the SEA 1995 provide that the codes of conduct applying to investment business firms or stockbroking firms may be applied in such a way or to such an extent as to take account of the status or experience of the person for whom the services are provided.

The code of conduct for investment business firms and for investment managers and conduct of business rules for stockbroking firms provide that before a firm enters into a relationship with a client, the firm shall assess whether the client is a professional client and maintain a written record of such assessment. Before a firm enters into a relationship with a private client they must take reasonable steps to obtain from the client the details of his investment objectives, investment experience and any other facts about his financial position which the firm reasonably believes it needs to know and ought to reasonably be expected to find out.

An investment business firm or stockbroking firm shall not be entitled to recommend to or undertake for a private client any transaction in any derivatives or any other transaction as the appropriate supervisory authority may stipulate from time to time, unless the private client has previously signed a statement acknowledging the risks resulting from such transactions. Any such statement must explain the risks of the transaction.

The authorisation requirement of the IIA 1995 may not be applicable at all to certain foreign investment business firms who are providing investment business services or investment advice from outside Ireland on a cross-border basis to Irish companies and Irish professional individuals only. Section 9(2) of the IIA 1995 states that an investment business firm will not be regarded as operating within Ireland and thus will not be subject to the authorisation requirement of the IIA 1995 where it has no branch in Ireland and where:

(a) its head or registered office is in a State outside an EU Member State; or

(b) its head or registered office is in an EU Member State outside Ireland and it is a firm which does not provide any investment business services requiring authorisation in its home Member State for the purposes of the ISD; or

(c) it is a firm authorised in a EU Member State outside Ireland under the ISD but is providing investment business services for which an authorisation under the ISD is not available; and

(d) such a firm is not providing services to individuals in Ireland unless they themselves provide one or more investment business services or investment advice on a professional basis.

Section 24 of the IIA 1995 provides that s 23 of that Act (which deals with the advertising requirements) shall not apply to a class of advertisement specified from time to time by the appropriate supervisory authority for the purpose of exempting from that section advertisements issued to persons appearing to the appropriate supervisory authority to be sufficiently expert to understand any risks involved. The CBI has indicated that as a matter of practice it will not expect advertisements issued only to persons who are considered sufficiently expert to understand any risks involved to comply with the advertising requirements issued by the CBI under s 23 of the IIA 1995. However, it has not specified any classes of advertisements for this purpose. Section 32 of the SEA 1995 provides for a similar exemption in respect of the advertising requirements under s 31 of the SEA 1995.

6.20 Branch of an investment firm having its registered office outside the EU or the European Economic Area that carries on investment services in Ireland on a cross-border basis

Foreign investment business firms or stockbroking firm which are authorised by a competent authority in another Member State of the EU pursuant to the ISD may carry on investment business services and give investment advice in Ireland pursuant to their ISD passport.

Stockbroking firms may not obtain authorisation from the CBI pursuant to the SEA 1995 unless their head or registered office is in Ireland. Branches of investment business firms, which have their head or registered office outside the EU, may obtain an authorisation from the appropriate Irish supervisory authority to act as an investment business firm in Ireland. Otherwise, non-EU investment business firms may not do business in Ireland unless they can bring themselves within the exemption in s 9(2) of the IIA 1995.

Investment business forms and stockbroking firms which have had their head or registered offices in the EU and which are authorised in their home Member State under the ISD are treated more favourably than firms which have their head or registered offices outside the EU, as the EU firms can carry on business in Ireland pursuant to their ISD passport.

CHAPTER 7

OFFERS TO THE PUBLIC

Dermot Cahill and Anne-Marie Mooney Cotter

7.1 Introduction

A company making 'an offer to the public' is required to publish certain information about itself, its directors, assets, liabilities and future prospects. This information document is called a 'prospectus', and is for the benefit of those who may be interested in taking up the offer. The purpose of the prospectus is to provide sufficient information to interested investors such that they are placed in a position to make an informed assessment of the prospects and financial status of the company making the offer.

The legal regimes that the offeror will have to comply with will vary, depending on whether the company is a listed or non-listed company, and will also depend on the particular type of offer being made. In the case of listed companies, they will be required to publish a prospectus complying with Council Directive 89/298/EEC ([1989] OJ L124/8) (the Prospectus Directive), Sched 3 to the Companies Act (CA) 1963, as well as the Stock Exchange's own rules, as applicable. A non-listed company on the other hand, will be required to publish a prospectus complying with the Prospectus Directive and/or Sched 3 to the CA 1963, as applicable.

Where more than one of the foregoing regimes applies to the particular offeror's offer, it will not be necessary to publish separate prospectuses under each regime. A composite prospectus, meeting the individual requirements of whichever regimes are applicable to the particular offer, will ordinarily suffice.

A separate regime, outlined in Pt XII of the CA 1963, applies for companies incorporated outside the State. This will be considered later in this chapter.

As a preliminary observation, it should be noted that the statutory provisions concerning prospectuses and offers to the public are drafted in opaque language, and are often difficult to interpret with a comfortable degree of certainty. Furthermore, the area is unduly complicated by the less than satisfactory intertwining of domestic and European Community legislation.

Whether or not an offer to the public requires a prospectus complying with some, or all, of the forgoing regimes, one feature is common to all regimes: the obligation to publish a prospectus is predicated on the making of an 'offer to the public'. The concept of offer to the public is a very nebulous term. It is often difficult to define, and furthermore, the requirement to publish a prospectus (being predicated on such an event) can vary from regime to regime.

7.2 Choice of legal regime governing the offer to the public

7.2.1 Third schedule prospectus

The CA 1963 does not define what is an offer to the public. Instead, it requires a prospectus to be published whenever a 'form of application' is issued for shares or debentures of a company (s 44(3) of the CA 1963). Section 2(1) of the CA 1963 provides that a prospectus means 'any prospectus, notice, circular, advertisement or other invitation, offering to the public for subscription or purchase any shares or debentures in the company'. In this roundabout fashion, reading ss 44(3) and 2(1) of the CA 1963 together, a prospectus is an information document required to be published whenever an offer in the form of a 'form of application' is made to the public for shares or debentures in a company. However, the wording used in s 2(1) reveals that the requirement for a prospectus is confined to where such an offer is an offer 'for subscription or purchase'. This means that the scope of the CA 1963 requirement for a third schedule prospectus is confined to where an offer of *new* shares or debentures of a company is made to the public, and does not apply to secondary offers of already issued shares.

Section 44(1) of the CA 1963 provides that the prospectus must contain information in accordance with the disclosure requirements of Sched 3 to the CA 1963. Schedule 3 requires information to be disclosed about the company, ranging from the existence of material contracts (contracts not involving the ordinary business of the company), the capital of the company, the number and amounts of shares issued, the property to be purchased with the proceeds of the offer, any interests the directors may hold in the property to be acquired, or directors' interests in any firm providing services to the company, other categories of information about the directors, as well as audited accounts.

This obligation to make the forgoing disclosure as required by Sched 3 is very onerous, because, *inter alia*, it requires the disclosure of audited accounts for the period of *five years* prior to the offer to the public (Sched 3 to the CA 1963, para 19).

Where the Prospectus Directive (see below) or Listing Particulars Directive (80/390/EEC) (see section 7.2.3 below) apply to an offer, the requirement for a third schedule prospectus may be superseded. This will now be considered in more detail.

7.2.2 The Prospectus Directive prospectus

Where possible, companies making an offer to the public will try and come within the scope of the Prospectus Directive regime, rather than the aforementioned CA 1963 third schedule regime. This is primarily because the Prospectus Directive regime requires disclosure of audited accounts for a *three* rather than a five year period prior to the offer (Reg 8(2) of the European Communities (Transferable Securities and Stock Exchange) Regulations 1992 (SI 1992/202) (the 1992 Regulations) which implements the Prospectus Directive). Such a prospectus will in many respects disclose information of a similar variety to that disclosed in a third schedule, though in some respects it will require disclosure of additional categories of information. Art 11 of the Prospectus Directive sets out the categories of information required, ranging from: information about those responsible for issuing the prospectus; information concerning the type of securities being offered; information concerning the issuer's capital structure and group companies; information on the issuer's business, assets, prospects and liabilities. The reader is referred to Art 11 of the Prospectus Directive for further particulars.

The events that trigger the obligation to publish a prospectus that complies with the Prospectus Directive varies from the event which triggers the requirement to publish a prospectus under the CA 1963 (see section 7.2.1 above). Under the Prospectus Directive, a prospectus has to be published whenever 'transferable securities' are offered to the public 'for the first time ... provided they are not already listed on a stock exchange in that State' (Art 1.1). 'Transferable securities' means 'shares in companies and other transferable securities equivalent to shares in companies, debt securities having a maturity of at least one year and other transferable securities equivalent to debt securities, and any other transferable security giving the right to acquire any such transferable securities by subscription or exchange' (Art 3(e)). Consequently, provided the securities being offered are 'transferable securities' offered to the public in an Art 1.1 context, then a company can draw up a prospectus which complies with the Prospectus Directive's requirements (three year audited accounts disclosure).

A third schedule prospectus (containing five years' audited accounts) will not be required because Reg 21(4) of the 1992 Regulations provides that a prospectus complying with the Prospectus Directive is deemed to be a prospectus within the meaning of the CA 1963, and in addition, Reg 21(3) provides that no third schedule prospectus is required.

However, this does not mean that the third schedule can be completely ignored. Regulation 8 of the 1992 Regulations provides that the prospectus drawn up under the Prospectus Directive must contain any information that the third schedule would have required to be disclosed, in the event that the Prospectus Directive does not require disclosure of that particular matter.

Furthermore, it may be that the offer is either to a group of persons, or is being made by a category of issuer, or is of a type of securities, which do not require a prospectus under the Prospectus Directive, but yet may fall within the obligation to publish a third schedule prospectus pursuant to s 44 of the CA 1963, as described at section 7.2.1 above. (Those instances where a prospectus is not required *under the Directive,* are considered later below.) Consequently, in those instances where the Prospectus Directive cannot apply, Sched 3, along with its longer more onerous disclosure period of five years prior to the offer, may still require to be satisfied.

7.2.3 The Listing Particulars Directive

A further complication is introduced by Council Directive 80/390/EEC ([1980] OJ L100/1) (the Listing Particulars Directive) (as amended by Council Directives 87/345/EEC, 90/211/EEC, and 94/18/EEC) and the Stock Exchange Listing Rules. The European Communities (Stock Exchange) Regulations 1984 (SI 1984/282) (the 1984 Regulations) implemented the Listing Particulars Directive. It provides that where the Stock Exchange has approved listing particulars for securities which are to be listed on the Exchange, then a third schedule form of prospectus is not required (Reg 12(2)). Such listing particulars are deemed to satisfy the CA 1963 requirement for a third schedule prospectus (Reg 12(3)).

Those issuing a listing particulars complying with the Listing Particulars Directive will have to also ensure that their listing particulars comply with the Prospectus Directive's requirements. This is because the domestic regulations (European Communities (Transferable Securities and Stock Exchange) Regulations 1992 (SI 1992/202)) implementing the Prospectus Directive appear to require a prospectus to comply with not only the Prospective Directive's requirements, but also the Listing Particulars Directive's requirements. In practice, therefore, the Stock Exchange requires listing particulars to be drawn up so as to ensure compliance with both Directives' respective regimes. Consequently, the Stock Exchange's requirements for the contents of listing particulars ensures that any content required under the Prospectus Directive is also required under the Exchange's Rules for Listing Particulars.

7.3 Offer to the public

Where an offer to the public falls outside the scope of the Prospectus Directive, the CA 1963 requires a third schedule-type prospectus to be published whenever there is an offer to the public of shares or debentures of a company for subscription or purchase (s 44 of the CA 1963) (see section 7.2.1 above).

For those offers to the public which fall within the scope of the Prospectus Directive, a prospectus is required whenever there is an offer to the public of unlisted transferable securities for the first time (Art 1 of the Prospectus Directive) (see section 7.2.2 above).

However, neither the CA 1963 regime nor the Prospectus Directive regime, defines what 'the public' means. Although the Directive does provide for a number of situations where those receiving the offer will not constitute the public, it also concedes that it was not possible to define 'the public' at Community level, given the disparity of the definition of 'the public' in the different Member State jurisdictions. The Directive gives only limited assistance in this regard.

For example, Art 2.1 of the Prospectus Directive provides that an offer is not an offer, to which the Directive applies, where the offer is:

- to persons in context of their trade or profession; or
- to a restricted circle of persons; or
- of securities, the selling price of all being not greater than €40,000; (and, or)
- of securities which can only be acquired at a minimum of €40,000 investment per investor.

In the case of the first two aforementioned categories, such vague and general language cannot have precise legal meaning attributed to it in the absence of further clarification at national level. For example, the Directive does not further elaborate on what 'a restricted circle' might mean. It is up to the national legislative authorities to complete this task. Regrettably, this was not done in implementing the 1992 Regulations.

The CA 1963 does not give a comprehensive definition of 'the public' either, but at least it does give some guidance, though as will be seen, even this is oblique in meaning and will require judicial interpretation to give it further clarity. Section 61(1) of the CA 1963 provides that the 'public' includes an offer to: any section of the public, whether selected:

- as members or debenture holders of the company; or
- as clients of the issuer of the prospectus; or
- in any other manner.

Section 61(2) further provides that where the offer is either:

- not calculated to result in securities becoming available to persons other than the initial offerees; or
- a domestic concern of the persons making and receiving the offer,

then the offer cannot be an offer to the public.

There is no Irish case law which interprets the meaning of 'the public'. Consequently, in order to try and understand better what this concept of the public might mean, one seeks to rely on case law from other common law jurisdictions, much of which predates the current domestic legislation. Notwithstanding, such case law is helpful as persuasive interpretation, because the concept of 'the public' has been employed in earlier company laws in the various common law jurisdictions. The trends that emerge in the case law are as follows.

First, in order for an offer to be an offer to the public, it must be 'an offer to anyone who should choose to come in'. So held Warrington J in the case of *Sherwell v Combined Incandescent Mantle Syndicate* (1907) 23 TLR 482 where the court held that where a company director had circulated an offer document to a large group of his friends, nevertheless it was not an offer to the public because the director's intention was very clear – he intended to confine the offer to that group, and not to any other person outside of that circle.

In another case, *Re South of England Natural Gas* [1911] 1 Ch 573, an offer of shares in a gas company was made to 3,000 shareholders of other gas companies on the basis that they were the persons *most likely* to take up the offer. By contrast with the *Sherwell* case, here the court identified a crucial difference. It was held that merely because an offer was made to those who were *most likely* to take up the offer, that of itself did not take the offer outside the offer to the public rubric because the terms of the offer did not preclude the offerees from passing the opportunity to accept the offer onto someone else.

In an Australian case, *Lee v Evans* (1964) 112 CLR 276, the court observed *obiter* that *Re South of England* demonstrates that merely because an offer is circulated to a select group, it does not necessarily follow that the offer is not an offer to the public, on that account. Indeed, s 61(1) of the CA 1963 would appear to adopt this position as it, *inter alia*, provides that the public can include:

> ... any section of the public, whether selected
> - as members or debenture holders of the company, or
> - as clients of the issuer of the prospectus, or
> - in any other manner ...

Therefore, the issue arises, how does one distinguish whether an offer – made to a selected group of persons who were selected because they are *most likely* to be interested in the offer – is an offer to the public or not? The answer is to be found in the *dicta* of the various judgments in *Lee v Evans*. In essence, the question to be asked is whether the offer is an offer 'to anyone who should choose to come in' (*per* Barwick CJ). In other words, is the offer only capable of acceptance *solely* by the group of persons to whom it is actually made, or could the offer be accepted by other persons who would not necessarily have received the offer from the offeror *directly*? In this regard, the reference in s 61(2) of the CA 1963 to an offer not being an offer to the public where it is not calculated to result in the shares becoming available to persons other than those receiving the offer, would appear to constitute a legislative illustration reflecting the *dicta* of Barwick CJ.

In another Australian case, *Corporate Affairs Commission (South Australia) and Another v Australian Central Credit Union* [1985] 59 ALJR 785, it was emphasised that just because an offer was sent to those *most likely* to take up the offer, this does not mean it cannot be an offer to the public.

This is an interesting case also because it illustrates how one arm of the two exceptions provided for in s 61(2) of the CA 1963 might be interpreted, that is, that an offer is not an offer to the public where it is '*of domestic concern to those making and receiving the offer*'. According to the Australian High Court, where a *rational connection* exists between those making and receiving the offer, then the offer can be said to be of 'domestic concern' to those making and those receiving the offer, and therefore not constitute an offer to the public.

In this case, the Australian High Court was called upon to consider legislative provisions similar in content to s 61(2) of the CA 1963. A credit union was issuing units in a unit trust to its members in return for their agreement to allow the union to purchase a property asset which the trust would manage. The court held that the offer to the union's members was of *domestic concern* to them in their capacity as members, because the offer by the union to its members had a rational connection with their membership of the union. By becoming holders of units in the trust, the members' ownership of the building (which was direct at the time of purchase, on account of their membership of the union) would be altered to indirect ownership status once the unit trust took over the property.

However, not every relationship between an offeror and a group of offerees will be of 'domestic concern' so as to bring the offer outside the definition of offer to the public. As Brennan J observed in the case:

> ... relationships, particularly commercial relationships, are various and not every relationship between an offeror and a group will suffice to take an offer out [outside the definition of offer to the public] ... [because] some relationships have no connection or only a tenuous relationship with the subject matter of the offer ... (Author's additional text added to clarify this rather disjointed quote.)

Therefore, to briefly summarise on the scope of s 61(2) of the CA 1963, a selected group of offerees can constitute 'the public' where there is no rational connection ('domestic concern' in s 61(2) language) between the offerees and the offer. However, where s 61(2) of the CA 1963 applies, that is, where either:

- the group selected are the only persons who can take up the offer (as opposed to being the group most likely to be interested in the offer); or
- the offer is of 'domestic concern' to the maker and receiver of the offer,

then there is no offer to the public.

One issue that can arise for consideration is whether an offer made by a company to its existing members constitutes an offer to the public. Section 44(7)(a) of the CA 1963 appears to provide that in such instance, no offer requiring a prospectus is required. However, s 44 has to be interpreted in light of s 61. If the offer of allotment of securities was capable of renouncement in favour of third parties, then it might well constitute an offer to the public on the basis that the offer was not only capable of acceptance by the company's existing members, but also capable of acceptance by anyone in whose favour a company member would renounce their *right of allotment*. In other words, the group selected would not be the only persons capable of accepting the offer.

7.4 Relaxation of requirement for a prospectus

7.4.1 Schedule 3 to the CA 1963

A third schedule prospectus is not required where:

(a) the Prospectus Directive applies (1992 Regulations);
(b) an offer is made to underwriters (s 44(4)(a) of the CA 1963);
(c) an offer is made to existing members (s 44(7)(a) of the CA 1963, though as noted above (see section 7.3), this may be subject to s 61 of the CA 1963);
(d) an issue of bonus shares;
(e) the Stock Exchange permits relaxation on account of its own disclosure requirements having been complied with in a similar offer, made in the previous two years (s 44(7)(b) of the CA 1963), or regarding a proposed issue of securities on the Exchange.

7.4.2 Prospectus Directive

A Prospectus Directive prospectus is not required where any of the following apply:

(a) Article 1.2 – split issues

Where the issue of securities is a split issue, that is, part is offered to the public and part is not, but is at a later date, a Member State has a discretion whether to require a fresh prospectus in the event that the latter part is subsequently so offered (Art 1.2). Ireland has exercised this option in the third schedule to the 1992 Regulations, by providing that no prospectus is required in respect of the offer to the public of the second portion of the securities.

(b)   Article 2.1 – offer to accept certain persons/securities at a certain price

Offers to certain persons to which the Prospectus Directive cannot apply:

- to persons in context of their trade or profession; or
- to a restricted circle of persons; or
- of securities, the selling price of all being not greater than €40,000; (and, or)
- of securities which can only be acquired at a minimum of €40,000 investment per investor.

(c)   Article 2.2 – types of securities

Although they may constitute 'transferable securities' (see section 7.2.2 above), offers of the following securities are nevertheless excluded from the Directive's regime because they are:

- securities offered in denominations of at least €40,000;
- units issued by collective investment undertakings other than those of the closed-end type;
- securities offered by the State or local authorities;
- securities offered on a take-over bid or merger;
- bonus shares;
- shares or equivalent securities that are offered in exchange for shares in the same company provided that the offer of the new shares does not increase the company's overall issued share capital;
- securities offered by employer or affiliated undertaking to employees or former employees;
- securities resulting from the conversion of convertible debt securities or from the exercise of warrants or shares offered in exchange for exchangeable debt securities (provided a public offer prospectus or listing particulars was published in the same State in respect of the convertible or exchangeable debt securities or warrants).
- securities offered by non-profit making bodies;
- securities offered by building societies or credit unions or industrial or provident societies;
- euro-securities which are not the subject of a generalised campaign of advertising or canvassing.

(d)   Article 5 – offers by certain categories of issuer

Article 5 is implemented by Reg 7 of the 1992 Regulations, which without adding any significant detail, merely states that there is no obligation to publish a prospectus in Ireland wherever securities are issued within the meaning of Art 5, that is:

- the securities are debt securities or equivalent thereto which are issued in a continuous or repeated manner by credit or other financial institutions equivalent to financial institutions which regularly publish their accounts, and are either set up or governed by a special law or are subject to public supervision intended to protect savings; or
- the debt securities or equivalent securities are issued by companies and other legal persons who are nationals of a Member State and which carry out their business

benefiting from State monopolies and are set up or governed by special laws or whose borrowings are irrevocably guaranteed by the State or local authorities; or
- debt securities issued by legal persons other than companies, which are nationals of a Member State and were set up by a special law and whose activities are governed by that law and consist solely in raising funds under State control for the purpose of financing production. Finally, such debt securities must be regarded under national laws applicable to admission to listing to be considered as securities that are issued or guaranteed by the State.

7.5 Penalties for failure to publish a prospectus

While it is outside the scope of this chapter to consider the many possible grounds for the imposition of *civil liability* against those responsible for issuing a prospectus containing negligent or otherwise misleading statements (for such consideration, the reader is referred to Cahill, *Corporate Finance Law* (Round Hall, Sweet & Maxwell, 2000, Chapter 3, pp 129–98)), we will briefly set out the *criminal* sanctions that can apply where there is a failure to issue a prospectus; where the prospectus fails to comply with statutory registration requirements; and where the prospectus contains false information.

Before considering specific offences enumerated in 20th century legislation, it should not be overlooked that s 84 of the Larceny Act 1861 provides for a prison term of up to seven years where a director, manager or other officer of a company knowingly issues or is a party to the circulation of a false prospectus. This heavy penalty was enacted to deal with deliberate fraud. However, fraud is difficult to prove, so prosecutions in this area under more recent legislation may have a better prospect of success as the focus is not on fraud as such, and consequently penalties are considerably lighter.

7.5.1 The third schedule (CA 1963) regime

Where the CA 1963 applies to an offer to the public, s 44(8) makes a person responsible for issuing a prospectus liable to a fine not exceeding €635, where there is a failure to comply with either the requirement to publish a prospectus or where the prospectus does not comply with the third schedule disclosure requirements. Statutory defences are provided, such as a plea of honest mistake or that the omission was of immaterial information.

Failure to register the prospectus with the Registrar of Companies pursuant to s 47 of the CA 1963 renders the company, and every person knowingly a party to the issue of the prospectus, liable to a similar level of fines as apply under s 44(8). If the prospectus contains 'untrue statements', then pursuant to s 50, the person who authorised such statements can be liable, upon summary conviction, to a fine not exceeding €635 or six months in jail, or both, or upon conviction on indictment, to a fine not exceeding €3,173 or two years in jail, or both. A statement is 'untrue' if it is misleading in the form and context in which it was used. In like fashion, a material omission can constitute an untrue statement.

7.5.2 The Prospectus Directive regime

The requirement to register the prospectus with the Registrar of Companies under s 47 of the CA 1963 also applies to a prospectus issued pursuant to the Prospectus Directive. Failure to do so is an offence, rendering the persons who knowingly were a party to the issue of the prospectus liable to a fine not exceeding €635 (Reg 11 of 1992 Regulations). Regulation 20 further provides that publication of information required by the Directive, that is of a misleading or false nature in a material respect, will render the person who knowingly was responsible for the publication of same liable to a fine not exceeding €1,269 or 12 months in jail, or both. The same regulation also provides that an officer or manager of a body corporate who consented or connived at, or whose neglect was responsible for, the body corporate committing an offence under the Regulations, will have similar sanctions and penalties attributed to them personally (that is, liable to a fine not exceeding €1,269 or 12 months in jail, or both).

Where a prospectus relates to an offer of shares or debentures that would otherwise require a third schedule prospectus (were it not for the application of the Prospectus Directive regime), s 50 of the CA 1963 (by virtue of Reg 21(4) of the 1992 Regulations) continues to apply to such a prospectus such that *if* the prospectus contains 'untrue statements' within the meaning of s 50, an offence is committed. Consequently, the person who authorised such statements can be liable, upon summary conviction, to a fine of not exceeding €635 or six months in jail, or both, or, upon conviction on indictment to a fine not exceeding €3,173 or two years in jail, or both.

7.5.3 The Listing Particulars Directive regime

So far as listing particulars are concerned, Reg 6(2) of the 1984 Regulations provides that the publication of information required by the Directive that is of a misleading or false nature in a material respect, will render the person who knowingly was responsible for the publication of same liable to a fine not exceeding €1,269. Regulation 6(3) further provides that an officer or manager of a body corporate who consented or connived at, or whose neglect was responsible for, the body corporate committing an offence under the Regulations, will have similar penalties attributed to them personally (that is, liable to a fine not exceeding €1,269). It is also an offence where late delivery of the listing particulars to the Registrar of Companies occurs (required pursuant to Reg 13), on the part of the issuer as well as every person who was knowingly a party to the publication. Where there is a failure to publish a listing particulars in conformity with the Listing Particulars Regulations (1984 Regulations), Reg 12(3) provides that s 44(8) of the CA 1963 makes a person responsible for the failure liable to a fine not exceeding €635.

Where a listing particulars relates to an offer of shares or debentures that would otherwise require a third schedule prospectus (were it not for the application of the Listing Particulars Directive regime), s 50 of the CA 1963 (by virtue of Reg 12(3) of the 1984 Regulations) continues to apply to such a listing particulars that *if* the listing particulars contains 'untrue statements' within the meaning of s 50, an offence is committed. Consequently, the person who authorised such statements can be liable, upon summary conviction, to a fine not exceeding €635 or six months in jail, or both, or upon conviction on indictment to a fine not exceeding €3,173 or two years in jail, or both.

7.6 Companies incorporated outside the State (Pt XII of the CA 1963) and the subsequent adoption of the principle of mutual recognition under the Prospectus Directive

Part XII of the CA 1963 provides a separate regime for companies incorporated outside the State. It provides that no company incorporated outside the State may offer securities to the public in the State unless accompanied by a third schedule-type prospectus. However, derogation exists for prospectuses first published or issued in a 'recognised jurisdiction'. To date, only the UK has been so recognised (Companies (Recognition of Countries) Order 1964 (SI 1964/42)).

However, to a large extent, Pt XII has been overtaken by events following the subsequent adoption of the Prospectus Directive at EC level in 1989. The Prospectus Directive, *inter alia*, sought to facilitate *mutual recognition* of prospectuses as between the various EC Member States in the circumstance where a public offer was being made simultaneously, or within a short time of a similar offer, in another Member State. In essence, the Prospectus Directive sought to facilitate issuers to access capital pools in more than one Member State, by requiring Member State authorities to recognise a prospectus which was drawn up to the Prospectus Directive's standards *and approved as such* in another Member State. This mutual recognition regime was designed to apply even if the public offer was going to be *listed* in one State, and made public, though not listed, in the other(s). With such offers, the Prospectus Directive sought to facilitate this objective by requiring the prospectus to be drawn up to comply with the disclosure requirements of the Listing Particulars Directive.

Consequently, notwithstanding Pt XII of the CA 1963, Reg 21(3) of the 1992 Regulations provides that a third schedule prospectus is not required if the offer is accompanied by a prospectus which complies with the Prospectus Directive's regime. (Consideration of the intricacies of the mutual recognition regime is outside the scope of this chapter: for a detailed consideration of this mutual recognition regime, see Cahill, *Corporate Finance Law* (Round Hall, Sweet & Maxwell, 2000, Chapters 1 and 2).)

7.7 Proposals for reform – EU Directive proposal on offers to the public

Issuers and investment banks have criticised the existing mutual recognition regime on the grounds that it has not allowed the fragmentation of capital markets in the EU territory to be easily overcome. It has been suggested that there should be only one set of disclosure documents, approved by the home country authority of the issuer, and accepted throughout the EU for public offers and admission to trading on regulated markets. An integrated market, properly regulated and prudentially sound, would deliver major benefits to consumers of investment products. Additionally, harmonised disclosure standards would promote investor confidence in the market. The proposed Directive on Offers to the Public provides for centralised filing in order to ensure easy access to prospectuses for all European investors irrespective of the Member State in which they reside. A single financial market will be a key factor in promoting the competitiveness of the European economy by lowering the cost of raising capital for companies of all size.

The proposal allows for a prospectus to be split into a registration document, a securities note and a summary note, each of which may circulate separately. The registration document (RD) would contain the information related to the issuer, the securities note (SN) would contain the information related to the specific securities issued, and the Summary Note would contain a résumé of the two documents and a risk warning. It is expected that this procedure would make the life of the issuer easier by lowering the costs of regulatory compliance without compromising investor protection. The prospectus would have to be approved by the home country authority of the issuer and be mutually recognised in all European markets, subject to a simple notification procedure and without additional information requirements. Issuers would also benefit from the introduction of a new concept of '*single passport*', that is, there would be only one prospectus approved by the home country authority of the issuer, which would have to be accepted throughout the EU for public offer and admission to trading on regulated markets. Compared to the existing regime, which is a system of mutual recognition subject to certain conditions, the new system would be based on compulsory automatic recognition of prospectuses drafted in accordance with the

Directive. The Directive therefore would have to apply to all public offers and admissions to trading on a regulated market.

Thus, the proposed Directive on Offers to the Public would consolidate the two existing Directives (that is, the Listing Particulars Directive and Prospectus Directive regimes, respectively). It would harmonise the requirements for the different types of public offers (that is, whether listed or non-listed) that have to be published when securities are offered to the public, thereby ensuring a level playing field throughout the Community.

The March 2001 Resolution of the Stockholm European Council on more effective securities market regulation in the EU, asked for implementation by the end of 2003 of the priorities set out in the February 2001 report by the Committee of the Wise Men chaired by Alexandre Lamfalussy. However, the benefits of the proposed Directive will be available in practice only once it has been implemented into the legislation of all Member States. Assuming the deadline for adoption is met, implementation should take place by the end of June 2004. This proposal is one more building block to help deliver the basis for the creation of an efficient internal market in financial services in the EU territory.

7.8 The American perspective

We will next briefly consider the American system as a means of comparison, and in light of recent important developments. The major federal statutes regulating the United States (US) securities markets are the Securities Act 1933 (15 USC §§ 77a–77aa (1988)) (the 1933 Act) and the Securities Exchange Act 1934 (15 USC §§ 78a–78ll (1988)) (the 1934 Act). The basic purposes of the Acts are the disclosure of information and the prevention of fraud. From a company's perspective, both the 1933 and 1934 Acts are primarily disclosure-mandating schemes. The Acts are administered by a federal government agency, the Securities and Exchange Commission (SEC).

The capital markets of the United States provide mechanisms for the purchase and sale of instruments, broadly known as securities, which represent claims of a contractual nature against the company that sells or issues the instrument (the issuer). The question of what constitutes a 'public' offering has a long judicial and administrative history, with the principal factor being whether the investors involved need the protection afforded by the Acts (*SEC v Ralston Purina Co* 346 US 119 (1953)). The SEC was created by the 1934 Act (s 4(a) of 15 USC § 78d(a) (1988)), which also contains its remedial and enforcement powers (see ss 21, 21A, 21B and 21C of 15 USC § 78u–1, 78u–2, 78u–3 (1988)). The 1933 Act is concerned with the process of capital formation through the public sale of securities, specifically the distribution of securities and the process by which securities are transferred from a company or other issuer into the hands of the investing public. Sound investment decision-making requires the investor to have certain information at the time of purchase, with the issuer being the most appropriate provider of that information. The 1933 Act centres on the public sale of securities. The preparation and dissemination of a registration statement is a sophisticated undertaking, with issuers and other parties exposed to liability risks for any material misstatement in a registration statement. The term 'prospectus' is broadly defined in s 2(10) of 15 USC § 77b(10) (1988), to cover all writings and all broadcasts which 'offer' a security for sale or confirm the sale of a security.

The 1933 Act, and specifically s 5, prohibits any person from offering or selling a security using the facilities of interstate commerce without a registration statement which contains within it the prospectus or selling brochure. These documents are prepared by the issuer and contain numerous lengthy disclosures about the company, its business operations, its finances, its owners, the securities being offered, and the distributors of those securities. There are a number of exemptions from the registration requirement, the broadest being in s 4(1) for transactions by persons 'other than an issuer, underwriter or dealer'. The incentive to push the securities onto the public can create the risk of misrepresentation or unwarranted pressure on potential buyers, which the statute is meant to regulate by exposing sellers to liability for material misstatements in connection with offers or sales.

The 1934 Act regulates market professionals, including the stock exchanges, brokers and dealers, and dealers in government securities, as well as companies whose securities are publicly traded.

Disclosure requirements for companies under the 1934 Act include the reports that companies file on a periodic basis. As a result, after the end of each fiscal quarter and the end of each fiscal year, a reporting company must publicly disclose all material information about the company then in its possession, including financial statements. Audited financial statements are required in the annual report.

An interim report must be filed if, during any fiscal quarter:

(a) a change in control of the company occurs;
(b) the company acquires or disposes of a significant amount of assets;
(c) the company goes into bankruptcy or receivership; or
(d) the company changes the accounting firm it uses to certify its finances.

Companies are also subject to the anti-fraud provisions of the Securities Acts at all times, which may require that they issue a public statement even when no periodic filing is then required, because of the risk of liability for a material misstatement or omission.

The greatest current challenge to the adaptability of the laws and the SEC is the increasing globalisation of capital markets.

7.9 Recent events

The SEC's primary responsibilities are to protect investors and to promote the fairness, effectiveness and efficiency of US capital markets. In light of recent scandals in the general services sector in the US impacting on the global economy, the US President George Bush demanded 'stricter accounting standards and tougher disclosure requirements', wanting corporate America to 'be made more accountable to employees and shareholders and held to the highest standard of conduct'. The initiatives include:

(a) a system of 'current' disclosure (that is, current information and affirmative disclosures);
(b) an updated and improved system of periodic disclosure that is quicker and more comprehensive;
(c) financial statements that are clear and informative;
(d) conscientious identification and assessment by public companies and their auditors of critical accounting principles that respond expeditiously, concisely, and clearly, to current and immediate needs and reflects business realities; and
(e) an effective and transparent system of private regulation of the accounting profession, subject to rigorous oversight.

The primary goal of the federal securities laws is to promote honest and efficient markets and informed investment decisions through full and fair disclosure that is transparent in financial reporting. Transparency enables investors, creditors, and the market to evaluate an entity in helping investors make better decisions and increase confidence in the fairness of the markets. Further, transparency is important to corporate governance because it enables boards of directors to evaluate management's effectiveness, and to take early corrective actions, when necessary, to address deterioration in the financial condition of companies. For financial statements to provide the information that investors and other decision makers require, meaningful and consistent accounting standards and comparable practices are necessary.

CHAPTER 8

INSIDER DEALING

John Darby

8.1 Introduction

Insider dealing refers to trading based on an imbalance of information resulting in an advantage of one person over his counter-party or over the public in general.

8.2 The statutory regime

The statutory provisions relating to insider dealing are to be found in Pt V of the Companies Act (CA) 1990. The enactment of Pt V was largely motivated by Ireland's obligation to implement Directive 89/592/EEC on insider dealing (the Directive).

8.3 Definitions

8.3.1 Dealing

Section 107 of the CA 1990 defines 'dealing' as:

> ... acquiring, disposing of, subscribing for or underwriting [or sub-underwriting], the securities, or making or offering to make, or inducing or attempting to induce a person to make or to offer to make, an agreement:
>
> (a) for or relating to acquiring, disposing of, subscribing for or underwriting [or sub-underwriting] the securities; or
>
> (b) the purpose or purported purpose of which is to secure a profit or gain to a person who acquires, disposes of, subscribes for or underwrites [or sub-underwrites] the securities or to any of the parties to the agreement in relation to the securities.

8.3.2 Securities

Securities is defined in s 107 of the Act as:

(a) shares, debentures or other debt securities, issued or proposed to be issued, whether in Ireland or otherwise, and for which dealing facilities are, or are to be, provided by a recognised stock exchange;

(b) any right, option or obligation in respect of any such shares, debentures or other debt securities in (a);

(c) any right, option or obligation in respect of any index relating to any such shares, debentures or other debt securities in (a);

(d) such other interests as may be prescribed by the Minister for Enterprise, Trade and Employment (the Minister); or

(e) securities issued by the Irish State.

The prohibition on insider dealing extends only to companies with a stock exchange quotation. It does not apply to private companies or unquoted public companies. Trading facilities must be provided on a 'recognised stock exchange'. The only exchange designated as a recognised Stock Exchange by the Minister is the Irish Stock Exchange.

The interpretation of a company in Pt V is restricted to mean companies incorporated in the State. However, insider dealing outside of Ireland in respect of securities covered by the CA 1990 appears to be prohibited.

8.3.3 Inside Information

Pursuant to the CA 1990, 'dealing' is prohibited if a party is in possession of 'inside information'.

Section 108 of the Act defines 'inside information' as being 'information that is not generally available, and which if it were so available, would be likely to materially affect the price of the securities of a particular company'.

8.3.4 Not generally available

The phrase 'not generally available', which is slightly different from that of the Directive 'which has not been made public', is not further elaborated upon and so is therefore open to quite a wide interpretation. The UK Criminal Justice Act (CJA) 1993 does, however, provide a non-exhaustive list of what it considers to be 'public' information. This might serve as a guide for the Irish courts, although it would appear that the Irish provision allows more scope for the inclusion of information within its wording than the corresponding UK legislation.

In *Kinwatt Holdings Ltd v Platform Ltd* (1982) 6 ACLR 398, information which was published in a newspaper and which was pleaded in a court case was held to be 'generally available'.

In *Johnson v Wiggs* 433 F 2d 803 (1971), information was held to be in the public arena where it had been reported in the local papers and on local television.

The extent to which publication may be deemed to bring information into the public domain and thus considered to be 'generally available' is largely dependent on the extent to which it has been published and its circulation. Even where information is published widely, it has been recommended by the Irish Association of Investment Managers that it is best practice to wait until the information has been published on the regulatory news services of the stock exchange before acting upon it.

8.3.5 Likely to materially affect the price of the securities

The phrase 'likely to materially affect the price of the securities' is the statutory interpretation of the Directive's 'likely to have a significant effect on the price of the securities'. It would appear that the wording of the CA 1990 is again more encompassing and allows for more information to be caught by it than the Directive. A Singapore court considered an identical provision in *Public Prosecutor v Allan Ng Poh Meng* [1990] 1 MLJ v, where it was said that:

> ... the standard by which materiality is to be judged is whether the information on the particular share is such as would influence the ordinary reasonable investor in deciding whether or not to buy or whether or not to sell that share ... If an insider has any doubt about the legitimacy of dealing while in possession of information gained by reason ... of

being a connected person ... then he should not deal. He should not deal because his doubts are in effect telling him that the information may well have a price impact.

8.4 The prohibition

Essentially the CA 1990 makes it unlawful for insiders to deal in securities on inside information, for them to cause or procure others to deal, or for them to communicate the inside information to another for the purpose of dealing. The common element making these activities unlawful is the possession of inside information. All these activities may give rise to civil liability and, additionally, dealing when it is unlawful to do so is made a criminal offence by the Act.

8.4.1 Primary insiders

Section 108(1) and (2) of the CA 1990 deals with the prohibition on 'persons' from using the benefit of 'insider information' to make gains regarding securities to which such information attaches.

Section 108(1) provides that a person must not deal in securities of the company if he is, or was at any time in the preceding six months 'connected to the company' where he is in possession of inside information by reason of his connection.

Section 108(2) provides that a person may not deal in the securities of another company if he is, or was in the previous six months 'connected' to a company which was proposing to enter into a transaction with the other company, and the connected person has inside information relating to that transaction by reason of his 'connection'.

A person is deemed to be 'connected to the company' if he:

(a) is an officer of the company, its subsidiary or holding company or of a subsidiary of its holding company. For this purpose an 'officer' includes the following persons: a director, including a shadow director, a secretary or employee, a liquidator, any person administering a compromise or arrangement made between the company and its creditors, an examiner, an auditor and a receiver; or

(b) is a shareholder in any of these companies; or

(c) occupies a position (including a public office), which may reasonably be expected to give him access to inside information by virtue of:

- any professional business or other relationship which exists between himself (or his employer or a company of which he is an officer) and that company or a related company; or
- his being an officer of a substantial shareholder in that company or in a related company.

8.4.2 Secondary insiders or tippees

Section 108(3) of the CA 1990 prohibits a person from dealing in securities of a company when in possession of inside information, where such was received directly or indirectly from another person, and is aware or ought reasonably to be aware that the other person is an insider who is himself precluded from dealing in the securities.

There is no requirement that the tippee be connected to the company and there must be some level of awareness on the part of the tippee that the information is coming from a primary insider.

There are three activities which an insider or tippee may not do while in possession of insider information about a company's securities:

1   Deal in those securities.
2   Cause or procure anyone else to deal in those securities.
3   Communicate the inside information to anyone else if the insider or tippee knows or ought reasonably to know that the other person will make use of the inside information for the purpose of dealing or causing or procuring another person to deal in those securities.

8.5 Exemptions

8.5.1 'Chinese Wall' structure

A 'Chinese Wall' structure is an artificial division with a firm, preventing the sharing or exchange of information between different groups within that firm, so as to prevent any conflict of interests.

Under s 108(7) of the CA 1990, the prohibition does not apply provided:

(a)   the decision to enter into transaction was taken on the company's behalf by a person other than the officer in possession of the inside information; and

(b)   written 'chinese wall' arrangements can be demonstrated to have been in position such that the insider officer could not have been able to communicate the inside information to the decision-maker in the company, nor give any advice to such person in relation to the transaction; and

(c)   the information was not communicated and the advice was not given.

8.5.2 Mere information that company proposes to deal

Under s 108(8) of the CA 1990, the company will not be precluded from dealing in securities of another company if the information in the possession of its officer was received by him in the course of the performance of his duties and consists only of the fact that his company proposes to deal in securities of the other company (for example, as part of a take-over bid).

8.5.3 Company dealing in its own securities

Section 223 of the CA 1990 provides that a company will not be prohibited from dealing in its own securities by reason merely that an officer of the company had information at the time, provided that the decision to deal was:

- taken by an officer of the company other than the officer who had the inside information; and
- there is no communication of the inside information to the decision maker; and
- the party in possession of the information gave no advice to the decision maker in relation to the transaction.

8.5.4 Exclusion of statutory liability

The following transactions are expressly exempted from the prohibition against insider dealing in Pt V of the CA 1990:

(a) the acquisition of securities under a will or intestacy of another person;
(b) the acquisition of securities in a company pursuant to an employee profit sharing scheme approved by the Revenue Commissioners for the purposes of the Finance Acts, the terms of which were approved by the company in general meeting, and under which all permanent employees of the company are offered the opportunity to participate on equal terms relative to specified objective criteria;
(c) transactions entered into in pursuit of monetary, exchange rate national debt management or foreign exchange reserve policies by any minister of the government or the Central Bank of Ireland, or by any person on their behalf;
(d) the obtaining by a director of a share qualification under s 180 of the Companies Act 1963;
(e) a transaction entered into by a personal representative of a deceased person, a trustee, or liquidator, receiver or examiner in the performance of the functions of his office;
(f) a transaction by way of, or arising out of, a mortgage of or charge on securities or a mortgage, charge, pledge or lien on documents of title to securities; or
(g) a transaction entered into by a person in accordance with his obligations under an indemnity agreement.

8.5.5 Agents

Although the definition of dealing includes transactions by agents, an agent will not be liable for insider dealing if while in possession of inside information he acts as agent on an execution only basis and has no reasonable cause to believe that the deal is unlawful for the principal.

To be excluded from liability, the agent must enter the transaction pursuant to a specific instruction of the principal to effect the transaction. He must not have given advice to him in relation to dealing in the class of securities or in rights or interests over them, which are the subject of his instructions.

Section 113 of the CA 1990 provides that where a person who is dealing as an agent has reasonable cause to believe or ought to conclude that the deal would involve insider dealing, he will be guilty of an offence if he does deal.

8.5.6 Seven day window

Section 108(10) provides that a person may deal in securities of a company if, while not otherwise taking advantage of his possession of price sensitive information relating to those securities, he complies with the following conditions:

(a) he gives at least 21 days' notice to the relevant authority of the relevant stock exchange of his intention to deal in the securities within a period beginning seven days after the publication of the company's interim or final results, as the case may be and ending 14 days after such publication;
(b) the dealing actually takes place during this period; and
(c) the notice is published by the stock exchange immediately on its receipt.

8.6 Liability

8.6.1 Civil liability

Section 109 of the CA 1990 provides that:

- an insider dealer is liable to pay compensation to any other party who is not in possession of the information for any loss sustained by that party by reason of any difference between the price at which the securities were dealt in that transaction and the price at which they would have been likely to have been dealt in such a transaction at the time of which the first mentioned transaction took place if that information had been available;
- an insider is liable to compensate the company in whose securities he dealt in contravention of s 108 for any profit accruing to the company from dealing in those securities;
- there is no requirement for the existence of a fiduciary duty between the parties; and
- s 109 is 'without prejudice' to any other forms of civil action which might be taken against the insider dealer.

The following requirements must be satisfied in order to successfully pursue either of the above causes of action:

- the claim must be taken within two years of completion of the transaction;
- the definitions contained in s 107 must be satisfied, namely that there has been 'dealing' in 'securities' by an 'officer' on the basis of 'information' which was not 'generally available' but would have been likely to 'materially affect the price of those securities'; and
- the issuing company in question must be incorporated within the State.

8.6.2 Criminal liability

Section 111 of the CA 1990 provides that a person who *deals* in securities in a manner declared unlawful by s 108 is guilty of an offence.

Section 112 provides that a person convicted of an offence under s 111 is automatically banned from dealing for 12 months from the date of conviction and it is an offence, subject to a fine and imprisonment, to so deal.

8.6.3 Enforcement of criminal liability

The Director of Public Prosecutions (DPP) in the High Court, which on conviction, will impose the criminal sanctions, presents cases for beaches of the insider dealing rules.

If in the course of any trial, it appears to the judge that a person has committed an insider dealing offence, then the court may of its own motion, or on the application of any person concerned with the proceedings, direct the management of the Irish Stock Exchange to make a report to the DPP. Furthermore, the Minister has authority to direct the management of the Irish Stock Exchange to make a report on any alleged breach of the insider dealing regulations to the DPP.

8.6.4 Insider dealing at common law

8.6.4.1 UK approach

The principal English judicial decision where insider dealing was the basis of the action is *Percival v Wright* [1902] 2 Ch 431. That was a case where a director of a private company was approached by a shareholder who wanted to sell his shares in the company. The director agreed to buy the shares but did not tell the shareholder that there was an imminent take-over bid for the company which would greatly increase the value of the shares. The take-over bid did not in fact occur but the shareholder found out about it and sought to have the sale of his shares set aside. In his judgment, Swinfen Eady J made the following statement, which has become the classic statement of English law preventing insider liability to shareholders:

> I am therefore of the opinion that the purchasing directors were under no obligation to disclose to their vendor shareholders the negotiations which ultimately proved abortive. The contrary view could place directors in a most invidious position as they could not buy or sell shares without disclosing negotiations, a premature disclosure of which might well be against the best interests of the company.

On the basis of this case, it has been accepted that directors of companies do not owe a fiduciary duty to shareholders of the company. Their fiduciary duties are owed to the company alone. Although the point does not seem to have been considered directly in Ireland, this appears to be the accepted principle.

The result of the *Percival* approach is that a director who has, by reason of his office, acquired in confidence a particular piece of information affecting the value of his company's shares incurs no liability to the other party at common law if he buys or sells such securities without disclosing that piece of information.

Notwithstanding *Percival*, there are instances where the shareholders have succeeded in lawsuits against directors when they have transacted in the company's shares with them.

Percival has generally only been departed from in circumstances where it has been found by the court that the directors have placed themselves in a fiduciary position vis à vis shareholders.

Directors are under a duty of care neither to mislead shareholders nor to make false representations to them. This issue has often been considered by the courts in the context of actions in fraud or deceit against directors by those who have acquired shares in a company on the basis of false statements in a prospectus. In *Nocton v Lord Ashburton* [1914] AC 932, Viscount Haldane LC considered the relationships between such action and breach of fiduciary obligations:

> Such a special duty may arise from the circumstances and relations of the parties. These may give rise to an implied contract at law or to a fiduciary obligation in equity. If such a duty can be inferred in a particular case of a person issuing a prospectus, as, for instance, in the case of directors issuing to the shareholders of the company which they direct a prospectus inviting the subscription by them of further capital, I do not find in *Derry v Peek* an authority for the suggestion that an action for damages for misrepresentation without an actual intention to deceive may not lie. What was decided there was that from the facts proved in that case no such special duty to be careful in statements could be inferred, and that mere want of care therefore gave rise to no cause of action. In other words, it was decided that the directors stood in no fiduciary relation and therefore were under no fiduciary duty to the public to whom they had addressed the invitation to subscribe.

In *Allen v Hyatt* (1914) 30 TLR 444 such a special relationship was found to exist. In that case, the Privy Council held that directors were in a fiduciary relationship with the shareholders on the basis that they had been acting as agents of the shareholders when they acquired from them options to purchase shares.

8.6.4.2 US approach

In the US, some courts have rejected the type of approach used in *Percival* and have held that directors have a fiduciary obligation when dealing directly with shareholders to disclose all material facts relevant to a transaction in the company's shares. Other courts have sought to get round the problem by finding 'special circumstances'. In *Strong v Repide* 213

US 419 (1909), the leading case in the US Supreme Court held that a controlling shareholder and general manager of a company were guilty of fraud in purchasing the shares of a minority shareholder without disclosing the then current negotiations for the sale of the company's property. The special circumstances were that the defendant had been entrusted with the negotiations to sell the corporate assets.

8.6.4.3 New Zealand approach

In New Zealand, Mahon J was somewhat blunter in *Coleman v Myers* [1977] 2 NZLR 225. He said:

> I reach the unhesitating conclusion that the decision in *Percival v Wright* directly opposed as it is to prevailing notions of correct commercial practice, and being in my view wrongly decided, ought no longer to be followed in an important transaction where a director dealt with identified shareholders.

Although the Court of Appeal upheld the decision that a duty was owed to shareholders, that Court preferred to circumvent it rather than to disagree with *Percival*. Woodhouse J said:

> In my opinion it is not the law that anybody holding the office of director of a limited liability company is for that reason alone to be released from what otherwise would be regarded as a fiduciary responsibility owed to those in the position of shareholders of the same company ... As I have indicated it is my opinion that the standard of conduct required from a director in relation to dealings with a shareholder will differ depending upon all the surrounding circumstances and the nature of the responsibility which in a real and practical sense the director has assumed towards the shareholder. In the one case there may be a need to provide an explicit warning and a great deal of information concerning the proposed transaction. In another there may be no need to speak at all. There will be intermediate situations. It is, however, an area of the law where the courts can and should find some practical means of giving effect to sensible and fair principles of commercial morality in the cases that come before them; and while it may not be possible to lay down any general test as to when fiduciary duty will arise for a company director or to prescribe the exact conduct which will always discharge it when it does, there are nevertheless some factors that will usually have an influence upon a decision one way or the other. They include, I think, dependence upon information and advice, the existence of a relationship of confidence, the significance of some particular transaction for the parties and, of course, the extent of any positive action taken by or on behalf of the director or directors to promote it.

8.6.4.4 Fiduciaries

The fundamental rule for fiduciaries was expressed by Lord Herschell in *Bray v Ford* [1896] AC 44:

> It is an inflexible rule of a court of equity that a person in a fiduciary position ... is not unless otherwise expressly provided entitled to make a profit; he is not allowed to put himself in a position whereby his duty and interest conflict.

It follows from that proposition that a fiduciary cannot keep a profit which derives from personal use of his fiduciary position. His liability to account arises from the fact of the profit being made. There does not have to be a fraud, bad faith or even damage to the beneficiary. Accordingly, a director of a company who personally takes advantage of a corporate opportunity is obliged to account to the company for his gain.

Insider dealing often involves a betrayal of a fiduciary duty or a relationship of confidence. A director, standing as he does in a fiduciary relationship to his company, cannot use inside information obtained in that capacity in order to make profits for him. If he does so, he is liable to account to the company even though the company could never have made those profits itself.

The high watermark of fiduciary liability appears to have been reached in *Boardman v Phipps* [1967] 2 AC 46. Boardman was a solicitor to a trust. Among the trust assets was a minority holding in a company whose profitability was not very satisfactory. An offer to buy the trust shares was made through Boardman but was rejected by the only active trustee. However, the trustee wanted something done to improve the value of the trust's shareholding and with consent Boardman attempted to get a beneficiary appointed to the board. This attempt was successful and Boardman advised the trust that the only way to improve the company was for a controlling interest to be purchased. The trust refused to buy more shares for themselves. Initially, they failed to gain control so they therefore attempted to negotiate a distribution of assets between the majority shareholders and the trust. The negotiations were conducted by Boardman on behalf of the trust and in the course of the negotiations he obtained useful information. The negotiations failed and Boardman and the beneficiary armed with this information acquired for themselves a majority holding with the consent of the trustees. In this position they were able to liquidate valuable assets of this company which profited the trust as well as themselves. The House of Lords held them liable by a 3:2 majority to account to the trust for their profit. The reasoning is unclear. Two members of the majority treated the information as trust property. Two members of the majority reasoned that Boardman's interest could have conflicted with his duty as he might have been asked by the trustees to advise on a court application to seek approval for the purchase of the shares. There was in fact no such request for advice and the minority took the view that no conflict of interest and duty had been proven.

No English or Irish case has analysed the fiduciary rule in relation to insider dealing. However, the ground upon which a liability to account to a company for the insider's profits will be if his duty and interest conflict.

CHAPTER 9

THE IRISH STOCK EXCHANGE

John Darby

9.1 Introduction

The Irish Stock Exchange (the Exchange) provides markets for equities, Government and corporate bonds as well as for investment funds. Currently, there are over 1,650 securities listed on the Exchange with the most significant volumes of trading in the equities and government bond markets.

The Irish Stock Exchange Limited is a company limited by guarantee under the Companies Acts (CAs) 1963–2001. The Exchange has a board of 12 directors, comprised of an independent chairman, four co-opted directors representative of wider market interests and seven directors elected by member firms.

9.2 Function

The main functions of the Exchange are twofold:

1. the provision of an efficient and effective market for Irish and overseas securities which meets the highest international standards; and
2. facilitating companies or other investment vehicles in raising capital for their businesses and bringing them together with private and institutional investors.

The Exchange provides a market where listed securities can be traded efficiently and on competitive terms. This market has been in existence for over 200 years and is currently used by a broad range of Irish and overseas companies and investors.

The securities listed on the Exchange	
Domestic Irish equities	Ordinary shares issued by Irish companies.
Overseas equities	Ordinary shares issued by non-Irish companies.
Irish Government bonds	Securities issued by the Irish Government to meet its exchequer borrowing requirements. They entitle the owner to regular interest payments and the repayment of the underlying capital sum at a given date in the future.
Bonds or fixed interest stocks	Usually issued by companies or local authorities.
UCITS and Investment Funds	Collective investment schemes that are established to passively invest in a portfolio of investments on the basis of spreading risk. The investment funds are both Irish and non-Irish domiciled and may take a number of legal forms or investment structures.
Specialist securities	Securities which because of their nature, are normally bought or traded by a limited number of investors who are particularly knowledgeable in investment matters. Securities which are listed include asset-backed debt, eurobonds, medium term notes and warrants.

The Exchange has four markets:

(a) the main market (the Official List);
(b) the developing companies market (DCM);
(c) the exploration securities market (ESM); and
(d) ITEQ® market (the technology market of the Exchange).

The Exchange regulates the market in Irish Government bonds. The National Treasury Management Agency is the body responsible for issuing new government debt instruments and for managing the existing portfolio of such debt.

The settlement system used for Irish equities is 'Crest'. The Crest settlement system has been in operation since July 1996 and is managed by CrestCo, an independent company. Member firms are directly linked to Crest which operates a rolling settlement on the underlying principle of guaranteed 'delivery versus payment' (DVP). This means that settlement only happens when a security's delivery is matched with payment. Irish Government bonds are settled by Euroclear.

9.3   Equity markets

Since its establishment in 1793, the Exchange has provided the main national market for Irish equity securities and Irish Government bonds. The Exchange is the designated competent authority for the listing of securities in Ireland and derives its standing from the European Communities (Stock Exchange) Regulations 1984 (SI 1984/282).

Companies seeking a quotation for their securities on the Exchange may apply to the Official List, the DCM, the ESM or the ITEQ® market. The Official List is the main market for listed companies and Irish Government bonds. The DCM is for new and developing companies. The ESM is confined to exploration and mineral companies. The ITEQ® market is the technology market of the Exchange.

9.4   ITEQ® – the technology market of the Exchange

The Irish Stock Exchange launched 'ITEQ® – the technology market of the Exchange' in September 2000 after extensive research and analysis into the needs of Irish technology companies.

ITEQ® provides a sectoral and geographical focus for Irish and European investors in Irish technology, particularly through its own ITEQ® index.

ITEQ® admission rules are specifically designed to meet the needs of high growth technology companies and are compatible with the regulation imposed by other technology driven markets (particularly NASDAQ®).

9.5   Irish Government bond market

Irish Government bonds are listed on the Exchange and may be bought or sold through any member firm. Government bonds are usually issued with a set redemption period and are always issued at par.

Institutional dealing in government bonds is done through primary dealers. These are certain exchange member firms which act as wholesalers in government bonds, quoting prices at which they are willing to buy or sell.

9.6 Regulation of the Exchange background

Until 1973 the Exchange, together with the stock exchange in London and the provincial UK stock exchanges, constituted the Federation of Stock Exchanges of Great Britain and Ireland. In 1973 all of these stock exchanges amalgamated, but there remained a distinct physical, although not legal, entity in Dublin, which retained a separate trading floor and a separate quotation function. This Irish branch was commonly called the Irish Stock Exchange, although its more formal name was the 'Irish Unit of the Stock Exchange'. In the mid-1980s, the Stock Exchange became a company limited by guarantee with the name 'the International Stock Exchange of the United Kingdom and the Republic of Ireland Limited'.

Since the Stock Exchange Act 1995, the Irish Stock Exchange has become legally independent.

9.7 Summary of the Stock Exchange Act 1995

The Stock Exchange is governed by the provisions of the Stock Exchange Act 1995 (the Act). The Act came into operation (with certain minor exceptions) on 29 September 1995.

9.7.1 Prohibition of unlawful stock exchange

Under s 8 of the Act, no person shall establish a stock exchange in Ireland unless it is an 'approved stock exchange', namely a stock exchange which has been approved by the Central Bank of Ireland (CBI). No person may operate a stock exchange established in Ireland unless it is an approved stock exchange. Contravention of either of these provisions is a criminal offence.

It should be noted that a stock exchange would not be regarded as established in Ireland if it provides services electronically to Irish clients and has its head office or registered office outside Ireland.

9.7.2 Approval to operate as an approved Stock Exchange

Under s 9 of the Act, the CBI may grant or refuse to grant to an applicant or 'proposed stock exchange' an approval to operate as an approved stock exchange, and any such approval may be given conditionally. Applications must be in a form specified by the CBI.

A proposed stock exchange will not be approved unless:

(a) it is a company incorporated under the Companies Acts;
(b) its memorandum and articles of association and its rules are in satisfactory form;
(c) it has the minimum level of capital as specified by the CBI;
(d) the CBI is satisfied as to the probity and confidence of its directors and managers;
(e) the CBI is satisfied as to the suitability of each of its qualifying shareholders;
(f) its registered office and its head office are in Ireland; and
(g) its rules provide for a written report to be made of any enquiry into any disciplinary matter and that the stock exchange will send a copy of the report to the Minister for Finance and the Minister for Enterprise, Trade and Employment if so requested.

In addition, the memorandum or articles of association or the rules of the proposed stock exchange must provide that the board of directors is broadly based and is composed so as to secure a balance between the interests of its different member firms and users of its services and the public interest.

For this purpose the CBI must be satisfied that the board of the proposed stock exchange includes a number of persons, including the chairman, who are independent of the operation or management of the stock exchange and independent of its member firms and its rules or memorandum or articles of association must provide either or both of the following provisions, namely:

(i) that the board can consider disciplinary matters involving, and complaints against member firms; and

(ii) that where the rules provide that such disciplinary matters or complaints can be considered by some members only of the board, the rules provide that in such cases board members will include at least one independent member.

CBI approval will be required for subsequent appointments of directors, chief executives or managers of the stock exchange and also for amendments to its memorandum of association, articles of association or rules.

An approved stock exchange must maintain procedures to investigate complaints against itself or its member firms.

9.7.3 Imposition of conditions or requirements

Under s 11 of the Act, when granting an approval under s 9 or consenting to an amendment of the memorandum or articles or the rules of a stock exchange, the CBI may, in the interests of the proper and orderly regulation and supervision of the stock exchanges and their member firms, impose conditions or requirements, provided that these do not contravene any guidelines issued to the CBI by the Minister for Finance with the consent of the Minister for Enterprise, Trade and Employment. Such conditions or requirements may be imposed in respect of an individual stock exchange or a class of stock exchanges or all stock exchanges or in respect of a class of member firms or all member firms. A stock exchange or member firm may appeal to the court against the imposition of any such condition or requirement.

9.7.4 Refusal to consent to amendment of rules

Under s 12 of the Act, the CBI may refuse to consent to any amendment of the memorandum or articles of association, or to the rules of an approved stock exchange on the basis of the proper and orderly regulation of the stock exchange or its member firms or in order to protect investors.

9.7.5 Appeal procedure

Under s 13 of the Act, a proposed stock exchange or, as the case may be, an approved stock exchange may appeal to the Minister for Finance where the CBI has refused to grant approval under s 9 or has refused to consent to an amendment of its memorandum or articles or rules under s 12.

9.7.6 Revocation of approval

Under s 14 of the Act, the CBI may revoke the approval of an approved stock exchange on its request, or if it:

(i) has failed to operate as a stock exchange within 12 months of its approval;

(ii) has failed to operate as a stock exchange for more than six months; or

(iii) is wound up.

The CBI may also apply to the court for an order revoking the approval of an approved stock exchange in various circumstances.

An approved stock exchange whose approval has been revoked (a former approved stock exchange) must cease to operate as such.

9.7.7 Maintenance of books and records

Under s 15 of the Act, an approved stock exchange must keep at an office within Ireland such books and records (including books of accounts) as may be specified by the CBI from time to time.

9.7.8 Prohibition of unlawful member firm

Under s 17 of the Act, it is an offence for a person who is not a member firm to claim to be a member firm or to hold himself out as a member firm.

9.7.9 Grant of authorisation

Under s 18 of the Act, the CBI may grant or refuse to grant authorisations to persons to operate as authorised member firms and such authorisations may be given conditionally or subject to conditions or requirements.

An applicant for member firm authorisation, called in the Act 'proposed member firm', may appeal to the court against a decision by the CBI to refuse authorisation.

An application for authorisation must be in a form specified by the CBI. A copy of the memorandum and articles of association or partnership agreement of the proposed member firm must accompany it. The form must also state the type of business proposed to be carried on by it and give particulars of any persons who have control or ownership of the firm, including any person whose shareholding or other commercial relationship with the firm might enable him to materially influence the conduct of the firm.

In order to be authorised:

(a) the firm must be incorporated by statute or under the CAs 1963–2001, or be a company made under charter or, if it is an unincorporated body of persons, it must have a partnership agreement;

(b) its memorandum and articles of association or partnership agreement must be in satisfactory form;

(c) it must have the minimum level of capital specified by the CBI;

(d) it must satisfy the CBI costs:
- the probity and competence of its directors and managers;
- the suitability of its qualifying shareholders; and
- its organisation and management skills and the adequacy of the numbers and expertise of its staff;
- it must have established procedures to enable it to supply the public with any required by the CBI and to enable it to supply the public with any information specified by the CBI;
- the organisation of its business structure must be such as to permit it to be adequately supervised by the CBI;
- its registered office and its head office must be in Ireland; and
- the CBI must be satisfied as to its conduct of business, its financial resources, etc.

The CBI may set out conditions and requirements, which may be constituted in the rules of an approved stock exchange, in order to monitor the solvency of an authorised member firm which is an unincorporated body of persons, and the solvency of its proprietor.

The CBI is required to impose conditions or requirements from time to time in respect of the level of capital to be maintained by an authorised member firm.

Any appointment of a director, chief executive or manager of an authorised or proposed member firm is subject to the approval of the CBI.

The CBI may direct an authorised member firm to alter its memorandum or articles of association or its partnership agreement on the basis of the proper and orderly regulation of stock exchanges and member firms or the protection of investors. No alteration of such documents may be made without the consent of the CBI.

An authorisation must specify the classes of investment services which may be provided by the relevant authorised member firm, and the authorisation may also specify additional services.

The CBI may amend the classes of investment services or other services which may be provided by the member firm.

The CBI may impose conditions or requirements on member firms in the interests of the proper and orderly regulation of stock exchanges and their member firms or the protection of investors or clients.

The CBI may also impose requirements on a proposed or authorised member firm to organise its business or corporate structure so that it is capable of being satisfactorily supervised by the CBI.

9.7.10 Firms doing business outside of Ireland

Under s 20 of the Act, an authorised member firm wishing to establish a branch in another Member State must notify the CBI who is required to communicate this to the relevant authority in the other Member States. Likewise, where an authorised member firm wishes to provide investment services in another Member State without establishing a branch.

9.7.11 Existing member firms

Under s 21 of the Act, every member firm of the Exchange on the day before the Act came into operation will stand authorised as an authorised member firm until the CBI has granted or refused to grant it an authorisation. This is provided that within three months it has drawn up a formal partnership agreement (where it is unincorporated and does not already have such an agreement) and that it applies to the CBI under s 18 of the Act for an authorisation.

Pending its decision, the CBI can impose conditions or requirements on the member firm and can issue directions under the Act.

Existing member firms may appeal to the court against any such conditions or requirements.

9.7.12 Imposition of conditions or requirements

Where the CBI grants an authorisation under s 22 of the Act, it may make it subject to conditions or requirements on the basis of the proper and orderly regulation and supervision of an authorised member firm. At any time after authorisation, it may impose conditions or requirements or amend any conditions or requirements previously imposed. However, no such conditions or requirements may contravene any guidelines issued to the CBI by the Minister for Finance with the consent of the Minister for Enterprise, Trade and

Employment in the interests of the proper and orderly regulation and supervision of stock exchanges and their member firms and the protection of investors.

Any condition or requirement may be imposed on an authorised member firm, all such firms or a class of such firms.

An authorised member firm may appeal to the court against the imposition of any such condition or requirement.

9.7.13 Refusal to consent to amendment of memorandum and articles

Under s 23 of the Act, the CBI may refuse to consent to the amendment of the memorandum or articles of association or partnership agreement of an authorised member firm.

9.7.14 Revocation of authorisation

Under s 24 of the Act, the CBI may revoke the authorisation of an authorised member firm on its request, or if the firm:

(i) has failed to operate as a member firm within 12 months following its authorisation;
(ii) has failed to operate as a member firm for a period of more than six months; or
(iii) is being wound up.

The CBI may apply to the court for an order revoking an authorisation in various circumstances.

A member firm whose authorisation has been revoked (called a former authorised member firm) must cease to operate as a member firm.

9.7.15 Register member firms

Under s 25 of the Act, the CBI must require an approved stock exchange to keep a register of its member firms which must be open to inspection by the public.

9.7.16 Asset/liability ratios

Under s 26 of the Act, the CBI may require an authorised member firm to keep a proportion of its assets in liquid form so that it can meet its liabilities as they arise. The CBI may also require an authorised member firm to maintain a specified ratio, or a maximum or minimum ratio, between its assets and liabilities.

Any such requirement may be imposed on all authorised member firms or a specified category of them and it may be applied to all assets or liabilities or to specified assets or liabilities.

The CBI may also specify, for an authorised member firm, requirements as to the composition of its assets or of its liabilities.

9.7.17 Maintenance of books and records

Under s 27 of the Act, an authorised member firm must keep at its offices in Ireland such books and records (including books of account) as the CBI may specify, in addition to any statutory books required to be maintained by it.

9.7.18 General function of the CBI

Under s 28 of the Act (subject to such guidelines as may be issued by the Minister for Finance with the consent of the Minister for Enterprise, Trade and Employment), the CBI is required to administer the system of regulation and supervision of approved stock exchanges and their member firms in accordance with the provisions of the Act. This is done in order to promote the maintenance of the proper and orderly regulation and supervision of approved stock exchanges and their member firms and the orderly and proper regulation of financial markets and the protection of investors.

The CBI may commission an independent assessment of the capacity of a proposed or approved stock exchange, or of a proposed or authorised member firm, to engage in an activity.

The Minister may, after consulting the CBI, prescribe the fee to be paid to the CBI by an approved stock exchange or member firm supervised by it under the Act, and different fees may be prescribed for different classes of approved stock exchanges or member firms. The Minister for Finance may make regulations for incidental or related matters necessary to give effect to such fees. The Minister for Finance must also give advance notice of proposed fees to the stock exchanges or member firms affected and he must consider any representations made by them.

9.7.19 Direction by the CBI

Under s 29 of the Act, the CBI may, in the interests of the proper and orderly regulation of approved stock exchanges or their member firms or the protection of investors, give directions to any or all approved proposed former approved stock exchanges or authorised proposed former authorised member firms or to directors and managers of approved stock exchanges and authorised member firms in relation to any matter related to the operation of a stock exchange or any matter related to its member firms or any matter related to an 'acquiring transaction'.

The CBI is specifically empowered to direct an approved stock exchange or an authorised member firm to suspend, for a period not exceeding 12 months:

(i) the carrying on of its approved or authorised business;
(ii) the making of payments not related to that business, the acquisition or disposal of any assets or liabilities;
(iii) the entering into specified types of transactions;
(iv) the soliciting of business from persons of a specified category; and
(v) the carrying on of business in a specified manner,

except as authorised by the CBI.

While a direction under s 29 remains in force, no winding up or dissolution proceedings may be commenced. No winding-up resolution may be passed and no receiver may be appointed in relation to the relevant approved stock exchange or authorised member firm without the prior sanction of the court.

The CBI may apply to the court for an order confirming a direction where the CBI believes that the direction is not being complied with.

Schedule 1 to the Act contains supplementary provisions relating to directions under s 29 of the Act. The relevant stock exchange or member firm may apply to the court for an order varying or setting aside the direction.

If the CBI is of the opinion that the relevant stock exchange or member firm is able to meet its obligations but that the circumstances giving rise to the direction are unlikely to be rectified, it may apply to court for an order directing the stock exchange or member firm to prepare a scheme for the orderly termination of its business and the discharge of its liabilities under the supervision of the CBI and to submit that scheme to the court for approval. If the stock exchange or member firm fails to comply with such a court order, the

CBI may apply to the court for a further order for the winding up or, as the case may be, dissolution of the stock exchange or member firm.

When a direction is given by the CBI the relevant stock exchange or member firm must take all necessary steps to ensure that its assets or client/investor assets are not depleted without the CBI's authorisation. In addition, the CBI may direct any credit or other financial institution which holds an account of the stock exchange or member firm to suspend payments from the account without the CBI's authorisation.

9.7.20 Winding up on application by the CBI to quit

Under s 30 of the Act, the CBI may petition the court for an order to wind up or, in the case of a partnership, to dissolve an approved stock exchange or an authorised member firm, or a former such exchange or firm, on certain grounds. For example, where in the opinion of the CBI, it is unable to meet its obligations or where its approval or authorisation has been revoked and it has ceased to operate as a stock exchange or, as the case may be member firm.

9.7.21 Restrictions on advertising

Under s 31 of the Act, it is an offence for any person to advertise the services of a stock exchange:

(i) where the stock exchange, if established in Ireland, is not an approved stock exchange; or
(ii) where the stock exchange, if established in a country other than Ireland, is not a stock exchange permitted to carry on business in accordance with the procedures, if any, prescribed by that country for the approval of stock exchanges.

It is an offence for any person to advertise or supply investment services and to hold himself out as a member firm if such person is not a member firm.

The CBI may impose conditions or requirements on an approved stock exchange or member firm. It may also set out rules or approve of rules in the rules of an approved stock exchange in respect of advertising by an approved stock exchange or member firm.

The CBI may require an approved stock exchange or its member firms to publish specified information or to display specified information at their premises. The Minister for Finance may also prescribe information to be displayed by an approved stock exchange or its member firms at their premises.

The CBI may give any member firm a direction in relation to the matter or form of any advertisement or other means of soliciting client money or investment instruments or business or in relation to the matter or form of any advertisement relating to any service provided for business being undertaken by the member firm, or to withdraw an advertisement or to cease advertising. The CBI is specifically empowered by this section to give certain types of direction, such as a direction:

(a) prohibiting the issue by a member firm of all advertisements or advertisements of a specified description;
(b) requiring the member firm to modify specified advertisements in a specified manner; or
(c) requiring the member firm to include specified information in any advertisements.

If a person, being neither an approved stock exchange nor a member firm or acting in contravention of a direction under this section, issues an advertisement inviting persons to enter into an investment agreement or containing information calculated to lead to a person doing so:

(a) he will not be entitled to enforce any agreement to which the advertisement related and which was entered into after the issue of the advertisement; and

(b) the other party to such an agreement will be entitled to recover any money or other property or investment instruments paid or transferred under the agreement together with compensation for any loss sustained by him as a result of having paid money or transferred property or investment instruments under the agreement. (If the property or investment instruments in question have passed to a third party, an amount equal to their value at the time of transfer should be paid to the other party.)

Similar provisions apply where such a person issues an advertisement inviting persons to exercise any rights conferred by an investment or containing information calculated to lead to persons doing so.

The compensation payable will be such amount as the parties agree or as the court may determine.

However, the court may allow such an agreement or obligation to be enforced and any money, property or investment instruments paid or transferred under it to be retained if the court is satisfied:

(a) that the other party was not materially influenced by the advertisement in making his decision; or

(b) that the advertisement was not misleading as to the nature of the investment, the terms of the agreement or, as the case may be, the consequences of exercising the rights and that it fairly stated any risks involved.

Where a person elects not to perform an agreement or an obligation or recovers money or property or investment instruments paid or transferred by him under it, he must repay or return any money, property or investment instruments received by him under the agreement or as a result of his exercising the relevant rights.

The CBI is specifically empowered to make further directions, such as a direction to a person:

(a) to publish a correction of a misleading advertisement concerning the services of an approved stock exchange or member firms;

(b) to publish the correction of an advertisement which contravenes this section; and

(c) to publish the fact that an offence under this section has been committed and that a fine, if any, has been imposed.

Under s 32 of the Act, the CBI may from time to time exempt a class of advertisement from the provisions of s 31.

9.7.22 Auditors

Under s 33 of the Act, the CBI may direct that an approved stock exchange or an authorised member firm does not appoint or reappoint a specified person as auditor. Such a person may apply to the court to have the direction set aside.

Under s 34 of the Act, an authorised member firm which is unincorporated must appoint an auditor satisfying the requirements of the CAs 1963–2001 to report on its accounts annually. The CBI may set out requirements in respect of the accounts and audit of such a firm and impose duties on the auditor.

The auditor of an approved stock exchange or an authorised member firm must report to the CBI in various instances, for example:

(a) if the auditor has reason to believe that circumstances exist which are likely to affect materially the ability of the stock exchange or member firm to fulfil its obligations to investors or clients or to meet any of its financial obligations;
(b) if the auditor has reason to believe that there are material defects in the accounting records or systems of control of the business and records of the stock exchange or member firm; and
(c) if the auditor decides to resign or not to seek reappointment.

The CBI may require an auditor to furnish a report to the CBI stating that whether in the auditor's opinion the stock exchange or member firm has complied with any condition or requirement set out in or imposed under the Act. The report may be required on an annual basis, and the auditor must send a copy of the report to the stock exchange or member firm.

Such a report must state if the auditor is of the opinion that:

(a) proper accounting records have not been kept;
(b) a satisfactory system of control of its business or records has not been maintained; or
(c) the rules or requirements relating to client money and investment instruments referred to in s 52 have not been complied with.

The report will be prepared at the expense of the relevant approved stock exchange or member firm.

An auditor will also be obliged to communicate with the CBI if he is concerned about:

(a) a person's competence having regard to his functions within an approved stock exchange or authorised member firm;
(b) a person's probity in terms of suitability to carry on the business of an approved stock exchange or authorised member firm; or
(c) whether disciplinary action should be taken, or a direction given, by reason of a contravention of any provision of the Act or of any conditions or requirements or directions imposed by the CBI.

The CBI may require the auditor of an approved stock exchange or member firm to supply it with information in relation to the audit of that stock exchange or member firm.

9.7.23 Employment of disqualified person(s)

Under s 37 of the Act, if the CBI becomes concerned about the probity or competence of an officer or employee of an approved stock exchange or authorised member firm, it may apply to the court to issue a direction to the stock exchange or member firm to dismiss him or (alternatively in the case of an officer or employee whose probity is not in question) to suspend him temporarily or remove him from a particular area of employment.

9.7.24 Codes of conduct

Under s 38 of the Act, except in respect of an approved stock exchange which has drawn up and maintains such rules of conduct, the CBI is required to draw up and issue a code of conduct for approved stock exchanges or member firms or both. The code must contain provisions to ensure that a member firm acts honestly and fairly and with due skill, care and diligence in the best interests of its clients and the integrity of the market, has adequate resources and appropriate procedures, obtains sufficient information from clients, makes adequate disclosure of material information to clients, avoids conflicts of interest where reasonably possible and, where this is not possible, ensures that clients are fairly treated and complies with all applicable regulatory requirements.

The CBI may also impose conditions or requirements on a member firm in respect of compliance with such a code of conduct.

9.7.25 Notification of certain transactions

Under s 40 of the Act, a person proposing to make an acquiring transaction or a disposal must notify the CBI immediately.

An 'acquiring transaction' is any direct or indirect acquisition by a person or persons acting in concert of shares or other interest in an approved stock exchange or an authorised member firm, provided that after the acquisition:

(a) his or their proportion of the voting rights or capital of the stock exchange or member firm would exceed a qualifying holding;

(b) the proportion would reach or exceed 20%, 33% or 50%; or

(c) the stock exchange or member firm would become a subsidiary of the acquirer.

A 'disposal' is any direct or indirect disposal by a person or persons acting in concert of a qualifying holding or a disposal which would reduce the qualifying holding so that his or their proportion of the voting rights or the capital held by that person or persons would fall below 20%, 33% or 50% or so that the stock exchange or member firm in question would cease to be a subsidiary of that person.

An approved stock exchange or authorised member firm must inform the CBI on it becoming aware of a proposed acquiring transaction or disposal which would cause a holding to exceed or fall below a qualifying holding or 20%, 33% or 50% of the voting rights or capital of the relevant stock exchange or member firm or would cause the stock exchange or member firm to become or cease to be a subsidiary.

On receiving a notification, the CBI may within one month request further information. The CBI may approve, with or without conditions or requirements, or refuse to approve an acquiring transaction.

Under s 41 of the Act, an acquiring transaction cannot proceed until the CBI informs the stock exchange or member firm in question and the proposed acquirer that it approves the transaction or three months have elapsed during which the CBI has not refused to approve the transaction, whichever first occurs. The three month period begins on the date of notification to the CBI or, if the CBI has requested further information, the date of receipt of that information.

Under s 44 of the Act, unless the CBI has specified a different period for implementation of an acquiring transaction under s 42, an acquiring transaction will be valid only if entered into within 12 months of the date of its approval or default approval by the CBI. If otherwise purported to be implemented, the transaction will be invalid, no title to shares or other interest will pass and any purported exercise of powers relating to the shares or interest will be invalid.

Under s 45 of the Act, the CBI is required to refuse its approval of an acquiring transaction where it is not satisfied as to the suitability of the acquirer or where it considers that the transaction is likely to be prejudicial to the sound and prudent management of the stock exchange or member firm or its proper regulation.

Under s 46 of the Act, an appeal may be made to the court against the CBI's refusal to approve an acquiring transaction or against any condition or requirement to which its approval was made subject.

Under s 48 of the Act, at least once a year, every approved stock exchange and authorised member firm must inform the CBI:

(i) of the names of its direct shareholders and members possessing qualifying holdings and the sizes of such holdings; and

(ii) (after making best efforts) of the identity of all indirect shareholders and members possessing qualifying shareholdings.

9.7.26 Investor compensation

Under s 51 of the Act, a member firm must not engage in business with clients and investors unless, and in accordance with any procedures set out in the rules of an approved stock exchange, it informs them of:

(i) whether or not there is a compensation fund; and

(ii) the nature and level of protection available from any such fund.

9.7.27 Client's money and investment instruments

Under s 52 of the Act, the CBI may impose requirements, or may approve of rules in the rules of an approved stock exchange, or both, with respect to clients' money and clients' investment instruments ('client money requirements'). Section 52 specifically describes certain types of client money requirements which the CBI may make, for example, requirement as to the types of accounts to be kept by a member firm, its rights, duties and responsibilities in relation to money and investment instruments received, held, controlled or paid by it, the circumstances in which money other than client money may be paid into accounts containing client money or in which money held in such accounts may be paid out, the use of nominee companies by member firms, etc.

All accounts containing clients' money must be designated 's 52 accounts' in all financial records of a member firm. The accounts must be kept with institutions specified by the CBI and the member firm must keep at its offices in Ireland such books and records in respect of client money and client investment instruments as the CBI may specify. An auditor must examine such books and records at intervals specified by the CBI and report to the CBI on whether in his opinion the client money requirements have been complied with.

No liquidator, receiver, creditor, etc of a member firm has any right against a client's money or a client's investment instruments held on behalf of a client until all claims of the client in respect of the money or investment instruments have been satisfied in full.

9.7.28 Powers of authorised officers

Authorised officers of the CBI are given powers under s 56 to enter premises believed to contain books and records of stock exchanges and member firms. They are given the power to inspect and take copies, and to require any person on the premises to produce books and records within his control or to prepare a report on a specified aspect of the business.

Section 56 imposes a general obligation on an approved stock exchange or member firm to furnish the CBI with such information and returns as it may specify.

9.7.29 Appointment of inspector by court

The CBI may apply to the court under s 57 to appoint an inspector to investigate the affairs of an approved stock exchange or an authorised member firm.

9.7.30 Inspectors' reports and proceedings

Under s 62 of the Act, an inspector appointed under s 57 is required to submit an interim report, if required by the court, and to undertake a final report on the conclusion of his investigation. The court must forward any such report to the Minister for Finance, the Minister for Enterprise, Trade and Employment, and the CBI. If the court thinks fit, a copy of the report must also be forwarded to the relevant stock exchange or member firm or to any other person specified by the court.

Under s 63 of the Act, following consideration of a report by an inspector appointed under s 57, the court may make such order as it thinks fit. This includes an order for the winding up of the relevant stock exchange or member firm or, in the case of an unincorporated member firm, for its dissolution.

9.7.31 Appointment of an inspector by the CBI

Under s 64 of the Act, the CBI may appoint an inspector to investigate and report on the affairs of an approved stock exchange or authorised member firm or its compliance with conditions or requirements imposed by the CBI under the Act, any rules or codes of conduct set out in or approved by the CBI under the Act, any rules of an approved stock exchange, any requirement of the Act or any client money requirements, etc.

On the basis of an inspector's report, the CBI may under s 65:

(i) apply to court in a summary manner for a determination that the relevant stock exchange or member firm has committed a breach of a condition or requirement imposed by the CBI under certain specified sections of the Act; or

(ii) send a notification to the stock exchange or member firm stating that the CBI will apply to court for such a determination unless the stock exchange or member firm requests within seven days that a committee be appointed, in which case the CBI may appoint a committee from a panel established by the Minister for Finance with the consent of the Minister for Enterprise, Trade and Employment.

Following an enquiry, the committee may dismiss the application or make a determination that there has been a breach of a relevant condition or requirement. In which case it may:

(i) issue a reprimand; and/or

(ii) direct the stock exchange or member firm to pay the CBI a sum in respect of any breach; and/or

(iii) publish details concerning its determination in *Iris Oifigiúil* and in one or more newspapers circulating in Ireland; and/or

(iv) make an order as to costs.

The stock exchange or member firm may appeal to the court against the determination of a committee.

The court, on hearing evidence in any proceedings under this section, may:

(i) issue a reprimand; and/or

(ii) direct the stock exchange or member firm to pay to the CBI a sum in respect of any breach; and/or

(iii) dismiss the application or make any other appropriate order; and/or

(iv) make an order as to costs.

Schedule 2 to the Act contains supplementary provisions relating to a committee appointed under s 65. The panel to be maintained by the Minister for Finance must consist of at least seven persons, at least two of whom must be barristers or solicitors. A committee must consist of not less than three persons, at least one of whom must be a barrister or solicitor.

CHAPTER 10

MUTUAL FUNDS

Joseph Gavin and Tracy Gilvarry

10.1 The main categories of Irish mutual funds

10.1.1 The main categories

The two main categories of Irish mutual funds, which are marketed to the public, are as follows:

1. mutual funds established under the Irish Regulations, which implements the EU UCITS Directive (EC Council Directive 85/611/EEC, as amended by EC Council Directive 88/220/EEC, implemented in Ireland by the Undertakings for Collective Investments in Transferable Securities (UCITS) Regulations 1989 (SI 1989/78)) (UCITS funds); and

2. mutual funds established under Irish law which do not benefit from the European cross-border marketing concessions provided for in the UCITS Directive (non-UCITS funds). (References in this chapter to UCITS and non-UCITS notices apply to the Central Bank UCITS and non-UCITS notices dated March 2002.)

Irish law imposes detailed investment and borrowing restrictions on retail funds. In contrast, a more liberal regulatory regime applies to institutional funds. An Irish mutual fund may be established under the following two categories of Central Bank regulations.

10.1.1.1 UCITS funds

A UCITS fund may only invest in transferable securities and is subject to investment and borrowing restrictions (see Pt VII and Reg 69 of the UCITS Regulations and UCITS notices 9.1 and 10.1). It may be established in one of the following legal forms:

(a) an open-ended investment company registered as a public company; and
(b) an open-ended unit trust.

10.1.1.2 Non-UCITS

In addition to UCITS funds, which may invest primarily in transferable securities, retail funds which invest in a wider variety of assets may also be established, subject to investment and borrowing restrictions (see non-UCITS notices 3.2, 13.6, 14.5, 15.3, 16.3, 17.3 and 18.2).

Non-UCITS mutual funds may be established as open or closed-ended funds in one of three legal forms:

(a) a unit trust;
(b) an investment company registered as a public company; or
(c) an investment limited partnership.

10.1.1.3 Retail and institutional funds

Retail funds may be created as UCITS funds or as non-UCITS funds. Institutional funds can be created as non-UCITS funds only.

10.2 Key features of unit trusts and investment companies

The unit trust and the investment company structures are the two most common forms of mutual fund established in Ireland, the principal features of which are set out below.

10.2.1 Unit trusts

10.2.1.1 Trust deed

The unit trust operates as an investment fund established under a trust deed between the management company and the trustee. The trust deed regulates the relationship between the fund manager, the trustee and investors in the fund. The trust deed defines the investment policy for the fund, sets out procedures for such matters as the issue and redemption of investors units in the fund, the meeting of investors in the fund, and the termination of the fund.

10.2.1.2 The manager

The management company may be incorporated as an Irish private limited company having a minimum paid-up share capital of €125,000 (UCITS notices 2.2, para 9) or the equivalent in another currency and a minimum of two directors who are Irish residents (UCITS notices 2.2, para 13).

10.2.1.3 The trustee

The trustee is the legal owner of the assets of the fund, which it holds for the benefit of the unit holders. The trustee also has a supervisory role to make sure that the fund's activities are carried out in accordance with Irish law and the provisions of the trust deed.

10.2.1.4 The investment advisor

The investment management function is typically outsourced by the manager to a third party asset manager, in its capacity as investment advisor to the manager. The investment advisor must be approved in advance by the Central Bank of Ireland (CBI).

The investment advisor is not required to have a presence in Ireland.

(a) **Investment companies**

The investment company is incorporated as a public limited company. The affairs of the company are subject to the direction of the board of directors. At least two of the directors must be Irish residents (UCITS notices 2.2, para 25). The articles of association of the company regulate such matters as the issue and redemption of shares in the company, the convening of shareholder meetings and the order of priority of distributions on the winding up of the company.

(b) **The administrator**

A third party administration company administers the activities of the company. The administrator's responsibilities include the pricing of shares in the company and arranging for issues, redemptions and transfers between shareholders.

(c) The custodian

The assets of the company must be deposited for safekeeping with a custodian company independent from the administrator. The custodian is responsible for overseeing compliance by the company with CBI conditions and the provisions of the company's articles of association.

(d) The investment manager

Typically, the company delegates the investment management function to a third party asset manager under the terms of an investment management agreement. The investment manager requires advance approval by the CBI.

The investment manager is not required to have a presence in Ireland.

(e) The board of directors

An investment company operates subject to the direction of a board of directors. Appointments to the board may only be made with the consent of the CBI by reference to personal characteristics of integrity and professional competence.

10.3 Retail funds established as UCITS funds

The European Community proposed the UCITS Directive in 1985 as one of many measures intended to liberalise the internal market for investment services among European Member States. The UCITS Directive was implemented in Ireland in 1989 by Ministerial Order, known as the UCITS Regulations 1989.

A UCITS is defined as an 'undertaking for collective investment in transferable securities'. It is an open-ended mutual fund investing in transferable securities, in compliance with specified retail investment restrictions, which may be marketed throughout the EU. A UCITS fund has attractive features, but important restrictions, as explained below.

10.3.1 Advantages of UCITS

The principal advantage of UCITS status is the ability of a UCITS fund to market its units or shares in all other EU Member States, without having to comply with the securities laws of each Member State.

In order to avail of this marketing advantage, certain conditions must be complied with:

(a) the fund must be approved by the CBI (although such approval is subsequently valid in all other Member States);

(b) information relating to the fund must be submitted to the CBI and the applicable supervisory authorities in each Member State in which units or shares are to be offered for sale;

(c) the various advertising documents which contain the information necessary to enable the public to make an informed assessment of the units or shares being offered must be submitted to all the relevant authorities;

(d) the fund must comply with the same advertising and marketing regulations imposed on local UCITS by the Member States in which the units or shares are marketed;

(e) marketing documents to be made available to the public in a given State must be printed in at least one of the languages recognised in that State; and

(f) paying agency arrangements must be established in each country in which units or shares are offered for sale.

10.3.2 UCITS as a retail fund structure only

Because of its nature as a retail fund structure, Irish law imposes extensive restrictions on the investment and borrowing policies of authorised UCITS funds. These investment and borrowing restrictions are described in detail in the UCITS Regulations 1989 (Pt VII and Reg 69).

A UCITS may be established under the UCITS Regulations 1989 in the form of an open-ended unit trust or as an open-ended investment company registered as a public limited company.

A UCITS must simultaneously satisfy the following requirements:

(a) the capital of a UCITS must be funded by means of an open offer to the public;

(b) the unit or shares of an investor must be redeemed on demand; and

(c) investments can only be made in transferable securities and in accordance with the detailed investment and borrowing restrictions set out in the UCITS Regulations.

10.3.3 Authorisation of UCITS

A UCITS fund is to be authorised by the CBI before it can be marketed to the public.

10.3.4 Professional duties of related parties

A UCITS fund, whether in the form of an investment company or a unit trust, is, in essence, a passive entity.

The operational aspects of a UCITS fund are outsourced to the various professionals comprising of the manager, the investment advisor or manager, the administrator and the trustee or custodian.

Irish law imposes minimum standards of professional care on these professionals which must be observed in carrying out their duties. Liability is also imposed on any relevant party for any losses suffered by investors due to a lack of professional care by that person.

10.3.5 Money laundering

A UCITS fund is subject to the provisions of Irish anti-money laundering regulations (Irish anti-money laundering regulations are implemented in the Criminal Justice Act 1994), which implement the EU Directive to counteract money laundering (EU Council Directive 91/308/EEC on the prevention of the use of the financial system for the purpose of money laundering). These regulations also apply to the related parties involved with a UCITS fund.

A UCITS fund and related parties are required to ensure that appropriate measures are put in place to ensure compliance with these Regulations.

10.3.6 Key features of UCITS funds

10.3.6.1 UCITS passport

A UCITS fund benefits from the European UCITS passport (ie, the UCITS fund may market its units or shares in all other EU Member States, without having to comply with the securities laws of each Member State) and, therefore, the distribution of UCITS funds to investors in the European Union is not subject to the Public Offer of Securities Regulations in each Member State in which the fund is distributed.

10.3.6.2 Transferable securities

A UCITS fund is restricted to investing in quoted debt and equity securities in compliance with the UCITS investment and borrowing restrictions (see Pt VII and Reg 69 of the UCITS Regulations 1989, and UCITS notices 9.1 and 10.1).

10.3.6.3 Efficient portfolio management

A UCITS fund may buy and sell derivative instruments for the purposes of efficient portfolio management and managing currency risk, subject to the conditions set out in the UCITS Regulations 1989 (see Pt VII and UCITS notices 11.1).

10.3.6.4 Umbrella fund

A UCITS fund may be created as an umbrella fund with several sub-funds having individual investment and borrowing policies.

10.3.6.5 Weekly dealings

A UCITS fund is required to have a sufficient degree of liquidity to permit dealings (subscriptions and redemptions) by investors in the fund at not less than weekly intervals.

10.3.6.6 Liquid assets

A UCITS fund is permitted to hold cash as an ancillary liquid asset to the investment policy of the fund, although investment in cash is not permitted as the investment policy for a UCITS fund.

10.3.6.7 Net asset value

The shares of investors in a UCITS fund must at all times equal the net assets of the fund and a UCITS fund may only incur limited borrowings (up to 10% of its net assets for temporary purposes including settlement).

10.3.6.8 Pooling techniques

A UCITS fund may not be constituted as a fund of funds or as a feeder fund into a masterfeeder structure, although certain pooling techniques, such as cloning, are permissible.

10.3.6.9 Multiple classes

A UCITS fund or a sub-fund of a UCITS umbrella fund may be established as a multiclass fund comprising of classes of shares with individual features applicable to the specific class, including currency specific classes and accumulating or distributing classes.

10.3.6.10 Securities lending

A UCITS fund is permitted to enhance yields by engaging in securities lending activities with prime brokers subject to conditions set out in the UCITS notices (UCITS notices 11.1).

10.3.6.11 Fund mergers

A UCITS fund is prohibited from converting into any other legal form. This prohibition is intended to protect the interests of retail investors in the fund.

10.4 Non-UCITS retail and institutional funds

10.4.1 Types of non-UCITS funds

Non-UCITS retail and institutional funds may be established using one of three legal forms:

(a) a unit trust authorised under the Companies Act (CA) 1990;
(b) an investment company established under the CA 1990; or
(c) an investment limited partnership authorised under the Investment Limited Partnership Act 1994.

Each of these legal forms may be used to create an open-ended fund (permitting redemption of shares or units out of fund assets), or a closed-ended fund (prohibiting redemption out of fund assets during the closed period).

10.4.1.1 Non-UCITS unit trust

A unit trust operates as an investment fund established under a trust deed between a management company and a trustee company. The trustee, on behalf of the investors, holds legal ownership of the fund's assets, who each have an undivided beneficial interest in the fund.

10.4.1.2 Non-UCITS investment company

A non-UCITS investment company is established as a public limited company. The company is operated subject to the direction of a board of directors, two of whom must be Irish residents.

10.4.1.3 Non-UCITS investment limited partnership

This form (which has only been used to date in a couple of isolated cases) has an advantage over unit trusts and investment companies in so far as a partnership may be regarded as a transparent entity for tax purposes.

10.4.1.4 Investment policies of a non-UCITS fund

The rationale for this category of Irish mutual funds is to provide fund promoters with fund structures that are capable of investing in a comprehensive range of investments.

The CBI imposes detailed investment and borrowing restrictions on non-UCITS funds which are targeted at retail investors. A more liberal regime applies to the investment and borrowing policies of an institutional fund.

10.4.1.5 Non-UCITS retail funds

(a)   **Retail funds**

The investment policy of retail funds are required to comply with detailed investment and borrowing restrictions, which are set out in the non-UCITS notices issued by the CBI (non-UCITS notices 3.2, 13.6, 14.5, 15.3, 16.3, 17.3 and 18.2).

A retail fund may be structured to invest in the following investments:

- quoted equity or debt securities;
- exchange traded futures and options on a capital protected basis;
- exchange traded futures and options on a leveraged basis;
- real estate;
- unquoted securities;
- cash and money market instruments;
- shares in investment funds in a fund of funds structure; and
- shares in a master fund in a master-feeder structure.

(b) Institutional funds

Institutional funds fall into two categories: qualified or professional investor.

(c) Qualifying investor fund

A qualifying investor fund is not bound by the investment and borrowing restrictions on retail funds as described above.

A qualifying investor fund is, however, subject to the following conditions (see non-UCITS notices 24.3):

- minimum subscription per investor €250,000;
- institutional investor owns or manages on a discretionary basis at least €25,000,000; and
- individual investor has a minimum net worth of €1.25 million (excluding principal residence).

(d) Professional investor fund

A professional investor fund may negotiate derogations from the investment and borrowing restrictions for retail funds described above; the rule of thumb typically operated by the CBI is to double the permissible limits for retail funds.

A professional fund is subject to a minimum subscription per investor of €125,000 (see non-UCITS notices 12.4).

10.4.2 Key features of non-UCITS funds

10.4.2.1 Open- and closed-ended funds

A retail or institutional fund may be created as open-ended (permitting periodic redemptions by investors) or a closed-ended fund (prohibiting periodic redemptions by investors).

10.4.2.2 Net asset value

The shares of investors in a retail fund must at all times equal the net assets of the fund.

10.4.2.3 Umbrella fund

A retail or institutional fund may be created as an umbrella fund with several sub-funds having individual investment and borrowing policies, provided that adequate measures are taken to segregate liabilities between individual sub-funds.

10.4.2.4 Pooling techniques

A retail or institutional fund may avail of a wide variety of legal and management pooling techniques including master-feeder structures, cloning, and global hub and spoke.

10.4.2.5 Efficient portfolio management

A retail fund is permitted to use derivatives for the purposes of efficient portfolio management and currency risk hedging, subject to the conditions set out in the non-UCITS notices issued by the CBI (non-UCITS notices 16.3).

10.4.2.6 Weekly dealings

A retail fund is required to have a sufficient degree of liquidity to permit dealings (subscriptions and redemptions) at not less than weekly intervals.

10.4.2.7 Share classes

A retail or institutional fund may be established as a single fund or as a sub-fund of an umbrella fund comprising of multiple classes of shares with individual features applicable to the specific class, including currency specific classes, fee specific classes and accumulating and distributing classes.

10.4.2.8 Securities lending

A retail or institutional fund is permitted to enhance yields by engaging in securities lending activities with prime brokers subject to the conditions set out in the non-UCITS notices (non-UCITS notices 16.3).

10.4.2.9 Fund mergers

A retail or institutional fund may be merged into another fund subject to the consent of investors in the merging fund.

10.4.2.10 Hedge funds

A hedge fund may only be structured as a professional investor fund or as a qualifying investor fund, subject to the conditions specified in the non-UCITS notices.

10.4.2.11 Risk spreading

An institutional fund established as a qualifying investor fund (in the form of a unit trust only but not in the form of an investment company) is not required to observe the principle of risk spreading.

10.4.2.12 Fractions of shares

Shares or units in a retail fund or institutional fund may be issued as fractions unless the shares or units are issued in bearer form.

10.5 Authorisation procedure for mutual funds

10.5.1 The CBI

The CBI is the responsible authority in Ireland for approving mutual funds which are offered to the public.

Applications for authorisation are handled by the International Financial Services Centre (IFSC) and Funds Supervision Department of the CBI.

10.5.2 Promoter approval

A promoter seeking to establish an Irish domiciled fund is required to obtain approval in its own right as a promoter of funds. The promoter must submit a promoter application addressing issues relating to the competence, integrity and adequacy of the promoter's financial resources.

A decision on the suitability of a fund promoter is made by the CBI based on the promoter's responses to the issues set out in the promoter approval questionnaire issued by the CBI.

10.5.3 Fund structure approval

In order to avoid the emergence of fundamental problems at a late stage in the approval process, the CBI has introduced an early warning system by requiring fund promoters to submit a detailed fact sheet outlining key aspects of the proposed fund structure in a fund fact sheet at the initial stage of the approval process.

The detailed fact sheet is to be submitted and approved by the CBI in advance of submission of fund documentation.

10.5.4   Approval process

Once the CBI has indicated its approval of the proposed fund structure, the promoter is next required to submit a complete file of documents and agreements (in draft form) to the CBI. The bank's policy is to issue comments on the documents no later than four weeks from the date of submission.

The process is conducted on a phased basis. Initial drafts are reviewed by CBI staff who reviews the documentation to ensure full compliance with applicable regulations and full consistency across all fund documents at a high level of detail.

The length of the process and the extent of CBI comments may depend on the quality of preparation of the initial drafts submitted to the CBI. Undoubtedly, the process is expedited in circumstances where the promoter is in a position to prepare documents on the basis of recently approved precedents.

10.5.5   Fund documentation

The fund documents fall into three categories: the prospectus, the organisational documents, and the agreements.

10.5.6   The prospectus

An offer to the public to invest in an Irish mutual fund can only be made on the basis of information concerning the fund contained in a written prospectus that must be approved by the CBI.

The prospectus is the document that pulls together information on the operation of the fund to enable investors to make an informed judgement of the investment opportunity presented to them by the promoter of the fund.

The prospectus must be offered to investors free of charge together with a copy of the organisational documents of the fund before an investment in the fund may be accepted.

The CBI must approve the prospectus and any amendments to it. Material changes to the information contained in the prospectus must be notified to investors in the periodic reports of the fund.

10.5.7   The organisational documents

The memorandum and articles of association (in the case of an investment company) and the trust deed (in the case of a unit trust) set out the rules governing the operation of the fund and the relationship between the fund and its investors.

Material changes to the organisational documents of a fund, which could have an adverse effect on the interests of investors in the fund, can only be made with the prior approval of the CBI and the prior consent of the investors in the fund. Any such changes may only be brought into effect after a specified time period, typically 15 days after authorisation, to allow investors sufficient time to redeem their holdings in the fund before the changes are implemented.

10.5.8 Other agreements

The duties of each of the parties involved in the operation of the fund are set out in various agreements:

(a) the investment management agreement;
(b) the investment advisory agreement;
(c) the global custody agreement;
(d) the administration agreement; and
(e) the distribution agreement.

The terms of these agreements set out in detail the duties, responsibilities and liabilities of the parties, the terms of remuneration and the notice provisions on termination.

10.6 Continuing requirements for mutual funds

Once a fund has been established, the relevant parties commence their respective functions to activate the fund. The distributor introduces investors into the fund. The manager or administrator administers the fund. The investment manager or adviser trades the assets of the fund in line with the fund's investment objectives and policies. The trustee or custodian settles trades for the fund and holds title to the fund's assets.

The focus of Irish law on mutual funds is to put in place measures to safeguard the interests of investors in the fund. This objective is achieved through a process of supervision at various levels, the dissemination of periodic information to investors and, ultimately, the exercise of control by investors over the direction of a fund through resolutions passed by investors in general assembly.

10.6.1 Supervision

Supervision of the activities of Irish mutual funds occurs at three levels:

(a) the fund operates subject to the direction of the board of directors of the fund (the board of directors of the company in the case of an investment company and the board of directors of the management company in the case of a unit trust);
(b) the operations of the fund are supervised by the trustee or custodian; and
(c) the CBI independently supervises the operation of the fund on the basis of reports supplied to it by the fund manager or administrator and the trustee or custodian.

10.6.2 The board of directors

The board of directors meets periodically (but not less than four times a year) to review the activities of the fund. Individuals may only be appointed to the board with the prior approval of the CBI based on criteria including personal integrity and professional competence.

10.6.3 The trustee or custodian

The trustee or custodian is required during each annual period to inspect the activities of the fund and to report to investors on the results of its annual inspection. If the trustee or custodian uncovers matters of concern (including a breach of the investment and borrowing restrictions), it is required to take remedial action and to report to investors on the action taken by it.

The individual members of the board of directors and the trustee or custodian may be held directly liable to investors for losses suffered by investors arising from their failure to carry out their respective duties with respect to matters within their control.

10.6.4 The CBI

The CBI seeks to ensure compliance by funds with the requirements of Irish law through a combination of meetings, inspections, reports and independent action.

The fund is required to submit detailed monthly reports to the CBI. Each of the parties which has a presence in Ireland is subject to periodic inspections by the CBI and key management personnel are required to attend half yearly meetings with the CBI.

The CBI relies on the home regulator to supervise the activities of a foreign investment manager or adviser of an Irish fund in its jurisdiction of incorporation. The CBI will only approve a foreign investment manager or adviser if it is satisfied with the regulatory regime imposed by the home regulator.

The CBI has the power to take action on its own initiative if it becomes concerned that the operations of a fund are not being conducted in accordance with Irish law and the interests of investors. Such independent acts may include a suspension of dealings by investors in the fund, removal of any of the manager or administrator, the investment manager or adviser, or the trustee or custodian, and, in some cases, liquidation of the fund.

10.6.5 Information to investors

An Irish mutual fund is required to publish certain periodic information to enable investors to make an informed decision to hold or sell their investment in the fund, including the publication of:

(a) issue and redemption prices of shares in the fund in a local newspaper; and

(b) annual reports and semi-annual reports of the fund detailing the fund's activities during the relevant period.

10.6.6 Control by investors

Certain changes in the operation of a fund can only be made with prior approval of the investors at a duly convened meeting of the investors in the fund (or of the investors in the applicable sub-fund in the case of an umbrella fund).

Changes to the risk profile of a fund requires approval of at least 50% of the investors in the relevant fund or sub-fund. However, certain other changes, such as increases in expenses payable out of a fund, can only proceed with the approval of at least 75% of the investors in the fund.

10.7 Taxation of mutual funds in Ireland

Taxation of a fund established in Ireland is primarily a matter of Irish law, although certain countries impose tax on their residents in certain circumstances on passive foreign investments made by them.

10.7.1 Taxation of public funds

Under Irish law, IFSC funds are transparent. UCITS and non-UCITS retail and professional investor funds established in the IFSC are exempt from all sources of Irish tax. No tax is levied on the fund but the non-resident unit holders may be liable to tax under the terms of the legislation in their own jurisdiction. Non-resident investors in collective funds in Ireland enjoy the following benefits:

(a) they are exempt from taxation on income and gains arising from their qualifying investment activities;

(b) no withholding tax applies to any distributions of income or gains or on any undistributed income;

(c) the issue of shares in a fund is exempt from capital duty; and

(d) non-resident investors are not subject to income tax, capital gains tax or capital acquisitions tax in Ireland on an investment in any of these funds.

A single institutional investor fund which satisfies certain eligibility criteria set out in s 36 of the Finance Act (FA) 1995 may also qualify for exemption from Irish taxes.

Since the introduction of the Finance Act (FA) 2000 the Irish tax regime applicable to non-residents is conditional upon valid declarations by investors (as to residency) at the time of subscription in the fund.

10.7.2 Taxation of private investor funds

A private investor fund established as an investment company under Pt XIII of the CA 1990 and operated from the IFSC is taxable at 10% per annum on income and gains from its qualifying activities. As a taxable entity, this type of fund qualifies for relief from double taxation under Ireland's tax treaty network.

10.7.3 Taxation of the fund's assets

Ireland has an extensive network of double tax treaties (that is, treaties for the avoidance of double taxation) which relieves the rate of withholding tax imposed by its treaty partners on receipts by Irish residents on assets located in those other countries.

The applicability of tax treaty benefits to funds located in the IFSC is determined by the treaty partner country in which the fund's assets are located and, typically, reduced withholding tax rates will not apply under the applicable treaty if the fund is exempt from tax under Irish law. Thus, public funds do not generally qualify for treaty relief under Ireland's tax treaty network.

10.7.4 Taxation of the investor

Tax treatment of income and gains received by a non-Irish resident investor in an Irish fund operated in the IFSC is typically a matter of the tax laws of the country of residence of the investor. It is important to note that tax deferral benefits arising from an investment in a fund located in the IFSC may be adversely affected by domestic tax laws that impute a tax on passive foreign investments.

The FA 2000 has essentially provided a new single tax regime for both domestic and IFSC collective funds. Prior to the enactment of this Act, collective funds established by IFSC-certified companies, and the non-resident unit holders in such funds, have not been subject to Irish tax on income or gains arising on the funds. The Act does not alter this policy, although it will be necessary for existing IFSC funds to submit a declaration to the Collector General regarding the residency of the unit holders. With respect to funds established after 31 March 2000, unit holders must submit a declaration of residency status to the investment undertaking. If a unit holder is neither resident nor ordinarily resident in the State no tax will be levied in Ireland.

10.7.5 Domestic funds

The FA 2000, however, has changed the tax treatment of any new domestic funds established after 1 April 2000. Prior to the FA 2000, existing domestic funds were taxed annually on a measure of income and gains. Unit holders were not liable for any further tax. The old regime will continue to apply for existing domestic funds.

In contrast, under the new regime, an Irish tax will be levied on the occasion of a 'chargeable event' if a unit holder in a domestic fund established after 1 April 2000 is resident or ordinarily resident in Ireland. In effect, the new regime provides for the continuance of the tax exemption for non-Irish resident unit holders in Irish funds while ensuring that investment income and gains accruing to Irish unit holders are subject to tax in Ireland.

10.7.6 Declaration of residency

An intermediary may make the declaration of residency, which must be made by non-Irish resident unit holders in order to be exempt from any Irish tax upon any distribution of income or gains by the fund, on their behalf.

In summary, the new taxation regime for funds in Ireland does not change the tax treatment of non-Irish resident investors in such funds. Non-resident holders will continue to be exempt from Irish taxation provided they make the appropriate declarations confirming their status as non-Irish residents. The tax treatment of income and gains received by a non-Irish resident investor will depend upon the terms of the tax legislation in their respective jurisdictions.

10.8 Listing of mutual funds on the Irish Stock Exchange

10.8.1 Introduction

The Irish Stock Exchange is a major listing centre for offshore mutual funds. The reasons for the success of the Irish Stock Exchange include the low cost involved in and the relative efficiency of the listing process.

10.8.2 Application procedures

An application for listing of a mutual fund will be processed by a sponsoring member firm of the Irish Stock Exchange. Generally, funds can be listed in approximately 4–5 weeks of the listing document being submitted to the Irish Stock Exchange for the first time.

10.8.3 Basic requirements for listing

The following basic requirements must be satisfied:

(a) the fund must be set up in accordance with the laws of the jurisdiction of its establishment or incorporation;

(b) the persons responsible for managing the fund must be shown to have integrity and suitable experience and expertise;

(c) funds that are regulated by the CBI are not required to have independent directors, but funds that are not so regulated are required to have two directors who are independent of, and who have no executive function with, the investment manager or adviser to the fund or a related entity;

(d) the trustee or custodian of the fund must be a separate legal entity from the investment manager, administrator or investment adviser to the fund, although it may form part of the same group of companies;

(e) the securities of the fund are required to be freely transferable and tradable but restrictions on transfer may be accepted for tax or regulatory reasons;

(f) the fund's investment policy should provide for an adequate spread of risk;

(g) a listing document must be prepared setting out all relevant information about the fund, demonstrating compliance with the Irish Stock Exchange's listing rules, including disclosure of potential conflicts of interest involving persons responsible for managing the fund and how these will be resolved;

(h) the application for listing must be sponsored by a member firm of the Irish Stock Exchange. The sponsoring firm must be satisfied that the fund is suitable for listing and that the directors of the fund (or directors of the fund manager in the case of a unit trust) understand the requirements of the Irish Stock Exchange; and

(i) the directors of the fund (or directors of the fund manager in the case of a unit trust) must take personal responsibility for the information contained in the listing document.

10.8.4 Investment policy and restrictions

The following general investment restrictions apply to listed funds:

(a) funds are not permitted to take legal or management control over underlying investments, although venture capital funds may exercise legal (but not management) control of underlying investments; and

(b) funds are not allowed to invest more than 20% of gross assets in the securities of any single issuer, although dispensations may be permitted up to 100% in the case of:

- securities issued or guaranteed by sovereign issuers or certain public bodies;
- currency and derivative funds; or
- index tracker funds which are confined to sophisticated investors.

Immediate corrective actions must be taken if it is discovered that any of these restrictions have been breached:

(a) except in exceptional circumstances and subject to shareholder approval, funds are required to adhere to the investment objective and policy statement set out in the listing document for a minimum period of three years following admission to listing; and

(b) funds which have commenced business prior to listing must disclose the initial investments made or to be made (if known).

10.8.5 Sophisticated investor funds

Funds must be confined to sophisticated investors if they are registered outside EU Member States, Hong Kong, the Isle of Man, Jersey, Guernsey and Bermuda or if they are property investment funds. Also, funds which have an investment manager with funds under management of less than US$100 million must be confined to sophisticated investors.

Sophisticated investors are defined as those whose investment in a fund is not less than US$100,000 or the equivalent in another currency. In the case of umbrella funds which are confined to sophisticated investors, there must be a minimum subscription of US$100,000 per sub-fund or US$300,000 to the umbrella fund in total (or the equivalent thereof in another currency).

10.9 Prime brokers

10.9.1 The role of the prime broker

Dr Joanna Benjamin in her publication 'Interests in Securities a Proprietary Law Analysis of the International Securities Markets' supplied the following description of the role and function of a prime broker:

> A typical prime brokerage service might be as follows. The hedge fund (through its manager) identifies securities (the assets) which it wishes to purchase. In order to fund the purchase (i) the prime broker lends the purchase price to the hedge fund. (ii) The prime broker purchases the assets on behalf of the hedge fund as broker. As the hedge fund's custodian, the prime broker (iii) settles the purchase by paying the purchase price to the vendor and receiving the assets, (iv) which it holds and administers as global custodian for the hedge fund. (v) The prime broker collateralises the debt of the hedge fund to it in respect of the purchase price by taking a security interest over the assets. (vi) In order to increase the hedge fund's gearing by enabling it to service the largest possible debt, the prime broker agrees to charge a rate of interest below commercial rates. As a *quid pro quo* for the low rate of interest, (vii) the hedge fund agrees that the prime broker may deliver the assets of the fund to third parties under repo, securities lending and other arrangements as part of the prime broker's business, retaining any profits for itself (onward dealing).

10.9.2 Requirements for prime broker funds

The CBI permits professional investor funds (PIF) and qualifying investor funds (QIF) to enter into relationships with prime brokers where the collective investment schemes can meet the following requirements:

(a) a PIF and QIF may pass assets of the scheme to a prime broker which assets the prime broker may pledge, lend, rehypothecate or otherwise utilise for its own purposes under the following conditions:

- the assets so passed shall not exceed the level of the scheme's indebtedness to the prime broker;
- the arrangement incorporates a procedure to mark positions to market daily, in order to meet the above requirement on an ongoing basis;
- the counter-party must agree to return the same or equivalent securities to the scheme; and
- the arrangement incorporates a legally enforceable right of set-off for the scheme;

(b) where the prime broker will hold assets of the scheme, other than as provided for above, the prime broker must be appointed as a sub-custodian by the trustee. While the prime broker may take a charge over those assets, the assets must remain in the segregated custody account of the scheme, in the name of the trustee;

(c) the prime broker, or its parent company, must have a minimum credit rating of A1/P1. In addition, the prime broker must be regulated as a broker by a recognised regulatory authority, and it, or its parent company, must have shareholders' funds in excess €200 million (or its equivalent in another currency); and

(d) there must be clear disclosure in the scheme's documentation of its proposed relationship with the prime broker.

10.9.3 Legal issues arising for prime brokers

10.9.3.1 Charge over fund assets

The prime brokers collateral comprises of a changing pool of assets. At any time particular securities may be removed from the portfolio under a repo/stock lending transaction between a prime broker and a third party and replaced at the end of that transaction by equivalent securities. The issue then arises as to whether the security interest in favour of the prime broker is a floating charge. A security interest over a changing pool of assets does not necessarily constitute a floating charge. The test for a floating charge is that the collateral giver retains control or freedom to deal in the collateral assets. On this basis, the fact that the collateral assets change from time to time under onward dealing raises no risk of re-characterisation as a floating charge, because onward dealing takes place at the instigation of the prime broker, and is beyond the control of the hedge fund and its advisor.

10.9.3.2 Rehypothecation of assets

Where a person has received assets as collateral under a security interest, that person may not rehypothecate or dispose of those assets to a third party in circumstances where the collateral giver is not in default, so as to protect the equity of redemption. If a prime broker rehypothecates or disposes of assets, the issue arises as to whether such actions affect the validity of the prime broker's interest in the collateral in the event of the hedge fund's insolvency. In such circumstances, if the collateral giver defaults, the equity of redemption does not prevent the collateral giver from enforcing its security interest, as in those circumstances the preconditions for the exercise of the equity of redemption has not been satisfied. Therefore in this instance rehypothecation should not weaken the positions of the prime broker in the event of the hedge funds insolvency.

Problems may arise, however, in circumstances where the prime broker becomes insolvent at a time when assets have been rehypothecated under onward dealing arrangements. This result is avoided in circumstances where the prime broker acquires title to the collateral by way of absolute transfer from the collateral giver and not by way of security interest. This results in the hedge fund having an unsecured credit exposure to the prime broker for the net value of the collateral in excess of the debt owing by it to the prime broker.

10.10 UCITS III

UCITS III comprises of two Directives which were published in the EU's *Official Journal* on 13 February 2002. The first Directive (01/108/EC) is known as the Product Directive (the PD). It expands the investment powers of UCITS. The second Directive (01/107/EC) is commonly referred to as the Management Companies Directive (the MCD). It gives managers of a UCITS a European 'passport' and simplifies the prospectus requirements.

10.10.1 Product Directive

The PD expands the investment powers of UCITS to enable them to invest in: (a) money market instruments; (b) funds of funds; (c) index tracker funds; and (d) financial derivative funds.

(a)   Money market instruments

The PD changes the definition of transferable securities to include: (i) shares in companies and other securities equivalent to shares in companies; (ii) bonds and other forms of debt securities; and (iii) other negotiable securities which carry the right to acquire any such transferable securities by subscription or exchange.

The PD also sets out a definition of money market instruments by providing that instruments normally dealt with in the money market must be liquid and capable of accurate valuation at any time and must be dealt in on a regulated market or the issuer must itself be regulated for the purpose of protecting investors.

(b)   Funds of funds

The PD provides that a fund can invest in the following:

- up to 100% of the net asset value of the fund in other UCITS. The investment in any one target fund is limited to 20% of the net assets value of the fund;
- up to 30% of the net asset value of the fund in non-UCITS; and
- a UCITS may acquire a maximum holding of 25% of the units or shares in another fund.

A restriction is also placed on the double charging of subscription and redemption fees when investing in funds in the same group.

(c)   Index tracker funds

The old rules placed a limit of 10% on the amount of assets that can be invested in any one issuer. The PD increases that limit to 20%, only where the objective of the fund is to hold securities which replicate the securities in the relevant index. This 20% limit can be increased to 35% in the case of a single issuer which is highly dominant in a particular market.

(d)   Financial derivative funds

The original UCITS Directive provided that derivative instruments can only be utilised for the purposes of efficient portfolio management. The PD provides that UCITS may invest in derivative instruments as part of its investment policy provided the underlying instruments are permitted investments for the UCITS fund.

10.10.2   Management Company Directive

MCD covers four main areas:

(a)   the provision for a wider scope of actions for management companies;

(b)   a passport for management companies;

(c)   new supervision or authorisation rules; and

(d)   a simplified prospectus.

(a)   Wider scope of activities

The original UCITS Directive provided that management companies were restricted to only managing funds authorised by the CBI. This new Directive provides that management companies may now manage segregated accounts for private and institutional investors and pension funds, and carry out ancillary services such as marketing, administration, safekeeping and investment advice.

(b)   Passport for management companies

The MCD provides that management companies may provide services or establish branches in other Member States. The home country regulator shall be responsible for the authorisation and regulation of the management company whether the management company establishes a branch or provides services in another Member State or not.

(c)   New supervision or authorisation rules

The MCD provides for minimum capital requirements for UCITS management companies. The CBI has always imposed such a requirement. The MCD provides that management companies must have initial capital of at least €125,000. Where the value of the portfolio exceeds €250,000,000, the management companies must provide additional own funds equal to 0.02% of the amount by which the value of the portfolio of the management company exceeds €250,000,000. The required total of the initial capital and the additional amount shall not exceed €10,000,000. The MCD also places a higher level of supervisory requirements in relation to shareholders, transfers of shares, appointment of directors and senior managers.

(d)   Simplified prospectus

The MCD requires that each UCITS must publish a simplified form of the prospectus in addition to the main prospectus. This simplified form must be investor friendly and capable of being understood by the average investor. The simplified form can be used in all Member States without alterations, other than translation.

CHAPTER 11

INTERNATIONAL BANKING AND FINANCIAL SERVICES

Niamh Moloney

11.1 Developments in EC financial services law

11.1.1 Introduction

The most striking recent developments in EC banking and financial services regulation concern the harmonised securities and investment services regulation regime. Major changes will be made to the EC banking regime, however, in the event that the negotiations currently underway in the Basle Committee on Banking Supervision are successfully completed on reform of the capital adequacy (or own funds) regime applicable to credit institutions (see section 11.1.10 below). EC securities and investment services regulation is, at present, a regime in transition. Since the adoption in 1999 of the ground breaking Financial Services Action Plan (COM (1999) 232) (the FSAP), the harmonised EC investment services regime and securities regulation regime, which opens up the integrated investment services and securities markets to domestic issuers, investors, and investment firms, has been undergoing a period of seismic change. Indeed, the volume of new regulatory proposals aside, a non-scientific review of the level of coverage of EC investment services regulation matters by the *Financial Times* since 1999, when the FSAP was presented, reveals considerable levels of reportage and editorial comment on the regime's recent evolution. The process of change initiated by the FSAP's schedule of proposals has been accelerated by the presentation of the seminal Lamfalussy Report on the Regulation of European Securities Markets in February 2001 and with the subsequent moves in the summer of 2001 to apply the Report's ground breaking, if controversial, law making model to FSAP proposals. The shape of the regime, which will emerge from this period of intense regulatory development, is still opaque. It appears, however, that the new EC regime will regulate the single market in securities and investment services, and as a result, domestic participants in the EC marketplace, considerably more aggressively and in significantly greater detail, thereby limiting Member States' discretion in this area, than is the case at present.

11.1.2 Investment services and securities regulation: the story so far

To date, three phases can be identified in the evolution of the EC securities and investment-services regulation regime. Phase 1 concerned the construction of a single deep and liquid securities market in order to facilitate pan-EC capital raising by issuers and promote economic growth. This was attempted via the detailed harmonisation of Member States' issuer disclosure (essentially prospectus, listing particulars, and interim disclosure) rules and admission-to-official-listing rules in order to bring about market integration through rule equivalence. Regulatory obstacles to pan-EC capital raising by issuers would, in theory, be eliminated as Member States would all operate the same regimes. This did not happen in practice as the directives were not sufficiently detailed, contained a number of exemptions, and allowed Member States to derogate from key provisions. Attention was also given to the pathology of market regulation with the adoption of the Insider Dealing Directive (Council Directive 89/592/EEC) (the IDD) to protect the embryo integrated securities market from insider dealing.

Phase 2 can be characterised by a focus away from the issuer and towards the secondary markets and, in particular, on the construction of the harmonised investment services regime via the adoption of the cornerstone Investment Services Directive (Council Directive 93/22/EEC) (the ISD) and its sister measure, the Capital Adequacy Directive (Council Directive 93/6/EEC) (the CAD). These key measures are designed to facilitate the construction of a single EC market in investment services via the twin pillars of single market construction: (a) mutual recognition by each Member State of the supervisory standards used by other Member States; and (b) home Member State control of the investment firm's activities. This device minimises the potentially obstructive regulatory role of the home Member State in which the passporting firm carries out activities. In particular, the ISD/CAD regime grants a regulatory passport to firms which have been authorised by the home Member State (essentially the Member State of registration or of headquarters) in accordance with that Member State's standards. These will conform to the Directives' common minimum standards; they include initial authorisation standards, ongoing capital adequacy requirements, ownership control requirements, and ongoing prudential requirements, such as record keeping and conflict of interest management rules. The ISD/CAD regulatory passport thus permits the firm to operate across the EC, subject to the supervision of its home Member State.

This integration mechanism had been pioneered some years previously in the securities regulation field. First, by the adoption of the Undertakings for Collective Investments in Transferable Securities (UCITS) Directive on the single market in collective investment schemes (Council Directive 85/611/EEC). Secondly, by the mutual recognition revisions to the issuer disclosure regime which allowed issuers, with certain significant limitations, to use a single disclosure document, approved in one Member State, in respect of capital raising operations across the EC (Council and Parliament Directive 01/34/EC (Securities Consolidation Directive) and Council Directive 89/298/EEC (Prospectus Directive)). In 1997, the investment services regime was bolstered by the adoption of the Investor Compensation Schemes Directive, which requires that investor compensation schemes be established in all Member States and which sets out the common minimum rules for their operation (European Parliament and Council Directive 97/9/EC).

After its adoption, and with the 1998 revisions to the CAD regime (European Parliament and Council Directive 98/31/EC), and the 1995 revisions to the ISD/CAD prudential supervision regime, which were designed to strengthen supervisory co-operation mechanisms across the EC in the wake of the collapse of BCCI (European Parliament and Council Directive 95/26/EC), the harmonised structure contained the very basic elements of securities regulation and investment services regulation. A common core of basic rules, largely covering, with respect to the investment firm, authorisation and prudential (or stability) regulation, including capital adequacy requirements, and, with respect to issuers, market access and interim disclosure requirements, applied across the Member States. A network of competent authorities had also been established which was designed to supervise the harmonised rules and to provide a pan-EC co-operation system on which the supervision of the integrated market and, in particular, the home Member State supervision system, could be based.

Nonetheless, the regulatory structure supporting the integration process was inadequate. Large areas of regulation remained unharmonised and thus presented significant obstacles, in terms of regulatory costs, to investment firms seeking to operate across the EC and to issuers attempting to access pan-EC pools of capital. The existing harmonised regimes were also deficient in a number of respects. The scope of the ISD investment services passport, for example, came to be regarded as restrictive given the growing range of investment services and market participants. For example, alternative trading systems (ATSs) which provide a similar bundle of services to traditional stock exchanges were not adequately catered for under the ISD passport. The issuer disclosure regime and its mutual recognition system came to be regarded as a failure in that, in practice, only a tiny number of very large issuers used the complex mutual recognition system to access the single marketplace. Small and medium sized issuers were particularly disadvantaged by the primary focus of the issuer disclosure regime's mutual recognition procedures on the official listing of securities, rather than on the public offer of securities, as many smaller issuers access markets outside the official lists of stock exchanges, such as the alternative investment market on the London Stock Exchange. More generally, implementation of the directives was inconsistent and often badly delayed and supervisory co-operation was underdeveloped, notwithstanding the dependence of robust home Member State supervision and the stability of the integrated market, which becomes more prone to systemic shocks and spillover effects from one Member State to another as it integrates, on effective pan-EC co-operation.

Phase 3, which is currently unfolding and is defined by the FSAP and the Lamfalussy law making model, will potentially dramatically increase the scope and sophistication of EC securities regulation and investment services regulation, and, accordingly, pave the way for more complete market integration. Concerted and urgent efforts are now being made to complete the single market in securities and investment services. This is evidenced not only by a series of path-breaking reports (including the pre-FSAP 1998 *Commission Communication on Financial Services: Building a Framework for Action* (COM (1998) 625) (the 1998 Communication), the FSAP, the 2000 ISD Communication (COM (2000) 729), and the 2001 Lamfalussy Report (Report of the Wise Men on the Regulation of European Securities Markets)), but also by its regular appearance in the conclusions of the biannual European Council meetings, which have recently prioritised the completion of the single market in financial services in general, and in investment services and securities in particular.

11.1.3 The FSAP and the Lamfalussy Report

The 1999 FSAP, which, following the 2001 Stockholm European Council, should be completed with respect to securities and investment services markets by 2003, sets out a programme of 42 legislative measures. If adopted, it will radically change the shape of EC financial services and securities regulation in general, and investment services regulation in particular. It is as significant for the single market in investment services as the 1992 programme was for the single market generally. The FSAP's proposals recognise that deficiencies in the harmonised regime are blocking greater integration and they are accordingly designed to remedy the major difficulties. A second theme of the FSAP is the need to protect the marketplace against the risks posed by greater integration, to meet the regulatory challenges posed by market developments, and to ensure the protection of retail investors in the integrated marketplace. The FSAP's investment services related proposals are grouped around four categories (wholesale markets, retail markets, prudential rules and supervision, and the wider conditions for an optimal single financial market). A number of the key proposals are outlined further in the paragraphs below.

While the FSAP sets out the substantive measures which must be adopted in order to complete the internal market in securities and investment services, its fate is closely bound up with that of the Lamfalussy Report's recommendations for more effective EC lawmaking in the securities and investment services sphere. In July 2000, a Committee of Wise Men on the Regulation of European Securities Markets, chaired by Baron Alexandre Lamfalussy, was constituted by the Council in order to assess the current state of integration in the EC securities and investment services market, and the harmonised structure supporting it. It was also to examine how the mechanisms for regulating the securities markets can best respond to developments such as stock exchange alliances and technological developments. Finally, it was to suggest proposals for adapting current practices, in order to ensure greater convergence and co-operation on the markets.

The findings of the Wise Men in the Lamfalussy Report amounted to a withering criticism of the current regime. The Report pointed to the inadequacy of the harmonised structure, to its inability to cope with market developments and to support greater integration and, in particular, to the failure of EC legislative procedures to deliver harmonised regulation quickly and effectively. It warned that unless steps were taken to complete the regulatory structure and open the marketplace and to revise the law making process:

> ... economic growth, employment and prosperity will be lower, and competitive advantage will be lost to those outside the European Union. And the opportunity to complement and strengthen the role of the euro and to deepen European integration will be lost. (Page 8.)

The Report found that the development of an integrated securities market was being held back by a number of factors including:

(a) gaps in the harmonised regulatory regime, which were preventing the operation of mutual recognition;
(b) an inefficient regulatory system;
(c) inconsistent implementation of rules;
(d) inefficiencies in clearing and settlement systems;
(e) differences in legal systems (such as divergences in how bankruptcy proceedings are dealt with);
(f) taxation differences;
(g) political barriers in the form of creative techniques designed to assist local suppliers and national markets;
(h) external trade barriers; and
(i) cultural barriers, such as different entrepreneurial cultures and different attitudes to regulation such as variations in approaches to corporate governance, disclosure, and the importance of competition.

In order to remedy this situation, it did not focus on substantive rule reform nor duplicate the Commission's work in constructing the FSAP, but focused instead on the inability of the EC law making process to deliver the FSAP reforms. The Report found that while there was a strong consensus on the need to deliver the FSAP as soon as possible, the current EC regulatory and law making framework was 'too slow, too rigid, complex and ill-adapted to the pace of global financial market change' (p 7).

Its proposed solution was to revise the EC law making process such that 'Level 1' principles, or basic political choices, would be adopted in framework measures (in the form of directives or regulations) in accordance with the normal EC legislative procedures set out in the Treaties. (In practice, most financial services and investment services measures are adopted under the co-decision procedure set out in Art 251 of the EC Treaty, which requires close contact between the Council and the European Parliament.)

'Level 2' measures, or detailed technical measures, which have not been seen hitherto in EC securities or investment services regulation, would be adopted by the Commission under a streamlined and accelerated delegated law making procedure in which the Commission would be supervised and assisted by two new institutional committees. One of these committees would supervise Commission law making under comitology procedures, as a regulatory committee, while the other would provide technical advice to that committee and to the Commission. The exercise of supervision by the primary law making institutions (the Council and the European Parliament) over the Commission in its exercise of delegated law making powers (the Commission is not, for the most part, a major law making institution but it is a key player in the law making process in that it proposes legislation), is governed by the Comitology Decision (Council Decision 99/468/EC). This Decision sets out three supervisory models, according to the degree of power available to the supervisory committee (or whether it is a regulatory, management or advisory committee). The scope of the measures to be adopted under Level 2 delegated law making procedures would be governed by the relevant Level 1 measure in which the delegation of power to Level 2 was granted. This delegation of law making to the Commission would allow the cumbersome, lengthy, and politically-captive primary Treaty law making process to be bypassed for the detailed technical rules necessary for securities and investment services market integration. Political accountability would be ensured by retaining the traditional procedures for the Level 1 measures which would set the scope of the delegation. Level 3 concerns the implementation process and requires enhanced co-operation between securities regulators across the EC in order to ensure consistent implementation of Level 1 and 2 measures. Level 4 addresses enforcement and calls for more aggressive enforcement by the Commission of EC rules.

In June 2001, the Commission established two Lamfalussy committees:

(a) The European Securities Committee (ESC), which will, as the political committee, composed of Member State representatives, supervise Commission law making.

(b) The Committee of European Securities Regulators (CESR), which will, as the expert committee, provide technical advice to the ESC and the Commission.

CESR is, in effect, FESCO, reconstituted and brought within the EC institutional structure. FESCO (the Forum of European Securities Commissions) was founded in 1997 and, composed of high-level representatives of European securities commissions and regulators, has been a driving force in securing extra-EC agreement between Member State securities or investment services regulators on harmonised standards. In recent years, it has produced important initiatives on harmonising standards with respect to issuer disclosure, market abuse, and conduct of business regulation, to name but three, all of which have had a major influence on proposal development by the Commission.

The first group of proposals in the form of Level 1 high-level principles and subject to amplification by Level 2 measures have now appeared (the Market Abuse Proposal (see section 11.1.8 below) and the Prospectus Proposal (see section 11.1.4 below)). The likelihood of detailed Level 2 securities and investment services measures appearing will depend in large part, however, on the European Parliament's willingness to agree to the extent of the delegation of law making power to the Commission in the relevant Level 1 delegating measure. The Council and the European Parliament under the co-decision procedure (Art 251 of the EC Treaty) adopt most securities and investment services measures. The European Parliament's position as a primary law maker in the EC has been hard won and it might be expected not to respond too kindly to attempts to curtail its powers by delegating law making functions to the Commission. Indeed, the inter-institutional negotiations on the Lamfalussy model revealed considerable resistance from the European Parliament, until the Commission agreed to a declaration in which an attempt was made to protect the Parliament's position. This included an agreement by the Commission that all delegations of power in Level 1 measures would be limited to four years. Nonetheless, the European Parliament's controversial rejection of the proposed Take-over Directive in July 2001 (after 12 years of negotiations) has revealed it to be a law maker of some volatility, independent of both the Commission and the Council.

Although recent Commission initiatives suggests the arrival of a vastly more comprehensive and interventionist investment services regime composed of detailed Level 2 measures, much will depend on whether inter-institutional tensions and power-broking will obstruct the Lamfalussy model. In addition, the July 2001 collapse of the proposed Take-over Directive following strong lobbying by national interests, particularly those of the corporate sectors in Germany and Italy that were fearful of exposure to Anglo-American predators, might signal a return to national interests driven law making which would be prejudicial to the development of the integrated market.

So far, the European Parliament, in its opinions on the securities regulation measures proposed to date by the Commission as Level 1 measures, has revealed an intention not to lose control of the Level 2 process. The Parliament has set out detailed guidance as to the principles under which the Commission, as law maker at Level 2 should exercise the delegated powers. For example, the guidance in the Parliament's revisions to the Commission's original Prospectus Proposal, which is to be adopted as a Level 1 measure (see further section 11.1.4 below), extended to 12 general principles. These included the need to ensure confidence in financial markets and the importance of reducing the cost of, and increasing access to, capital, as well as to the more specific guidelines applicable to specific delegated powers set out in the Prospectus Proposal.

11.1.4   Issuer disclosure: the Prospectus Proposal

The Commission's Prospectus Proposal (COM (2002) 460 – it revises an earlier Commission proposal presented in June 2001), which fundamentally reforms the current harmonised disclosure or prospectus regime applicable to official listing and public offers, is one of the FSAP's most dramatic legislative proposals. Presented as a Level 1 measure, which will be fleshed out by detailed Level 2 rules adopted by the Commission, it is currently going through the EC legislative process and is generating considerable controversy, with the marketplace proving hostile to certain of its core provisions.

The proposal is structured around the introduction of a full issuer-disclosure passport, which includes a shelf-registration mechanism. In a shelf-registration system an issuer registers a basic or foundation disclosure document which is then updated by means of a shorter document each time the issuer wishes to access the capital markets. Such a system supports issuers who access the capital markets on a regular basis and allows them to benefit from changes in market conditions. This new regime would, therefore, obviate the need to produce major disclosure documents each time an offering was launched or a listing application made. The current EC regime, however, does not provide for a shelf-registration system and allows Member States to impose additional conditions on disclosure documents that have been approved in another Member State, which adds considerable costs to the pan-EC capital-raising process. The mutual recognition system for market access disclosure documents is not complete, it is complex and does not provide issuers with a full passport mechanism. The new regime is designed to overhaul the current system in order to facilitate the widest possible access to investment capital for all issuers, including small and medium sized enterprises (SMEs), while strengthening protection for investors by ensuring that all prospectuses, wherever they are issued across the EC, provide investors with clear and comprehensive information with which to make investment decisions.

In a major change to the current official list focused regime, the distinction between the disclosure or prospectus regime applicable to securities admitted to official listing (Directive 01/34/EC) (the Securities Consolidation Directive which consolidates the official listing Directives), and securities admitted to trading on markets which do not require official listing or public offers generally (Directive 89/298/EEC) (the Prospectus Directive), is removed.

The proposal has five key features. First, it proposes the adoption of updated and enhanced disclosure standards in line with international standards for public offers of securities and admission to trading, adapted according to the nature of the issuer and the securities. The upgrading of the current disclosure requirements will be in accordance with the International Disclosure Standards adopted by IOSCO (International Organisation of Securities Commissions) in 1998. The current distinction in the EC regime between admission-to-official-listing and admission to other trading markets (such as the London Stock Exchange's alternative investment market) is thereby removed and, it appears, a 'one size fits all' approach adopted.

Secondly, it reformats the structure in which disclosure is provided to the marketplace. Under the proposed regime issuers could choose to draw up the prospectus as a single document (which includes a summary), or, where admission is sought to trading on a regulated market, as separate documents consisting of a registration document (containing general information on the issuer and the financial statements), a securities note (containing information on the securities offered), and a summary note. A third format would be made available for frequent issuers, such as those which offer securities under programmes. Issuers of securities that trade on a regulated market would also be required, in the interests of investor protection, to update the information in the prospectus or registration document annually.

Third, the proposed new regime offers the possibility for issuers to offer or admit securities to trading across the EC on the basis of a simple notification of the prospectus once the prospectus has been approved by the home Member State competent authority (the full passport system). Issuers would be required, however, if the host Member State in which the securities were offered or traded so required, to publish a translation of the prospectus summary.

Fourth, controversially, it proposes the concentration of responsibility for review of the prospectus in the home Member State independent competent authority and the removal of the ability of securities trading markets to review listing particulars (or the disclosure document or prospectus required for admission-to-official-listing). The marketplace is proving to be hostile to this innovation, which represents a major change to the current regime. It would mean that a German or Irish issuer raising capital on the London Stock Exchange only, for example, would be required to have the disclosure document approved by the German or Irish authorities. The argument in favour of permitting issuer choice as to the approving authority rests in part on the implications for competent authority resources and expertise and the lack of incentive for competent authorities to provide more efficient services. Where the home Member State always reviews its issuers' prospectuses, regardless of where the offer is to be made in the EC, there may be the danger of a domestic monopoly developing for each competent authority and of a lack of efficiency arising, as there would be little incentive for the authority to seek efficiency gains. In addition, there would be little opportunity for the various competent authorities to specialise with respect to particular markets. Intermediaries and advisers would be required to become familiar with all Member States' approval procedures, and could not concentrate, as they can at present, on the major centres, for example, in London and Luxembourg.

Finally, the Commission has proposed extensive use of the comitology process in line with the Lamfalussy Report's findings in developing the detail of the new disclosure regime at Level 2.

The proposal is tailored to reflect the needs of particular issuers and investors. In particular, a special regime would apply to offers of high minimum denomination securities designed to be traded by professionals where issuers could choose the competent authority which would approve the prospectus and a tailored regime would apply to the content of the prospectus. Offers to qualified investors in the form of a private placing would be exempt from the requirement to produce a prospectus. This feature reflects a key theme of the Commission's proposal, which is to ensure that the wholesale capital markets, where trading occurs between professional investors, operate efficiently. Small and medium sized issuers are catered for by an exemption from the prospectus requirement where the offer falls below €2,500,000. Where a prospectus was required from such issuers, its content would be adapted.

The management in the EC of disclosure, particularly financial disclosure, has also become more high profile in the wake of the Enron collapse. In April 2002, the Commission published an analysis of the repercussions of the Enron collapse in which it outlined the steps that were needed to avoid a similar problem in the EC. Its main recommendations included the need for rapid adoption of the International Accounting Standards Regulation (which followed in July 2002). It also called for the issuing of a recommendation on auditor independence (adopted in May 2002).

In addition, the Commission recommended the expansion of the mandate of the EC's High-Level Group of Company Law Experts to address corporate governance and auditing questions. In this regard, the Council and the Commission agreed in September 2002 that an EC action plan be adopted in respect of corporate governance reform, particularly on reform of executive remuneration and auditing practices, as a core component of the EC's response to the repercussions of Enron. In November 2003, the High-Level Group presented its proposals for review of company law in Europe in its important and wide ranging Report on a Modern Regulatory Framework for Company Law in Europe. The Commission also called for an examination of the effectiveness of the supervision of derivatives.

Finally, it recommended that an assessment be made of the measures required to protect the marketplace from false or misleading signals from financial analysts' recommendations. (This is taking place in the context of the current reform of the EC's insider dealing regime (see section 11.1.8 below) and the reform of the ISD (see section 11.1.7 below).)

Other initiatives in the disclosure field include the adoption of a regulation, which requires that all publicly-quoted companies in the EC report their financial information under international accounting standards (IAS) by 2005 (European Parliament and Council Regulation EC/1606/02). (The new standards to be adopted in the future by the new international accounting standards harmonisation body, the International Accounting Standards Board, are to be called International Financial Reporting Standards (IFRS).) A review of the ongoing reporting regime is also underway.

11.1.5 The E-Commerce Directive

The E-Commerce Directive (European Parliament and Council Directive 00/13/EC) (the ECD) is a general measure, not specific to financial or investment services, but it has important implications for the integration and regulation of the EC financial services and investment services market.

The provision of investment services via the internet represents one of the most significant of the challenges currently faced by the EC's investment services regime. EC investors are not, as yet, taking to the internet for investment services in vast numbers. The number of trades executed online is, however, increasing steadily. This development, and the cross-border nature of online services, has aroused concern that investor protection, in the form of common minimum protective rules in all Member States, is not sufficiently robust. From the investment firm's perspective, however, the internet is a powerful marketing and delivery tool, given the dematerialised nature of investment services and products and the delivery of online services across the EC should not be made subject to duplicative and onerous regulatory burdens.

The ECD has had a critical impact on the EC's approach to pan-EC conduct of business regulation and investor protection, and on the current push to move the investment services regime as a whole away from home Member State control and its obstructive effects. It introduces a new market construction device: the Member State of establishment or Member State of origin. Under Art 3(1) of the ECD, each Member State is to ensure that the information society services provided by a service provider 'established on its territory' comply with the national provisions applicable in the Member State in question which fall within the area covered by the Directive. Under Art 3(2) of the ECD, which has been termed the internal market clause, Member States may not for reasons falling within the co-ordinated field (the field harmonised by the Directive), restrict the freedom to provide information society services from another Member State. The ECD is, therefore, based on the principle that online services that do not have a physical connection to another Member State are most effectively supervised by the Member State in which the service provider is established, and that online service providers should be protected from the imposition of regulation by each Member State in which the services are accessible. Article 3 of the ECD does not specify how the Member State of establishment is to be determined, but Art 2(3) of the ECD provides that an 'established service provider' is a service provider that effectively pursues an economic activity using a fixed establishment for an indefinite period. This formula would include branches. As a result, online services of any kind, investment services or otherwise, which are supplied from a branch, are subject to the regulatory regime of the Member State in which the branch is located.

This general Directive has had two important consequences for the provision of online investment services and the investment services regulatory regime.

First, it largely eliminates the Art 11 ISD conduct of business problem (section 11.1.6 below) for online investment services: Art 11 subjects investment firms to the conduct-of-business rules of all the Member States in which they operate, and thus generates considerable regulatory costs for passporting firms. All online investment services are now regulated, certainly as far as conduct of business rules are concerned, from the Member State in which the service provider is established, which can include the Member State in which a branch is located. In this respect, it is a very positive development with respect to market access by investment firms.

Second, it generates a considerable potential problem with respect to investor protection in the single market. Up to now, any attempts to tie the investment services regulatory system to one Member State (usually the home Member State) in the interests of minimising the burdens faced by firms operating across the EC and maximising the effectiveness of the regulatory passport, have been undertaken together with minimum harmonisation of the rules over which the home Member State would exercise control. Market stability and investor protection demand that all Member States operate to the same minimum if the home Member State is to have sole control over the investment firm and the host Member State in which the firm operates is to be ousted. Harmonisation of investor protection regulation is, however, embryonic at present. Accordingly, the host Member State generally governs protective regulation, as is seen in Art 11 of the ISD. The ECD breaks this link between single Member State control and minimum harmonisation and, in doing so, reveals the impact a general measure can have on a highly regulated area such as the investment services field.

Due to the poor state of conduct of business harmonisation, considerable concern was generated following the ECD that investors would be subject to a Member State of establishment regime without the cushion of common, minimum, investor protection rules. The possibility, therefore, exists of investors losing the protection of their own rules and being subject to unfamiliar controls (of the firm's Member State of establishment) and, depending on the market conditions and regulatory culture of the investors' Member State as compared to the firm's Member State of establishment, potentially being subject to less than optimum rules. Post-ECD, the conduct of business regime has, therefore, shifted away from host Member State control to the Member State of establishment, but without the protection of minimum harmonisation.

Three important areas of protective regulation are excluded from the Member State of origin principle by Art 3(3), which provides a derogation from the internal market clause for the areas listed in the ECD Annex. These include contractual obligations concerning consumer contracts and rules concerning the permissibility of unsolicited communications by email. More generally, an investor protection or consumer protection derogation is available for the host Member State under Art 3(4)(a) of the ECD. This is designed to minimise the risk of prejudice to investors. Over-reliance on this derogation, however, cuts against the market access benefits of the Directive as it exposes firms that supply investment services on an online basis to the regulatory regimes of the Member States which rely on the derogation, as well as to the regulation imposed by the Member State of establishment.

The adoption of the Distance Marketing Directive (see section 11.1.6 below) and the revisions proposed to the ISD (section 11.1.7 below), however, suggest that the EC system will shortly contain more comprehensive harmonised investor protection standards.

11.1.6 Distance marketing of financial services

In September 2002, the important Distance Marketing of Financial Services Directive (European Parliament and Council Directive 02/65/EC) was finally adopted after lengthy and difficult negotiations between the Member States. The proposal was originally presented by the Commission in 1998. The new distance marketing of financial-services regime will impose a harmonised set of disclosure, marketing, and contractual term requirements across the EC on all suppliers of financial services (including investment services, insurance services and banking services) who use distance methods (for example, the telephone, fax, and internet) of communication with consumers. A consumer is defined under the Directive as any person who, in a distance contract covered by the Directive, is acting for purposes outside his trade, business or profession. Suppliers will be required to supply consumers with extensive disclosure requirements, prior to the conclusion of a contract, concerning: the supplier, the financial service, the contract, and forms of redress.

The substantive disclosure required under these categories includes the requirement that a risk warning be given where the financial service is related to instruments which involve special risks or where the price depends on fluctuations in the financial markets which are outside the control of the supplier, and that the supplier give notice that historical performances are not a guide to future performance.

These disclosure requirements must all be provided in a clear and comprehensible manner and in good time before the consumer is bound by the distance contract or offer. The contractual terms and conditions, as well as the specified disclosure required under the new marketing regime, must be provided to the consumer, again, in good time prior to contract conclusion. A less onerous information regime applies to telephone communications, but only where the explicit consent of the consumer is given. Withdrawal rights will also be imposed, with consumers given the power to withdraw from distance financial services contracts within 14 days of contract conclusion, without penalty and without giving any reason (a 30-day period applies to life insurance and personal pension operations).

The Directive also imposes restrictions on cold-calling and other aggressive forms of unsolicited communication, although it does not go so far as to ban cold calls. Member States, where they allow such calls to take place, must ensure that either they are not authorised unless the consent of the consumers concerned has been obtained, or that they may only be used if the consumers have not expressed a manifest objection. This is the opt in or opt out mechanism of controlling aggressive marketing techniques. The Directive also requires Member States to promote the setting up or development of effective and adequate out-of-court complaints and redress procedures, as well as to ensure that adequate and effective means exist to ensure compliance with the Directive.

The Directive marks a major step forward for EC securities and investment services regulation in that it represents the first serious attempt to deal with investor protection in the integrated market, albeit it in the specific context of distance contracts. Up to now, the focus of the harmonisation programme has been almost entirely on the market-access rights of an investment firm or the issuer, and only rarely on the protection of the investor, particularly the retail investor, who accesses the increased risk environment of the integrated marketplace.

11.1.7 Revisions to the ISD

The investment services regime as set out in the ISD is based on the single market principles of home Member State control of investment firm regulation (in accordance with minimum EC standards) and mutual recognition. This serves as the basis for the ISD passport. Considerable structural problems have, however, emerged with passport. Full home Member State control is only achieved with prudential or stability based rules (for example, the Art 10 ISD operational prudential rules (such as asset protection rules) and the capital adequacy rules set out in the CAD). Host Member State control (essentially control by the Member State within which the firm operates), which is highly prejudicial to integration due to its obstructive effects, still dominates in micro or protective regulation, particularly conduct of business regulation. The infamous example of this structural weakness in the investment services passport is the delphic formula of Art 11 of the ISD which grants jurisdiction with respect to conduct of business regulation to the 'Member State in which the service is provided'. It does not harmonise in any detail the conduct of business rules which must be applied by Member States under Art 11. Investment firms that use the ISD passport to access the integrated marketplace are thus potentially exposed to 15 different sets of conduct of business regulation. The investment services passport is also increasingly being seen as limited in scope and unable to cope with new market developments and market actors, such as the growth of alternative trading systems (ATSs).

ATSs provide similar trading and information services to those provided by the traditional stock exchanges but are often constituted and regulated as investment firms. In order to pave the way for a massive overhaul of the ISD in order to ensure the final integration of the investment services markets, the Commission in July 2001 presented an extensive working paper setting out its preliminary orientations on how reform should proceed. This was superseded in March 2002 by a second working paper which took into account extensive consultations with the marketplace. A formal proposal on reform of the ISD was presented in November 2002.

One of the major revisions concerns Art 11 of the ISD. The proposal contains a new and much more detailed set of conduct of business standards, which Member States must ensure investment firms comply with. These standards include marketing rules, documentary record requirements, best execution obligations, risk warnings, and suitability requirements. These standards are much more advanced than the minimal conduct rules contained in the current Art 11 regime. The Member State of establishment control device is also incorporated in the new regime. In other words, branches of investment firms will be subject to the conduct rules of the Member State in which the branch is based. Other forms of cross-border services provision will be subject to home (rather than host) Member State control, another major change in policy, given the high degree of rule harmonisation which will allow conduct of business regulation to be managed by the home Member State alone. Finally, the new Art 11 regime is tailored and differentiated to reflect different risk profiles; retail and professional investors will be treated differently.

Dramatic changes are also be made in the proposal to the regulation of investment firms and stock exchanges in order, *inter alia*, to take into account the activities of ATSs as well the rise of in-house trading of securities (internalisation) by investment firms.

11.1.8 A new market abuse regime

The Market Abuse Directive (not yet published in the *Official Journal*) drastically overhauls the EC's insider dealing regime. While the EC had taken steps to address the problem of insider dealing with the IDD, there remained a wide spectrum of egregious behaviour in the trading markets outside the scope of the EC's insider dealing formula. They ranged from the misuse of information to manipulative trading practices which have a detrimental effect on the integrity of the marketplace.

The Market Abuse Directive brings together the former insider dealing regime (while updating its provisions) and a new market manipulation regime in a new directive. In line with the approach commonly taken, market manipulation has been defined in terms of trading practices and the dissemination of false or misleading information. Member States are required to prohibit market manipulation, which covers:

> ... [t]ransactions or orders to trade, which give, or are likely to give, false or misleading signals as to the supply of, demand for, or price of financial instruments, or which secure, by a person, or persons acting in collaboration, the price of one or several financial instruments at an abnormal or artificial level, unless the person who entered into the transactions or issued the orders to trade establishes that his reasons for doing so are legitimate and that the transactions conform to accepted market practices on the regulated market concerned.

Market manipulation also covers transactions or orders to trade which employ 'fictitious devices or any other form of deception or contrivance'. Disclosure is also brought within the scope of market manipulation in that the dissemination of information through the media, including the internet, which gives, or is likely to give, false or misleading signals as to financial instruments, including the dissemination of rumours and false or misleading news, where the persons who disseminated the information knew, or ought to have known, that the information was false or misleading, is brought within the prohibition. In a controversial provision, this rule applies to journalists, although whether a journalist has breached the rule is to be assessed taking into account the rules governing the profession, unless the journalist derives an advantage from the dissemination of the information. Journalists therefore benefit from the general intention qualification, as well as from a profit rule.

The scope of the new regime is set by broad definitions of the markets and securities covered. Both the insider dealing and market manipulation prohibitions are subject to a common (and in the case of the insider dealing regime significantly upgraded) enforcement regime, which includes provisions on administrative and criminal sanctions.

Finally, the new regime introduces a supervisory co-operation system which again represents an advance on the insider dealing regime. A particular (and likely to be controversial) innovation is the introduction of operating controls on the dissemination of information by issuers and market professionals, in order to enhance the effectiveness of the new market abuse regime. Like the Prospectus Proposal (section 11.1.4 above), the Directive provides for the adoption of technical, implementing, Level 2 measures via comitology procedures and so reflects the new Lamfalussy decision making model.

11.1.9 Financial conglomerates

Ensuring appropriate and adequate supervision of financial conglomerates, which have enjoyed enormous growth in the integrated investment services market in recent years, has emerged as a dominant theme of discussions on reform of the EC banking and investment services regime. The supervisory difficulties posed by financial conglomerates centre on ensuring the effective supervision of the constituent conglomerate entities (such as banks, insurance companies, and investment firms), each of which generate a variety of risks that impact on the group as a whole. Risk can be aggravated given the likelihood of considerable divergence of supervisory approaches across the different regulatory sectors. A 2002 Directive has been adopted which is designed to ensure that the stability of the integrated market is not prejudiced by gaps in the supervision of financial conglomerates by different sectoral supervisors.

11.1.10 Credit institutions and capital adequacy

Drastic revisions can be expected to the EC capital adequacy regime which currently applies to credit institutions and, although to a lesser extent, to the EC investment firm capital adequacy regime. These revisions will track the changes at international level under discussion in the Basle Committee, which are not projected to come on line until 2006 (see section 11.2.2 below).

11.2 International developments

11.2.1 Trends

The management of systemic (or system wide) risk is increasingly a pre-occupation of financial and banking regulators internationally. A number of initiatives are being undertaken to ensure effective co-operation between national supervisors and the containment of risk globally. These include initiatives on the management of financial conglomerates. In 1996, a joint forum on financial conglomerates was set up at international level and constituted by representatives of the International Organisation of Securities Commissions (IOSCO), the Basle Committee on Banking Supervision, and the International Association of Insurance Supervisors. It was established to build on the work of the Tri-partite Group of Banking, Insurance and Securities Regulators which was established in 1993. In 1999, the joint forum produced a number of extensive papers concerning the supervision of financial conglomerates which cover:

(a) capital adequacy;
(b) the application of 'fit and proper' principles;
(c) a framework for information sharing;
(d) supervisory co-ordination;
(e) intra-group transactions and exposures principles; and
(f) risk-concentration principles.

Increased levels of online trading are also generating concern internationally. The major body for international co-operation between securities regulators, IOSCO, has issued a number of communications designed to ensure that retail investors, in particular, are adequately protected in the online marketplace. IOSCO has identified a number of the features of the 'new economy' which provoke concerns. These include the rapid development of short term trading over the internet and its impact on investors' risks. It has recommended that investors who trade online be made aware that an order may not be executed more quickly than it would be were it given to a broker in the traditional manner. Furthermore, investors are to be made clear as to the risks and costs involved, and online brokers, notwithstanding the different relationship they have with investors, are to continue to be subject to the duty to act in the best interests of the investor.

11.2.2 Capital adequacy and the Basle Committee

One major international development concerns how the own funds or risk (or regulatory) capital of credit institutions should be measured. Risk capital is designed to provide a cushion for credit institutions against risks, such as the risk of mass withdrawal of deposits, which could undermine solvency, given that credit institutions typically have debts which can be instantly withdrawn, but a relatively illiquid asset base in the form of credits or loans. Proposals are under discussion at international level through the Basle Committee for a new Basle Capital Accord.

The Basle Committee on Banking Supervision is the international banking regulator. It adopted internationally agreed standards for credit risk capital in 1988 (Basle Committee on Banking Supervision, International Convergence of Capital Measurement and Capital Standards (the Basle Accord)). The basic credit risk capital requirement is that credit institutions maintain a minimum ratio of 8% of eligible own funds (the assets it may hold as own funds) to risk-weighted balance sheet and off-balance sheet items.

The Accord categorises how assets are to be risk-weighted and applies weightings of 0%, 20%, 50%, and 100% according to the category to which the asset belongs. Negotiations are currently underway, however, to revise this approach and so allow credit institutions to adjust asset risk-weightings to reflect more closely the actual economic risks incurred by the credit institutions. The current Basle approach of classifying assets according to four broad risk of default categories has been categorised as too crude and costly. The first sets of proposals were issued in June 1999 and were followed by a second set in January 2001. Adoption of a new Accord is not expected until 2006 and is likely to be held up by negotiations on translating the proposals into the EC capital adequacy regime for credit risk for credit institutions. It is expected that the revised EC framework and the new Basle Accord will be implemented at the same time in the interests of financial stability and in order to ensure that a level playing field is maintained.

The proposals also address capital requirements for risks other than credit risk, such as operational and other risks which are not currently covered. In addition, the proposals will examine the supervision structure underpinning the international banking system, including the extent to which disclosure and market discipline can be used to manage risk. Overall, the new regime is based on a three pillar structure which is designed to ensure that the risk capital regime adequately reflects the risks to which credit institutions and the financial system are exposed: minimum capital requirements, supervisory review, and market discipline.

In line with its FSAP objectives and the Basle Accord developments, the Commission first presented a paper reviewing the current EC regulatory or risk capital requirements in 1999 which was followed by a second paper in 2001 (issued after the revised Basle Accord proposals were presented). These papers, which reflect the Basle proposals while fine tuning them to the Community environment (and to the application of the Community capital-adequacy regime to investment firms as well as credit institutions, in particular, as well as to the reality that the Basle rules are designed to apply to large, international credit institutions and not all credit institutions), are designed to provide the basis for a proposed directive for a new capital adequacy framework and to facilitate the ongoing development of the internal market. Underlying the review is the need to update the capital regime to ensure that standards reflect market developments, and that they accurately reflect the risks run by credit institutions and investment firms. The review has recognised that while credit and market risk (market risk is the principal risk run by investment firms) are the predominant focus of the capital adequacy regime, a range of other significant risks are not subject to capital requirements. To that end, a key and controversial feature of the review, reflecting the Basle discussions, is the proposal that capital requirements be introduced for risks other than credit and market risk, such as operational risk, as part of the overall objective to produce a more comprehensive and risk-sensitive approach to risks.

INDEX

Agricultural Credit Corporation (ACC)	1.1
Auditors	1.7
Automated teller machines	2.1.1
Basle Committee	1.3, 11.2.2
Building societies	1.1.1, 1.5, 1.5.1
Banking	
activities	1.1.1
business	
definition of	1.1.1, 4.5
confidentiality, duty of	2.1.5
bank's own interests	2.1.5
customer's consent	2.1.5
legal compulsion	2.1.5
public duty and	2.1.5
cheques	
See Cheques	
customer relationship and	2.1
fiduciary duties	2.1.4
liability under contract law	2.1.1
liability under law of torts	2.1.3–2.1.3.3
licence	1.1.1
Capital adequacy	1.3, 4.1.1.3, 5.6.4, 6.7, 11.1.1, 11.1.7, 11.1.10
Charges	1.7, 3.4–3.4.6
fixed	
See Fixed charges	
floating	
See Floating charges	
registration	3.2.4, 3.6
company incorporated outside State and	3.2.4.3
late	3.2.4.2
process	3.2.4.1
Cheques	2.2.1
bank's liability and	2.2.1.4, 2.2.1.5
crossings on	2.2.1.3
nature of	2.2.1.1
property as	2.2.1.2

Central Bank of Ireland (CBI)	1.2, 4.5
See also Investment advisors	
codes of conduct	2.1.6
See Investment advisors	
disclosure of information by	1.7
establishment of	1.1.1
legislative code of	1.1
mutual funds	
See Mutual funds	
notices	1.2
powers of	1.1.1, 1.4
role of	5.2
stock exchange and	9.7
See also Irish Stock Exchange	
Credit unions	1.1.1, 1.5.1, 5.2
Credit transaction	3.2.2.1
Consumer credit	2.1.7, 2.1.7.1
Deceit	2.1.3.3
Defamation	2.1.3.1
refer to drawer	2.1.3.2
Deposit protection	1.7
Directors	
common law duties	4.3.2
fiduciary duties of	8.6.4
fraudulent trading	4.3.2
qualifications	5.5.3.3
reckless trading and	4.3.2
transactions with	3.2.2–3.2.2.4
connected persons	3.2.2.2
expenses	3.2.2.3
group exemption	3.2.2.3
minor transactions	3.2.2.3
whitewash procedure	3.2.2.3
E-Commerce	11.1.5
EU financial services law	11.1–11.1.10
Financial Services Action Plan (FSAP)	11.1.1, 11.1.3, 11.1.4, 11.1.8
market abuse	11.1.8
credit institutions	11.1.10

distance marketing of financial services	11.1.6
e-commerce	11.1.5
financial conglomerates	11.1.9
investment services	11.1.2, 11.1.7
See also Investment services	
issuer disclosure	11.1.4
Lamfalussy Report	11.1.3, 11.1.4
securities	11.1.2
See also Securities	

Euro

introduction of	1.1.1

Financial Services Ombudsman	**1.1.2**
Financial transfers	**1.7**
Fixed charges	**3.4.3, 3.4.6**
See also Charges	
book debts	3.4.5
Floating charges	**3.4.1**
See also Charges	
avoidance of	3.2.5.4
book debts	3.4.4
crystallisation	3.4.2
Fraudulent preferences	**3.2.5.1, 3.2.5.3**
Friendly societies	**1.1**

Insider dealing	**5.6.3, 8.1–8.6.4**
definitions	8.3
dealing	8.3
inside information	8.3
likely to materially affect the price of securities	8.3
not generally available	8.3
securities	8.3
exemptions	8.5
agents	8.5
Chinese Wall structure	8.5
company dealing in its own securities	8.5
exclusion of statutory liability	8.5
mere information that company proposes to deal	8.5
seven day window	8.5
liability	8.6
civil	8.6.1
common law	8.6.4
criminal	8.6.2, 8.6.3
primary insiders	8.4.1
prohibition on	8.4
secondary insiders	8.4.2
statutory regime	8.2
tippees	8.4.2
Interbank money transfers	**2.2.3**

International developments	**11.2, 11.2.1, 11.2.2**
Internet services	**2.1.1, 5.6.11, 11.3.1, 11.1.6**
Investment advisors	**5.1–5.8**
See also Investment services	
activities carried on outside Ireland	5.8.1.2
authorisation process	5.5
application form	5.5.1.1
capital requirements	5.5.3.2
director's qualifications	5.5.3.3
fee	5.5.1.2
information required	5.5.2
financial	5.5.2.2
general	5.5.2.1
individual questionnaires	5.5.2.3
Irish and non-Irish applicants	5.5.1.4
refusal of	5.5.3.1, 5.5.4
time	5.5.1.3
authorisation requirements	5.3–5.3.5
affiliates	5.4
investment advice	5.3.3
investment business firms	5.3.1
investment business services	5.3.4
Central Bank of Ireland	5.2, 5.4, 5.5.3.3, 5.5.4, 5.6.1, 5.6.2, 5.6.4, 5.6.6.1–5.6.9, 5.7.1.2–5.7.2.2
See also Central Bank of Ireland	
enforcement	5.7
breach of condition	5.7.1.5
civil liability	5.7.1.8
directions	5.7.1.4
mechanisms of	5.7.2
authorised officers	5.7.2.1
inspectors	5.7.2.2
warranties	5.7.2.3
penalties	5.7.1.1
personal liability of officers	5.7.1.7
probity of employees	5.7.1.6
revocation of authorisation	5.7.1.2
winding up	5.7.1.3
See also Winding up	
investment instruments	5.3
regulation of	5.6, 6.1
advertising	5.6.9
capital adequacy	5.6.5
See also Capital adequacy	
code of conduct	5.6.2
anti-fraud	5.6.2.1
books and records	5.6.2.6

client disclosure	5.6.2.3	Irish Stock Exchange	4.2, 4.6, 5.2, 6.14, 9.1–9.7.31
conflicts	5.6.2.2		
consent requirements	5.6.2.3	*See also* Stock exchange	
private assessment	5.6.2.4	Act governing	9.7–9.7.31
professional assessment	5.6.2.4	approval of stock exchange	9.7–9.7.31
soft common		auditor and	9.7
arrangements	5.6.2.5	Central Bank of Ireland and	9.7
insider dealing	5.6.3	*See also* Central Bank of Ireland	
See Insider dealing		function of	9.1, 9.2
internet	5.6.11	listing rules	4.6, 7.2.3
investment compensation	5.6.8	markets	9.2
mandatory	5.6.1	Developing Companies	
money laundering	5.6.10	Market (DCM)	9.2
prudential rules	5.6.7	equity	9.3
administration matters	5.6.7.1	Exploration Securities	
qualifying holdings	5.6.6	Market (ESM)	9.2
appeal	5.6.6.3	Irish Government bond	9.5
disapproval of		ITEQ®	9.2, 9.4
transactions	5.6.6.2	Official List	9.2
prejudicial influence	5.6.6.4	mutual funds	
safeguarding client assets	5.6.7.2	*See* Mutual funds	
Investment services	**6.1–6.20**	types of securities listed on	9.2
See also Investment advisors		*See also* Securities	
appeal against refusal of			
authorisation	6.8	**Letters of credit**	**2.2.2**
capital adequacy	6.7		
See also Capital adequacy		**Mistaken payments**	**2.2.4**
capital requirements	6.7	**Money laundering**	**1.6, 5.6.10**
Central Bank of Ireland	6.2.3, 6.6, 6.8	civil liability	1.6.2
See also Central Bank of Ireland		categories of	1.6.2
		Criminal Assets Bureau	1.6.2
codes of conduct for	6.13, 6.16–6.19	criminal liability	1.6.1
conflicts of interest	6.13	offences	1.1.6
criteria for authorisation for	6.9	reporting obligations	1.6.1
distinct authorisation	6.3	secondary	1.6.1
EC developments and	11.1.2, 11.1.3, 11.1.7	UCITS	10.3.5
		See also Mutual funds	
firm, definition of	6.10	**Mortgages**	**3.3**
firms providing	6.2	creation of legal	3.3.1
harmonisation of	11.1.1	freehold unregistered land	3.3.1
investment instruments	6.2.1, 6.2.2, 6.10	leasehold unregistered land	3.2.2
Member States	6.12	registered land	3.3.1
natural persons providing	6.5	equitable	3.3.2
prudential rules	6.11, 6.14, 6.15	mortgagee	
		duties of	3.3.3
registered offices outside EU	6.20	rights of	3.3.3
stock exchange rules	6.14	mortgagor	
See also Stock exchange		duties of	3.4
suitability of shareholders	6.6	rights of	3.4
two-man management rules	6.4	priorities	3.3.5
unincorporated bodies providing	6.5	equitable interests	3.3.5
Irish Financial Services		legal interests	3.3.5
Authority (IFSA)	**1.1.1, 1.1.2**	registered land	3.3.5
Irish Financial Services Centre	**4.2**	unregistered land	3.3.5

Mutual funds 10.1–10.10.2, 11.1.1
  authorisation procedure 10.5–10.5.8
    approval process 10.5.4
    fund documentation 10.5.5
    fund structure approval 10.5.3
    organisational documents 10.5.7
    other agreements 10.5.8
    promoter approval 10.5.2
    prospectus 10.5.6
  Central Bank of Ireland 10.1.1, 10.2.1.4, 10.3.1, 10.4.1.4, 10.4.1.5.1, 10.4.2.5, 10.5.1, 10.6.4
    See also Central Bank of Ireland
  continuing requirements for 10.6
    board of directors 10.6.2
    Central Bank of Ireland 10.6.4
    control by investors 10.6.6
    information to investors 10.6.5
    supervision 10.6.1
    trustee/custodian 10.6.3
  institutional funds 10.1.1.3, 10.4, 10.4.1.5.2
  Irish Stock Exchange, listing on 10.8
    See also Irish Stock Exchange
    application procedures 10.8.2
    basic requirements for 10.8.3
    investment policy and restrictions 10.8.4
    listing centre 10.8.1
    sophisticated investor funds 10.8.5
  main categories 10.1.1
  non-UCITS 10.1.1, 10.1.1.2, 10.4
    key features 10.4.2
      closed-ended funds 10.4.2.1
      efficient portfolio management 10.4.2.5
      fractions of shares 10.4.2.12
      fund mergers 10.4.2.9
      hedge funds 10.4.2.10
      net asset value 10.4.2.2
      open-ended funds 10.4.2.1
      pooling techniques 10.4.2.4
      risk spreading 10.4.2.11
      securities lending 10.4.2.8
        See also Securities
      share classes 10.4.2.7
      umbrella fund 10.4.2.3
      weekly dealings 10.4.2.6
    notices 10.4.1.5.1
    types of 10.4.1
      investment company 10.4.1.2
      investment limited partnership 10.4.1.3
      investment policies 10.4.1.4
      professional investor fund 10.4.1.5.4
      qualifying investor fund 10.4.1.5.3
      retail funds 10.4.1.5
      unit trust 10.4.1.1
  prime brokers 10.9
    legal issues and 10.9.3
      charge over fund assets 10.9.3.1
      rehypothecation of assets 10.9.3.2
    requirements for funds 10.9.2
    role of 10.9.1
  retail funds 10.1.1.3, 10.3, 10.3.2, 10.4.1.5.1
  taxation 10.7
    declaration of residency 10.7.6
    domestic funds 10.7.5
    fund's assets 10.7.3
    investor 10.7.4
    private investor funds 10.7.2
    public funds 10.7.1
  UCITS funds 10.1.1, 10.1.1.1, 10.3.2, 10.10
    advantages of 10.3.1
    authorisation of 10.3.3
    definition 10.3
    key features of 10.3.6
      effective portfolio management 10.3.6.3
      fund mergers 10.3.6.11
      liquid assets 10.3.6.6
      multiple classes 10.3.6.9
      nest asset value 10.3.6.7
      notices 10.2.1.4
      pooling techniques 10.3.6.8
      securities lending 10.3.6.10
        See also Securities
      transferable securities 10.3.6.2
      UCITS passport 10.3.6.1
      umbrella fund 10.3.6.4
      weekly dealings 10.3.6.5
    Management Company Directive 10.10.2
      authorisation rules 10.10.2
      new supervisor rules 10.10.2
      passport for management companies 10.10.2
      simplified prospectus 10.10.2
      wider scope of activities 10.10.2
  money laundering 10.3.5
    See also Money laundering
  professional duties of related persons 10.3.4

Product Directive and	10.10.1	industrial design	3.6
financial derivative funds	10.10.1	patents	3.6
index tracker funds	10.10.1	trade marks	3.6
money market instruments	10.10.1	land *See* Mortgages	3.3
UCITS III	10.10	law issues	4.4
unit trust	10.2.1, 10.4.1.1	maturity date	1.1.1.1, 1.1.1.2
investment advisor	10.2.1.4	Irish Stock Exchange	9.2
manager	10.2.1.1	*See also* Irish Stock Exchange	
trust deed	10.2.1.1	public offer of	4.4
trustee	10.2.1.3	*See* Offer to the public	
		Non-UCITS	10.4.2.8
Negligence	2.1.3.1	*See* Mutual funds	
Netting	3.5.3	*ultra vires*	3.2
See also Set-off		*Bell House* clause	3.2.1
agreement, definition of	3.5.3	enforcing contract	3.2.1.2
		improperly transferred assets	3.2.5.2
Offers to the public	7.1–7.9	independent objects clause	3.2.1
See also Securities		judicial interpretation	3.2.1.1
American perspective	7.8, 7.9	main objects rule	3.2.1
companies incorporated outside the State	7.6	whitewash procedure	3.2.2.3
definition of	7.3	UCITS	10.3.6.10
listing particulars	7.2.3, 7.5.3	*See* Mutual funds	
See also Irish Stock Exchange		**Securitisation**	4.1–4.7
meaning of	7.1	*See also* Securities	
prospectus	7.1, 7.2.1, 7.2.2, 7.3, 7.4.2, 7.5.2	collateral loan obligation programmes	4.1.1.3
certain categories of user	7.4.2	definition of	4.1
failure to publish	7.5	insolvency	4.3–4.3.2
mutual recognition	7.6	jurisdiction of courts	4.3.2
split issues	7.4.2	protection of creditors' rights	4.3.1
types of securities	7.4.2	noteholder	4.1, 4.3
reforms	7.7	perspective	4.1.2–4.1.2.5
third schedule prospectus	7.2.1, 7.2.3, 7.4.1, 7.5.1	direct asset claim	4.2.1.4
		higher yield	4.1.2.1
Pension funds	4.1	insulation from corporate originator credit risk	4.1.2.5
Restitution	2.2.4	standardised rating	4.1.2.2
		tailored securities	4.2.1.3
Securities		taxation	4.2
See also Securitisation		notes	4.1, 4.4, 4.5
allowing	3.1.2	maturity of	4.5
asset covered	1.7	originator	4.1, 4.1.2.5, 4.3, 4.3
definition	8.3	perspective	4.1.1–4.1.1.3
directors	3.2.2	capital adequacy	4.1.1.3
See also Directors		*See also* Capital adequacy	
EU developments and	11.1.2, 11.1.3	capital raising	4.1.1.1
forms of	3.1–3.6	improved balance sheet	4.1.1.2
insider dealing		special purpose company (SPV)	4.1, 4.1.2.5, 4.2, 4.3, 4.3, 4.4, 4.5, 4.6
See Insider dealing			
insolvency	3.1.1		
intellectual property rights	3.6		
copyright	3.6		

stock exchange	4.2, 4.6
See also Irish Stock Exchange	
taxation	4.1, 4.2
Set-off	**2.1.9, 3.5**
See also Netting	
bankers' combination of accounts	3.5
bankruptcy	3.5
contractual	3.5
contingencies	3.5
flawed assets	3.5.2
insolvency	3.5.1
mutuality of debts	3.5
permission to combine	3.5
equitable	3.5
legal	3.5
Shares	
classes	10.4.2.7
financial assistance for purchase of	3.2.3
fractions	10.4.2.12
Statute of Limitations	**2.1.8**
Statutory regulation of banks	**1.1**
Stock exchange	
See also Irish Stock Exchange	
London	4.6, 9.6
Luxembourg	4.6
Taxation	
See Mutual funds; Securitisation	
Trustee savings banks	**1.1**
Ultra vires	
See Securities	
Unfair terms in consumer contracts	**2.1.2–2.1.2.6**
core terms	2.1.2.5
good faith	2.1.2
house building contract terms	2.1.2.1–2.1.2.6
meaning of	2.1.2
Winding up	**2.1.9, 3.2.5.1, 5.7.1.3**